Renewing Research Practice

Renewing Research Practice

Edited by

RALPH E. STABLEIN *and* PETER J. FROST

STANFORD BUSINESS BOOKS
An imprint of Stanford University Press
Stanford, California
2004

Stanford University Press
Stanford, California
www.sup.org

Library of Congress Cataloging-in-Publication Data

Renewing research practice / edited by Ralph E. Stablein and Peter J. Frost.
    p.   cm.
    Includes bibliographical references and index.
    ISBN 0-8047-4676-1 (alk. paper)—ISBN 0-8047-4677-X (pbk : alk. paper)
    1. Business—Research. 2. Management—Research. I. Stablein,
Ralph E. II. Frost, Peter J.
HD30.4.R4595 2004
338.5'072—dc22   2004006011

Printed in the United States of America on acid-free, archival-quality
paper.

Original Printing 2004

Last figure below indicates year of this printing:

13   12   11   10   09   08   07   06   05   04

Designed and typeset at Stanford University Press in 10.5 / 12 Bembo.

To Bill Hicks with deep appreciation;
to Joy, Hohepa, Lily, Nola, Paul,
Caitlin, and Maeve with affection

Contents

viii   Contents

8. How Projects Lose Meaning: The Dynamics of Renewal
    KARL E. WEICK   183

    Commentaries on Chapter 8
    Mountain Dancing: A Reflection on Karl Weick's Work
        DAVID BARRY   205
    The Process of Renewal: Breathing New Life into Old Projects
        JAMES D. LUDEMA   209

*Toxins and Antidotes: Parting Thoughts on Researcher Resilience
and Renewal*   217

        References   227
        Contributors   241
        Index   245

Acknowledgments

WE WANT TO acknowledge the generosity of the contributors. Their willingness to reflect openly and publicly on the backstages of academic life has made this book possible. Because the book took a long time to complete, we thank them for their patience, as well.

Massey University and the University of British Columbia provided partial support for the project, and the support staff of both institutions helped us deliver the manuscript. Many thanks go to Brigit Eames, Josie Grace, Ming Guo, Cynthia Ree, and Catherine Toulis. Josie patiently shepherded the manuscript through the final formatting process.

We want to offer a special thank you to Bill Hicks, who provided wise advice, support, and enthusiasm for us throughout the project, and who accepted the book at Stanford University Press. After Bill's retirement, Kate Wahl and Tony Hicks ably guided us through the rest of the publication process.

We accept responsibility for any errors and omissions in the manuscript.

Ralph Stablein Peter Frost
Palmerston North Vancouver
New Zealand Canada

August 2003

Renewing Research Practice

New Beginnings

As winter descends on my garden, the earth gets crusty, plant stalks wilt, colors fade, and signs of life disappear. Many years ago—I can't recall exactly when—my career and research life had the feel and the look of a garden in winter. I was crusty and critical in my thoughts and my deeds as they concerned my own research and the research of others. While research projects were still progressing (sometimes they have a life of their own), they were not sustained by stalks that felt very generative or alive. Finally, my writing and my expressions of what I was learning from my work felt colorless and dead.

Jane Dutton

If you've never felt like Jane, then this book is not for you—yet. Alas, few of us can claim to never experience these thoughts and feelings, some of us more deeply or for longer. This is a book about renewal. The book is driven by the stories of scholars who have been stuck, who have gotten lost, who have been confused, but who have managed to nurture and sustain their work. They have rebounded to make multiple significant and varied contributions to our understanding of organization and management.

The good news is that low points need not be end states. Experienced scholars have developed routines and resources that allow comebacks, breach impasses, encourage creativity, stimulate energy, and resolve dilemmas. The genre of academic writing often continues to hide the processes and practices of the author in doing the research—the "tricks of the trade" (Becker 1998). In editing this volume, we have tried to create a venue that stretches the academic genre to allow the sharing of these backstage research practices. Now, we all can benefit from the willingness of the contributors to discuss their research choice points, transitions, and renewals.

As in our previous book, *Doing Exemplary Research*, we describe research as a journey. In the earlier book, we followed the journeys of seven research projects as told by the authors. Now we return to the subject matter, but not to the case method. We expand the notion of journey to encompass the research life. In this book, we aim to capture the tacit wisdom of active scholars on their personal research journeys. Journeys have beginnings and ends. Each research project, the exemplars of our earlier book, is embedded in the longer and more complex journey of a working lifetime.

Jane Dutton suggests above that journeys are not easy all the time. The special interest of this book is to offer aid and support to our colleagues on difficult, confused, or stalled journeys. Neither the editors nor the contributors to this volume know the trials of your journey. But we are committed to exploring the possibilities of development, to help you find a better way. In this book, we look back to help you move forward. An odd strategy; yet, we hope these accounts and commentaries of past journeys will stimulate your personal processes of development and renewal.

Each researcher enters the field with a particular background and set of concerns at a particular moment in history. A variety of personal and scholarly changes require the renewal and development of our research practice as we live the research life. Each person's entry point into the academy conditions, but does not determine, the researcher's assimilation of, and responses to, change.

Anne Huff (1999) encourages us to think of scholarship as a conversation. The research literature is a buzz of multiple conversations amongst the many subgroups of the field. Our goal, as scholars, is to participate in the relevant conversations. Our research contributions (articles, chapters, books) raise the standard of conversation. We shift and shape the subject and direction of discussion. Each of us starts in a different place, with a different voice to add to a research conversation. We need to find our voice, and sometimes we lose our voice.

When we do lose our place in the research conversation, we cannot parrot or emulate the research practice of our eminent colleagues. In a changing world, what worked for our contributors cannot work for our readers. Yet, we are confident that experienced colleagues can stimulate the renewal of our contemporary research practice. We may rarely mimic successfully, but we may reverse, revise, reinterpret, or reflect on their experiences to inform our own research practice in our own unique contexts. Further, we know that the reflections of our colleagues who have witnessed and participated in the development of our field can inform our research practice as we attempt to build on the foundations of earlier contributions.

Our goals are not limited to assisting the journeys of individual scholars. We also hope to influence the collective journey of the academy. We hope that the explicit acknowledgment and exploration of these issues will expand our notions of scholarly community. The research work of the community of scholars is an intellectual enterprise that cannot be easily severed from the social. As Andy Van de Ven recently reminded, "We ARE the Academy" (Van de Ven 2002, 171). As a community of scholars we must acknowledge the social and moral dimensions of community. We sincerely believe that the more that we do, the more we improve the intellectual performance of individual scholars, the community as a whole, and increase our understanding of the various phenomena we study. The stories told here vitalize the abstract notion of scholarly community—bridging the intellectual, the social, and the personal in concrete detail.

The book is organized around series of chapters prepared by well-recognized scholars in the field. Our contributors, in many, different ways have touched the lives of others: through their writings, their teaching, and their advising, they have guided others successfully through their formative doctoral years. Some draw on their extensive experience of collaborating with other scholars to offer ideas for keeping one's spirit of research alive. All our authors have logged many "manuscript years" as authors and as reviewers for major publications in the field. They know the agony and the ecstasy of writing up one's work and of keeping going in the face of tough feedback. Two authors add senior administrative experience as leaders of the Academy of Management to their reservoir of insights for making one's way as a scholar. We asked the contributors to share their tacit knowledge of scholarly renewal gained in the doing of exemplary research.

Following each chapter are two commentaries. We have invited colleagues to become readers of each journey. In this role of reader, we have asked them to develop a response that invites or even nudges you, as a fellow reader, to interact with the ideas presented. We set them the task of creating a reflection that would encourage the reader to apply or extend the themes of the chapter to the reader's own personal journey. These commentaries function in several ways. Sometimes they provide a context for the chapter. Sometimes they add another layer of subtlety and insight. Several of the commentaries suggest hands-on activities for the reader to do. We invite you, the readers, to react. Your reaction is valid! Your reaction is primary! Use the thoughts and experiences of these scholars as you will on your journey, as fodder for your mill, to intrigue, to evaluate, to inspire, to reform, to divert your scholarly journey.

Woven between these chapter/commentaries sets, we discuss broader issues that we believe are important to the development of a successful research practice over time. These include discussion of scholarly community, ethics, the changing intellectual terrain of organizational studies, images of scholarship, the intoxication of the research journey, rethinking the notion of discipline in the context of the new production of knowledge (Gibbons et al. 1994), and reflection on the American-centrism of management research.

We would encourage the reader to start at the beginning with Jane Dutton's story. However, the ordering of the chapters is somewhat arbitrary. The reader could enter at any account. Similarly our editorial weavings refer to the adjacent chapters but address issues that are somewhat independent of them.

One Scholar's Garden
A Narrative of Renewal

AS WINTER DESCENDS on my garden, the earth gets crusty, plant stalks wilt, colors fade, and signs of life disappear. Many years ago—I can't recall exactly when—my career and research life had the feel and the look of a garden in winter. I was crusty and critical in my thoughts and my deeds as they concerned my own research and the research of others. While research projects were still progressing (sometimes they have a life of their own), they were not sustained by stalks that felt very generative or alive. Finally, my writing and my expressions of what I was learning from my work felt colorless and dead. The research was not generative in the sense of inspiring new ideas or, more significantly, of having the feel of something important, creative, and alive.[1]

This is a tale of trying to bring a research garden back to life. In this sense, it is a tale of renewal, although renewing one's research process and research outputs seems continuous, and not a one-time event. I use the garden metaphor for its potential in conveying research as an earthy, grounded process of trying to coax life out of seeds and soil. In the metaphor, most times I am the gardener, toiling away trying to grow worthwhile research projects that affect the conversation in organization studies. Like most gardeners, I am learning to live with long time horizons, acceptance of only limited control, and the joy of unexpected growth in places that were not tilled or planted by me. The garden metaphor lets me talk about the conditions that enable growth and abundance in the garden, and about the conditions that seemed to encourage the opposite. Of course, looking back, there is never an isolatable set of forces that makes a garden flower. There are good years, and there are bad ones. The more I garden, the more humble I be-

---

1. I have benefited greatly from the helpful reactions and comments of Monica Worline.

come about what it takes to make a truly magnificent garden that is sustainable over many years.

Rarely in the Garden Alone

Most of my research is collaborative. A glance at my resume would show that few of my research products are singly authored. Even for those single-authored products, their foundation and inspiration derive from collaborations and interdependent work done with others. Since my early days as a graduate student I have always enjoyed the energy, coaxing, and contact made possible by doing research with other people.

Not all of my collaborations have been easy. I seem to have to learn over and over again that every collaboration involves difficult work. My estimates about how long it takes to get a task done collaboratively are usually off by at least a factor of three. Even with people with whom I have collaborated for several years (and there are several), we relearn the difficult lessons of unrealistic time frames, unarticulated assumptions, unmet expectations, different styles in working with graduate students, and misalignment in writing times.

I have and continue to grow tremendously in the collaborations of which I am a part. They are the soil from which I grow my garden. As I reflect on how collaboration has contributed to a sense of renewal (or at least the hope that my scholar's garden is becoming more fertile), three points stand out. First, I feel more alive in some collaborations than I do in others. I take this sense of "life" in collaboration seriously as evidence that I am growing in the collaboration. Second, collaborations have lives of their own—there are seasons in a collaboration process that I am learning to work with and accommodate to as opposed to fight or change. Third, there are certain routines in collaboration that help to avoid perilous detours or bumps in the road. I am learning to at least discuss these routines more explicitly and be conscious of how they are working or not keeping the collaboration alive. I turn to each of these points about renewing in collaboration below and where possible try to provide concrete examples that illustrate my general points.

GROWTH-IN-COLLABORATION

Jean Baker Miller (1991) and her colleagues at the Stone Center at Wellesley College have this idea that human beings experience growth in some connections and decay or at least nongrowth in others. I find their idea incredibly helpful in making sense of my experience in some collaborations and not others. Not all collaborations are the same. In some I feel authentic, challenged, and zestful (Miller's term); in others I feel academic, tested, and pressured. In both types of collaborations, I usually produce something.

However, in the former type of collaboration I literally feel myself growing as a person.

I use three signs as evidence that I am in the kind of collaboration in which I am growing. First, I notice that I shed my "expert" mask and find myself saying "I don't understand," "I don't know," and "help me out" a lot. I feel intellectually vulnerable and emotionally open. Second, when I am in these collaborations, the boundaries between my "professional" and "personal" life are highly permeable; in fact, they almost disappear. In my growing collaborations, I am unafraid to reveal my "wholeness" as a person and my collaborators do likewise. Third, the work in the collaboration is work about life as opposed to work about organizational behavior or some narrow academic topic. While not always conceived of this way, through the collaboration, the research question becomes a question about life, and the collaboration becomes a safe and exciting vessel in which to explore this life question.

I'd like to share two examples of this form of collaboration. One is ongoing, and one just finished. One is with colleagues who are peers; the other is being done with two graduate students (one who is now a professor at a business school). One took almost six years to complete; the other is heading on a similar trajectory in terms of time taken from conception of the original research idea to acceptance of a paper in a refereed journal. It is important to note that this six-year time frame seems how long it typically takes me from conception of an idea to eventual publication of something from the idea.

The first example is a collaboration with Connie Gersick and Jean Bartunek, and it is a collaboration on a research topic about which none of us had done any prior research. We were drawn together by a chance meeting on a panel at the Academy of Management meetings, and through our separate comments on the topic of what is a good research question we recognized a similar resistance to the question, and a framing that focused on relationships as central to defining good research questions. While we did not know each other initially beyond acquaintance, we began a series of phone conversations that eventually moved to a commitment to collect data on the meaning of relationships in professional lives. The inspiration for taking this focus came partially from our sense that our experience as female academics in business schools was very different from that of our male colleagues. Our research became a way to play with and explore this question.

The research collaboration was very much a harbor for making sense of our own career experiences and a place for playing with how we might recreate and refocus ourselves as we were moving forward in our own academic journeys. It was a harbor that survived some storms and some moments of zero movement. However, there were real moments of personal revelation as we talked with each other and talked about the data that we collected, and as we tried to make sense of the result. We learned about how one's relational landscape shaped the logic that one employed for one's career. We used this research insight to reflect on our own career trajectories. Often the boundaries between "our lives" and the research were paper thin or absent altogether. While I did not always feel that I was "growing-in-collaboration," the majority of the time I did. I felt I could easily admit my ignorance and could laugh at and question what I was bringing to the collaboration. It felt safe to be vulnerable, and the collaboration allowed for the simple fact that life and its demands sometimes got in the way of linear research progress. As I write about this collaboration and its inevitable ups and downs, I am reminded that we never considered the quality of our collaborative connections as a source of energy when we were being trained as graduate students.

A second example of growth-in-collaboration is a project with Gelaye Debebe and Amy Wrzesniewski that focuses on what we can learn from the stories of people who clean hospitals. This is a project that began from a very different place—from an interest in studying a particular occupation and from letting the people we were studying shape the research question that became our focus. This project is also very different from any research I had done in the past both in terms of topic and in terms of method. It is a collaboration in which none of us are subject experts, and despite the faculty-student distinction, hierarchy and status differences interfere less than they have on other faculty-student collaborations of which I have been a part. In this collaboration, our research meetings would vacillate between discussions of what we were learning about organizations and how we were changing how we viewed people in support roles, how we viewed our roles as women and how we might conduct ourselves differently. In this collaboration as in the one described above, we collaborators were conscious that the research was teaching us about life as much as about organizations. Although I was sometimes more uncomfortable because of a sense that as professor "I should know," more often than not, we shared vulnerabilities about our own ignorance about how to make sense of the data, the overall teachings of the research, and how to position it.

SEASONS OF COLLABORATION

I am coming to see collaborations as having their own rhythm that is related to the clocks, pressures, and prods from the persons participating in the collaboration. It is as if each collaboration develops its own pattern of movement that we as collaborators must honor and adjust to. There are seasons to collaborations—springs when ideas are budding, summers when efforts are in full bloom, falls when the flowers of the efforts are most visible yet not really moving, and winters when the collaboration is dormant. The rhythm of the collaboration is not fully controllable by any one collaborator, which thus requires awareness and explicit conversation about where the collaboration is and when it is likely to move to the next season. I have had the best experiences when there is explicit talk and agreement about the movement of the collaboration, and when people comply with their promises about when the collaboration will be dormant and when there will be activity. Most of my collaborations pass through multiple seasons of growth-withering-dormancy. Part of my growing ease in collaboration I think comes from simply realizing that this is the case.

ROUTINES FOR COLLABORATION

Along with rhythms, I am learning that there are certain routines that help me to avoid some of the pain that is inevitably a part of every collaboration. The first routine involves explicit talk about the kinds of products expected from the collaboration and how we might deal with authorship. I have found it most helpful to think of as many products as there are collaborators and to give everyone a chance to own or "drive" a product as first author. At the same time, I have learned that making authorship talk a normal part of what is discussible also allows for flexibility as the product evolves and drivers may chose to move into passenger seats.

I've also learned about the importance of making space for talking about life (and non-task-related events, ideas, and issues) as an important prelude to doing the work in the collaboration. While I should know the importance of this routine, of course, I mostly forget to apply any of this wisdom to my own life. However, I have watched my colleague Bob Quinn, and his artful sensitivity to the socioemotional needs of any group, and learned from this modeling, about the importance of making this part of collaborative meetings. So far, it seems to have made a difference.

Weeding

Our academic lives afford infinite ways of being choked and drowned by excessive demands. There have been several times when I have seriously considered leaving academe because it seemed the only way to escape the oppressive weight of giant "to-do" lists, promises, and professional obligations that seemed inescapable and brought no joy. I have tried all kinds of solutions along the way—for example, taking a year off after my third year as a full-time academic and going halftime after I got tenure. None of these solutions solved the problem of suffocating demands that I felt I could not escape.

I realize now that this set of suffocating obligations did not just appear overnight. They were the gradual result of not carefully weeding the garden of demands that composed my professional life. The poor weeding job was sometimes due to my own cowardice about saying "no." Other times, the rapid growth in demands arose from seemingly benign commitments that others made for me (for example, committee assignments, delegated administrative duties) and because I was not paying sufficient attention, they mushroomed into giant, energy-depleting obligations that were difficult to escape. Like uncontrolled weeds, these obligations sometimes grew to such a level that they screened out the light and energy needed for the discretionary activities (for example, research), doing major damage to the activities that brought me joy. Thus, poor weeding not only resulted in having to tend to tasks that I did not care for, but also it sapped crucial light and energy from the activities that sustained and nourished me.

I have become a much better weeder of late. I think this has allowed a lot more light into the garden. First, I have decided, sometimes with regret and other times with guilt, that there are certain activities that I am simply not going to do, at least not for now. One activity is teaching in executive education. While this decision has the feel of being a bad citizen by not "carrying my weight" in a domain that is critically important in my local environment, I realize the drain this would be on my emotional energy store. Thus, I chose for now to say no to these opportunities. Similarly, I have decided to not take on major administrative duties in my local environment. I did my three-year stint as chair of my department and actually enjoyed it (after initial major resistance). I have had several opportunities to take associate dean roles at the school and the university levels. However, for now at least, I have decided that these roles divert my limited energies away from research and working with PhD students, who are my real battery chargers. Third, I am much more limited with reviewing manuscripts than I used to be. I now turn down manuscripts to review unless they are definitely in my research area or I am on the board for the requesting journal. I also have limited the number of editorial boards of which I am formally a part. I am also being much more careful about agreements to write letters of recommendations for graduate students, for promotion and tenure reviews, and for colleagues.

Beyond perfecting my skills in saying no, my weeding acumen also has included withdrawing from certain research projects that were no longer feeding or nourishing me. This has probably been the most difficult part of the weeding process because pulling out of research projects has often meant breaking promises, admitting defeat, implying unhappiness or disaffection, sometimes doing temporary damage (at least) to relational ties that have significance in my life. In addition, it is sometimes very difficult to tell what are weeds and what are vital plants, particularly in the early stages of a project.[2]

2. Thanks, Monica, for this suggestion.

Despite the difficulty of this form of weeding, it has probably generated the most yields in terms of restoring energy. It has been news to me to learn that one can actually exit a research project and have the research project continue to chug along. My own reluctance to pull out of projects often was the result of an overinflated sense of how important I was to the project's sustainability.

Some collaborations can be major sources of corrosion of the spirit. If a research collaboration is corrosive, it is energy depleting and it severely restricts the supply of energy available for other aspects of our professional lives. Thus, the importance of attending to what projects need weeding because the research collaboration is corrosive is a lesson I keep relearning. I am also learning to take seriously the bodily signs that collaboration is corrosive. Upset stomachs, defensive body language, little energy to connect: all are critical signals that the collaboration needs help at a minimum, or may need to be weeded as a last resort. Using my body as a sensing device to judge restorative or depleting professional situations is also something that we never discussed in graduate school, yet it is part of what I am doing on my renewal journey. I am finding it really helpful.

Breaking Down Fences

In my earlier days there were fences that separated various aspects of my professional duties and neatly walled my professional from my "personal" life. I don't know why I was so insistent about these fences, but at this stage in my career, I am doing everything I can to break them down. The fences, while keeping things nice and tidy at the surface, kept my work and my life fragmented and differentiated, prohibiting the experience of living my work and working my life. I think some of the reintegration that has occurred has fed the sense of renewed energy that I feel as I see so many more pieces of my life as connected to and enriching each other. Some examples might help illustrate what I mean.

One obvious fence that I am trying to eradicate is the barrier that separates the content of what I am teaching from the ideas that I am researching. In the course of seventeen years of doing this career there have only been three out of thirty-four semesters when there has been a close connection between what I teach and what I research. Most of this separation has been my own construction. Most of the classes that I have taught (core MBA, core undergraduate organization behavior, and corporate strategy classes) have some degrees of latitude in what is covered. Moving forward I am challenging myself to fold into core teaching more of the working premises of what I am studying and what I am naturally excited about. By doing this, I start to see who I am and what I care about as part of what I would like to explore with students in class. I have found this integrative move, even at a small scale, joyful and fun. Following the metaphor, the integration has let sunlight bathe my work. I literally feel its restorative quality. The integration between teaching and research became even more extensive when I more recently taught and designed a doctoral class that centered on my research interests (relationships and organizations) and a new MBA elective on managing professional relationships at work.

A powerful but more invisible fence has been the divider that sustains the premise that what I believe in my research is separate and distinct from what I believe as a human being just trying to get through the day. Thankfully, there has been a gradual meltdown in the false distinction between my research ideas and ideas about life more generally. In fact, the growing fusion between the learning as a "scholar" and the learning as person-wife-mother-daughter-sister has brought major healing and energy to how I think about my work. My work is my life in a very different way than I understood this phrase before. The fence barrier that had protected each separate sphere and kept them from mutually enriching each other has disappeared. I don't believe I ever made a conscious choice to remove this fence. Rather it is an aftereffect of doing research that really matters to me and doing it with people in collaborations that allow me to grow as a human being.

An example of this fusion is in an ongoing project with Peter Frost that plays with trying to describe, honor, explain, and understand compassion in the workplace. We just finished one piece of this work with two graduate students, Monica Worline and Annette Wilson, in which we interviewed people we knew in academe (students, faculty, and staff) and asked them to share stories of witnessing and of experiencing compassion. The interviews themselves were transformative. They challenged us to face the limits of our own compassionate responding, opened us to the possibilities of organizations and professions as sites of healing, and put us face to face with the depth of suffering that is entwined with the conduct of our work lives. In discussions of the interviews and how we were processing them to write, it was sometimes difficult to know when we were talking about our lives or about the narratives told by our study participants. We remarked often about how listening, thinking, and writing about this topic felt like life—with its light and its darkness. For me, this project continues to breathe light into my life, and my life feels like it breathes light into the project. The fence of separation was never desired or achieved in this project. Thank goodness.

Tools for the Tilling

I was trained in a very traditional way. As a graduate student I took lots of methods courses with some terrific teachers and became quite proficient with all the latest multivariate techniques and tools of experimental design. Never once did I question what these tools did to the data I was collecting and to me the data collector. However, I now see a very close connection between the kinds of tools I use to collect, analyze, and write data and who I am becoming as an individual. This point was driven home to me in my colleague Karl Weick's gripping account of the disaster at Mann Gulch, where the firefighters did not drop their tools. Karl's haunting question of why this was so has resulted in his argument that the tools are part of the firefighter's identity. Dropping the tools would have meant letting go of the firefighters' core identity (Weick 1993). I have dropped tools and added tools that allow me to conduct my professional work. I have been much more conscious of the tools that I use as expressions of who I am, what my identity is, and what I can become. As a gardener, this means paying closer attention to the tools that I am using to till the garden.

I am learning that different tools allow for different types of connections with others. I believe deeply in the claim of the self-in-relation theorists that we are cocreated in dialogue with others. As Edward Sampson so eloquently puts it, "We gain a sense of self only in and through a process of interaction, dialogue and conversation with others in our social world" (1993, 106). If this is so, different tools create different kinds of dialogues. Different kinds of dialogues enact me in ways again that I find energy depleting or energy generating. In addition, different tools make me a part of different communities of practice (to use Jean Lave's wonderful idea) and afford different paths of becoming.

Here are two examples of tools I am currently using that are taking me down paths that I treasure in terms of giving me energy and fitting who I would like to become. One tool/perspective was introduced to me through Dave Cooperrider and his colleagues and students at Case Western. I collaborated with Dave on a conference in 1995 that fully immersed me in the possibilities of transformation (personal and organizational) of using an appreciative inquiry lens. It is difficult to put into words what it has meant to me to be exposed to and been a small part of the Appreciative Inquiry community. It enabled me to see a totally different way of being an academic and has given me new hope about how to think about this role as contributing to society.

At the heart of appreciative inquiry, as Dave and Suresh Srivastva have articulated it, is the core premise that "the appreciative mode of inquiry is a way of living with, being with, and directly participating in the varieties of social organization we are compelled to study. Serious consideration and reflection on the ultimate mystery of being engenders a reverence for life that draws the researcher to inquire beyond superficial experiences to deeper levels of the life-generating essentials and potentials of social existence" (Cooperrider and Srivastva 1987, 131).

At the heart of the appreciative inquiry effort was Dave Cooperrider, who in his modest and self-effacing way, truly inspired me to think differently about the ways that organizations and theories of organizations could make a difference. Dave's inspiration came in at least two ways. First, there was his writing and his practice of appreciative inquiry that teaches you about the transformative potential of using the affirmative question. It has changed how I do my research, how I conduct my classes, and how I think about small interventions in my work and family life. It has changed how I think and act, period.

Second, I had the opportunity to collaborate with Dave on an edited book (Cooperrider and Dutton 1999) that came from the conference called Organizational Dimensions of Global Change. In the practice of putting together this book I was able to see the way that Dave used appreciative inquiry as a means of interacting with the authors. In particular, I saw him transform the mundane task of briefly introducing chapters written by authors into a way of affirming and enacting the positive possibilities of the authors and the authors' messages. Prior to doing this book with Dave, I had edited six other books where we wrote introductory texts that summarized authors' contributions. I had never seen the positive possibilities of using this small narrative space as a place to construct the other in the most positive possible light and to see what this did to the readers of the book and the writers of the chapters. The tools that come from appreciative inquiry continue to generate great yield in my garden.

A second set of tools that has taken me into a community of practice that is transforming me is a set of dilemma-dialogue techniques introduced to me in the Nag's Heart conferences developed by Faye Crosby. I went to my first Nag's Heart conference five years ago, and it is one of the most memorable turning points in my professional life. The conference is theme-based and is designed around the simple idea that a conference should be restorative, nurturing, and fun, and should help you with meaningful dilemmas in your professional-personal life. At the heart of the conference is a method that I call the "group dilemma method," where each person has an equal share of the group's time to both share a dilemma and get undivided attention and help from the group on working with the dilemma. This format enacts the dilemma sharer as someone vulnerable, who needs help, and enacts the group as a set of collective helpers. This construction of the foundation for the dialogue is highly generative. Whenever I have been a part of a group that has used this method, we immerse quickly into meaningful dialogue that is instrumentally helpful, emotionally open, and often conceptually reframing. Beyond being really useful for generating ideas that seem to be meaningful to people's lives, this tool enacts a community in a particular way that I find really inspiring. It brings people to the table (literally and figuratively) in positions to provide constructive helping to each other. This is a practice I can live with and that gives me life. Again, did anyone in graduate school talk about which tools put you in touch with what people and with what effects? The more I have changed my toolkit to fit my current and desired identity, the more fully my garden has grown.

Crucial Nutrients

Finally, no tale of renewal from a gardening perspective would be complete without some reference to the nutrients that enable ideas and energy to grow. At least two kinds of nutrients seem critically important: one is the university environment; the other is my family environment. As a conclusion to my narrative of renewal, let me share a few comments on each.

First, I am deeply fortunate to be in the Department of Organizational Behavior and Human Resource Management at the University of Michigan. I see no better academic location for my garden. My local university environment has provided critical nutrients for renewal. The University of Michigan truly values interdisciplinary work. As someone who does this kind of work, this is fantastic fertilizer! Michigan is also a mecca for organizational studies. I have the opportunity to codirect ICOS (the Interdisciplinary Community of Organizational Studies) at Michigan that has more than three hundred faculty and PhD students from more than ten different schools as part of its community. I have had the privilege of codirecting it with both Mayer Zald (from sociology), Diane Vincokur (social work), and Michael Cohen (from the School of Information). All three have been inspirational and fun to work with as codreamers of the possibilities born from creating a vibrant organizational community. Each is a humble but terrific scholar who lives the commitment to doctoral education. In a way ICOS has provided an opportunity to be an institutional entrepreneur with a partner who complements and inspires. ICOS has weekly seminars, funds small grants and conferences, and basically builds bridges between intellectual locales for people interested in organizations. (See our website at http://www.si.umich.edu/ICOS/.) For a fence sitter, for someone who sees herself as having a very hybrid intellectual identity, ICOS is truly an intellectual home.

The University of Michigan also is a wonderful place for women faculty.

This is an important element in my own renewal process. For years my gender identity was something I buried or worked actively to disassociate from, fearing the consequences of a feminist stereotype (especially in a business school), and at some level, denying that my gender mattered. However, the more senior I become the more central is my identity as a woman faculty member, and the more thankful I am to be at the University of Michigan Business School and the university more generally. Structurally, Michigan is a supportive place for women. Women are in significant positions of power at the university. There are institutes such as IRWG (Institute for Research on Women and Gender) that are seedbeds for excellent interdisciplinary work on gender and issues of diversity. Beyond structure, there is a norm for an extension of informal support to each other that I increasingly realize is rare. For example, when I became department chair of OBHRM in the Business School, women department chairs from other places around the university offered to meet me and share their experiences. Women faculty in the Business School meet for informal dinners once a term. These occasions have brief programs that are designed to facilitate connection and career enhancement. Neighbors, as the self-organizing group calls itself, is a subtle but vital source of emotional and pragmatic support that keeps my garden growing.

Finally, I have a family—a wonderful partner and two daughters—who pour steady light into the garden. Like all families, we have our ups and downs, and they have certainly seen me through the dark days of winter, but their abiding love is a nutrient for which there is no substitute. I have been married to Lloyd Sandelands and we have had children since we started this career, so it has very much been a journey together. I have finally decided that I will not find a solution to the "work-family" tug, ever, and that this is okay. I would not trade having them in my life for anything. We refurbished an old barn into a house several years ago, and for the first time in my life, the physical family place feeds my soul. I have no idea how to factor the love of living space into my own renewal journey, but I believe it is significant.

Concluding Thoughts

Having taken the time to write this piece, I wonder why we rarely think about renewal journeys. I realize I have never considered renewal as an essential part of my own or others' professional life journeys. Yet, upon reflection, it is a stunning gap. It is a gap that can be eased through the sharing of practices, ideas, and inspirations extracted from our own and other's attempts to reenergize. For the chance to reflect and share, I thank you Ralph and Peter.

My reflections remind me of the relational component of our professional work. "Much more than the meeting rooms and offices where we work, our relationships with individuals and groups constitute the environment in which we live our professional lives" (Gersick, Bartunek, and Dutton 2000, 1026). Exercising care in how we chose our relational environments seems an important professional skill for renewal. For me this means remaining mindful about my collaboration partners and practices as vital contributors to my personal and professional growth. At the same time, it reminds me that I contribute to or take away from others' growth by how I participate with them in collaboration.

Beyond being mindful, this renewal story has inspired some new commitments. I now teach a three-part piece on "building effective relationships" as part of a required course in our doctoral program. I see this sequence as an attempt to encourage reflection about the relational competence needed to survive and thrive in this profession. I have designed workshops to give people space and an opportunity to talk about collaboration dilemmas in our professional practice. I am deeply committed to trying to help in creating safe space to learn and grow in ways that make the collaborations that compose our professional lives more growth enhancing.

The reflections also shed light on the importance of tools for doing our work and for constructing who we can become. They remind us to be careful and reflective about the tools we use to create our professional practice. This realization keeps me open to the identity-creating possibilities afforded by some tools over others. For me this is a radical and liberating frame for thinking about what practices undergird my professional work now and what practices I might like to add in the future.

Renewal means subtracting as well as adding. My weeding skills need constant honing so that I use them to balance my penchant for planting. It seems we would all benefit from supporting each others' attempts to weed our respective gardens. Perhaps the collective soil of the field would benefit from norms that endorsed rather than discouraged weeding.

In sum, the garden metaphor provides a generative way of thinking about how we grow ourselves in growing our work. It reminds us that there are real limits to how much we can control the conditions for growth. At the same time, it reminds us to pause, reflect, feel, and smell the roses that inhabit this privileged place that we call our work home. It helps us see that after winter, comes spring.

JEAN M. BARTUNEK

The Stuff in Jane Dutton's Garden

I'M IN AWE of anybody who can successfully plant a garden even once, let alone "perennially." I think I kept a ficus plant alive for a couple years once. But that was more than twenty years ago. Even my cactus plant died. (From too much water? Too little water? I could never tell.)

So when I first started reading Jane Dutton's chapter based on the image of a garden, of planting and weeding it so it can grow year after year, so the rhythms of fallow and fertile time can be sustained, I felt a little daunted and put off and—well—envious. Maybe *Jane* can have the sense of timing necessary to keep creating a lovely garden, but not me. Maybe *Jane* knows how to nurture something beautiful year after year after year, but that skill is way beyond my aspirations. And besides, I don't feel particularly comfortable in gardens that look perfect, especially when their beauty appears to be almost effortless.

But then I started reading Jane's chapter more carefully, and I let myself recognize that Jane was helping readers to see much more than something pristine and perfect. There is a bunch of other stuff in her garden besides an exquisite sense of timing and beautiful flowers. I found perilous detours and bumps, clocks, decay, a harbor or two, fences, passenger seats, giant to-do lists, corrosion, broken fences, a fair amount of construction, unreviewed manuscripts, a few defeats, life, death, lots of tools and a toolkit for them, ultimate mystery, some tables, Mecca, bridges, an old barn, and some basic arithmetic. Now *this* begins to look interesting. This I can relate to.

I heard recently that at the Animal Kingdom theme park in Florida there's a "tree" that's been created entirely out of ruined tires. The tree looks great. If ruined tires can be worked with to create something lovely, then imagine what can be done with all this other stuff in Jane's garden. Some of what's buried there may not seem like the usual fertilizer. But it certainly does an effective job.

The stuff buried in Jane's garden evokes several bipolar contrasts for me, and I want to use these as my own tools for digging. The contrasts that stand out for me are cyclical versus linear growth (detours, clocks, decay, fences, and a harbor), community versus individual attention (another harbor, unreviewed manuscripts, weeding, defeats, adding and subtracting), and life versus death (ultimate mystery). It is important to see these contrasts within the context of what has been created from them—the creative, generative, contributions that have been nurtured for years and continue to flower in Jane's garden—but those contributions will not be my emphasis.

Detours, Clocks, Decay, Fences, and a Harbor—Cyclical versus Linear Growth

Jane talks about the experiences that have been renewing for her, focusing primarily, though not exclusively, on difficulties she has experienced in the past and solutions she is finding in the present. Her approach appears at first blush to be linear: after times of great struggle she has finally figured out what she needs in order to find ongoing growth in her work.

In fact, though, when I dig deeper into Jane's narrative, her garden imagery, including the garden's detours, perilous bumps, decay, and clocks, is more cyclical than linear. Gardens need to be redeveloped every year. Renewal can only happen if there's something that needs it. There's a lot of snow every winter in Michigan, and so a lot of germinating that has to take place beneath the surface each year.

It can be easy to assume that cycles are circles. But this is not necessarily the case; spheres are cyclical as well, and Jane's depiction can be understood using spherical imagery. Although Jane encounters some of the same detours and bumps again and again, she has learned better to anticipate them and to develop routines to respond to them more effectively. Thus, she—and her garden—are not in exactly the same place with each new research collaboration. Maybe, in fact, the detours and bumps she experiences contribute to her garden's growth, as she learns to develop ways to deal with them.

At this juncture in her life Jane finds herself trying to break down fences, between her research and her teaching, between her professional and personal life, between her body and her mind. As she removes the fences she's learning that these different spheres of her life do enrich each other pretty well, and thus renew her research life.

Ecclesiastes said that there is a time to tear down and a time to build. Right now this is a time in Jane's life to tear down—at least in terms of fences. There have been and there will be other times to build fences, when each sphere of her life, her teaching, her research, her professional, her personal life, her mind, and her body will need continued development on its own terms as well. This pattern will be necessary not only for renewal in her research but also for renewal of the rest of her life, so that her research arises out of something deeper in her.

So—Jane experiences cyclical seasons and rhythms in the collaborative research process that she doesn't have control over. She learns that she's helped if she can find some harbors to protect her from the storms she now knows are going to come at some time or another. She has learned the importance of doing enough weeding to secure space for herself. She learns, over and over again, that it's important that she include herself as a person, as well as a researcher, in research collaborations. If a cyclical imagery holds true, she will, as she notes with respect to including herself as a person, need to learn these lessons again and again, but hopefully at deeper and more profound levels of understanding.

Another Harbor, Unreviewed Manuscripts, Weeding, Defeats, Adding, and Subtracting—Community versus Individual Attention

Jane's chapter is about her own renewal as a researcher. Yet she doesn't come to the garden alone much; she's usually there with others. Moreover, her work gets done in a much larger setting: in a large university and with multiple colleagues, some at her university and some elsewhere as part of her academic profession. What does individual renewal mean in a context like this?

This question invites another image: How much of what Jane's tilling is in an individual garden? How much is it part of a community garden in which many individuals have plots, and what one person plants is intertwined (both metaphorically or literally) with what others do?

Jane talks about how much she enjoys collaborating with others; she feels more alive in collaborations (at least in some of them) than when she's working independently. She also talks about how much she values working at the University of Michigan, how nurturing an environment that is for her. Since Jane works so much with others, her renewal processes are not hers alone; they affect and are affected by those of her collaborators and her larger academic setting.

Thus, if Jane brings all of herself into a collaboration that might stimulate and legitimate more personal sharing by her collaborators, it might stimulate their own more whole expression. If she doesn't, that might put a damper on such sharing.

My experience of working with Jane and Connie Gersick on the research that Jane alluded to was of gradually becoming more comfortable talking honestly and nondefensively about our own lives in conjunction with our study, and learning from both at the same time. Sometimes it was easier for us to talk about ourselves than to challenge each other to get on with the analyses that were awaiting attention before the study could go anywhere. But the study definitely was important for me in terms of learning to meld personal sharing with professional work.

Jane emphasizes the importance for her of weeding things out so that more light can get into the garden. She's doing a lot of weeding—of executive education, department chairing, reviewing manuscripts, recommendation letters, and some research projects, sometimes with a sense of defeat. Much of what she's weeding is requests that come to her from others and that, cumulatively, could probably consume her whole life if she let them. Many women have to learn that it's okay to put limits on such requests in order to have some time for themselves and their own contributions.

This is one area where the community versus individual garden is pertinent, and where I find myself feeling a little twinge as I read. Our profession depends on people who write reviews and recommendation letters and serve as chairs of departments and committees. This work is necessary for the community garden that enables individuals to have our own plots. Some people, like Jane, are asked to do much more of this than others are. What are appropriate boundaries for her, or for anyone, to establish regarding this type of work? How much should individuals think in terms of community even as they think of their own plots?—and vice versa? What's the role of a larger community in nurturing the ongoing growth of its most productive members, while not harming other members who need more assistance to develop?

Ultimate Mystery: Life versus Death

Taking her cue from David Cooperrider and Suresh Srivastva, Jane reflects on how the "ultimate mystery of being engenders a reverence for life that draws the researcher to inquire beyond superficial experiences to deeper levels of the life-generating essentials and potentials of social existence" (Cooperrider and Srivastva 1987, 131). This brief inquiry into the life-generating essentials in Jane's garden has suggested that they are certainly not all what we would likely imagine as life generating. In fact, some of them appear, on the surface, at least, to be pretty awful.

There is excitement and energy in Jane's garden, but there has also been death. Sometimes the garden has been full of colors; sometimes it has been colorless. Sometimes Jane has loved her work; sometimes she has wanted to leave academia. Sometimes she has felt free; sometimes she has almost suffocated. Sometimes she has experienced corrosive research relationships; sometimes she has experienced research relationships that invigorate her and take her to the limits of her compassionate responding.

A couple days after September 11, 2001, the wife of one of our BC doctoral students, Jegoo Lee, gave birth to their second child. Jegoo wrote me a wonderful note in which he said his wife and he "felt the mystery of nature again." They experienced this mystery even at a time when there was death and destruction around them. It seems to me that Jegoo's comment is quite apt for Jane's garden.

A garden requires both death and life on a regular basis; without one the other won't happen. Moreover, while a gardener can be sure that both processes will occur, he or she can't control the precise circumstances of the occurrence. Growth in the garden or elsewhere, however we may try to help it along, is, ultimately, a mystery of nature in which we are privileged to participate, a mystery of birth that may take place even in the midst of destruction. Perhaps there have been times when as Jane felt her research life was deadening she didn't recognize the small beginnings of personal and professional growth that were taking place and that are now blossoming. Perhaps at a time when a garden appears most alive it is particularly crucial to look for the seeds of decay and to accept them as inevitable. Perhaps attention to, and acceptance of, both processes is necessary for research and other parts of our lives to renew themselves on a continuous basis.

At the beginning of her chapter Jane talked about her garden in winter; at the end she spoke of smelling the roses. Bette Midler sang, "Just remember in the winter, far beneath the bitter snows, lies the seed, that with the sun's love, in the spring becomes the rose." This is the ultimate mystery: life results in death, and death gives forth life. While I might have started my reading of Jane's chapter feeling envious, I ended it feeling grateful. This chapter, by its deep reflection, by its willingness to explore issues that are not easy to talk about in public, by its honesty, by its creativity, by its expansive imagery, opens the way to appreciation of mystery and renewal not only in Jane's life and work but also in our own.

KEVIN CORLEY

Preparing to Be a Gardener

Renewal in Transition

A BIT OF CONTEXT for my thoughts before I share them. As I write this, I am in the process of finishing my dissertation and looking for my first faculty position. Graduation is less than six months away and there is a bit-tersweet feeling of losing and gaining at the same time. As I stand here on the threshold of my academic career, Jane's garden analogy really clicks for me. I feel as if I'm about to leave the fertile garden of my doctoral program and research advisor (where the dirt was rich, the history of abundant sea-sons great, and the potential for future harvests bountiful) and strike out into my own little patch of dirt with a lot of fertilizer (the really smelly kind) and a few seeds. Am I ready to be a gardener? What will my garden grow? Is it too much to hope that my garden plot sits on top of a lucrative gold mine?

The thing about the garden metaphor is that while it is extremely realis-tic in its depiction of the research life, it is also somewhat daunting. As Jane points out, gardeners must accept long time horizons and limited control (tenure review in only five years?), not to mention back-stiffening work and getting a lot of dirt under your fingernails. I know several real gardeners and it's hard work. Yet every one of them finds it rewarding. That is an interest-ing balance to think of as I commence my gardening—hard yet rewarding work. How does one strike this balance? What ratio of "yes, I'll do that" to "no, I don't have the time" results in hard but rewarding? Have I been prop-erly prepared to strike this balance?

Jane's chapter highlights for me how little of the academic process I will face in the coming years is learned in the formal aspects of a doctoral pro-gram. This is both exciting and frightening. From where I stand now, I can see that the seminars one takes as part of a doctoral program are extremely limited in what they offer (albeit very successful within their limited pur-pose). Much more is gained through a strong mentoring relationship with an experienced professor (which I was lucky enough to have) and from social interactions with others in the field (conferences, research projects, and so on). But feeling a distinct sensation that my brain is full after five years of doctoral study and that I couldn't possibly stuff another thing in it right now if I tried, what does it mean that a doctoral program teaches you so little about what is really important in having a successful career?

That is where Jane's thoughts and the others offered in this book provide bona fide insight. I see plainly now that this transition I am preparing for (from doctoral student to assistant professor) needs to be a transition mixed with a healthy dose of renewal. For if renewal is not part of the transition, the conditions will be ripe for the growing of weeds, the building of fences, and the deterioration of the soil which all good research projects depend. Renewal is not just for those with well-cultivated gardens, it is necessary throughout one's career, even near the beginning. Making renewal a part of every transition (whether from one rank of professorship to another, or from one stage of family life to another, or even from one research project to another) helps guarantee those walls and weeds will not appear as quickly and that the garden will remain vibrant and strong.

To those other doctoral students and junior faculty just starting their gardens, I urge you to think about what you would write about yourself and your research colleagues twenty years from now. What do you want your garden to look like? Who do you want to have toiled with you in your garden? Will your garden be recognized for its exotic plant life, for its immaculate pathways, or for its diversity in species? Obviously, the people in this book have done quite well for themselves and they all have taken different approaches to that success. But a commonality among all of them, and one explicitly discussed by Jane, is that they depended on others and were dependable for others in the projects that truly mattered to them as humans. They grew as much as the "plants" in their "gardens" did and they were an integral part of the growth of others. What will you and I do to engender this type of growth in others? What will you and I do to recognize the need for renewal and some focused growth of our own? When we're asked to look back on our careers twenty years hence, what type of legacy will you and I be writing about? To think about these questions now is not too soon, because, after all, in the garden of life, the seed you plant today becomes the tree you rely on for shade and comfort tomorrow.

The Community of Scholars

The "community of scholars" is a good familiar phrase. Most of us will have encountered the phrase while studying philosophy of science. Whether we identify with Kuhn or Lakotos or Feyerabend or Dewey or Campbell or Merton or Lyotard or Foucault, we are all familiar with the concept. We enact our community of scholars daily when we frame our papers for our colleagues, check on citations, write peer reviews, or direct our students to the literature.

The community of scholars is an intellectual enterprise focused on contribution to knowledge. We collectively determine the research agenda. We adjudicate on successful contributions to that agenda. We collectively decide just what we know about organization and management when we endorse the views of our colleagues in our own papers.

A community of scholars is personal. It is a small group of academics, most of whom know each other. There was (arguably) a single community of American organizational scholars, that is, the Academy of Management of the 1970s. As the field grew, attempts to map the developments were rampant (Pfeffer 1982; Astley and Van de Ven 1983; Burrell and Morgan 1979). Today we tacitly accept the fragmentation of the community into the many subcommunities of management and organizational studies.

Because community is personal, our induction into the community of scholars still bears the imprint of apprenticeship and personal mentoring. The formal task interdependent of coauthored research is often the cause (or the effect) of friendships. It is difficult to separate work life and home life. Jane suggests it may not be such a good idea anyway.

The community of scholars is hierarchical. It is characterized by an interplay of individual effort and decision making and community-level outcome and judgment. As authors (or more commonly as collaborating coauthors;

Bozeman, Street, and Fiorito 1999) we do the work of the community. We make the decisions on research design or research reporting. We make these decisions within our own understandings of the community standards. But these decisions always involve a trade-off of resources (time, dollars, access) against the criteria (rigor, relevance) of the community.

Then, we must subordinate ourselves to community judgment in the peer review process. Peer review acts as both a filtering process and a tempering process. In the first instance, peer review is a quality-control mechanism (see Campanario 1998a, 1998b, for a comprehensive review of the literature). Reviewers enforce the minimum standards of the community. They attempt to eliminate manuscripts that are unlikely to represent a contribution to knowledge. It is important to note that rejection of manuscripts reflects resources as well as quality standards. For example, rejection rates in organization and management journals are much higher than in the more affluent natural sciences. Acceptance by peer review signals to the community that a particular manuscript has the potential to contribute to knowledge. Acceptance in a peer-reviewed journal does not indicate a contribution has been made. Our colleagues make that decision when they read and incorporate the new insights and findings in their own teaching, writing, and understanding of organizational life. In fact, we know that a very large proportion of published journal articles are rarely cited; thus, these articles may not have much influence on the body of knowledge.

Peer review has developed as an important tempering process, as well. There is a strong developmental component in the peer review process, which can enhance the quality of journal articles. Beyer, Chanove, and Fox (1995) suggest that this effect may be the most important effect of the review process. Many authors attest to the ultimately helpful input of reviewers, while universally acknowledging the initially negative emotions associated with receiving reviews (Cummings and Frost 1985; Frost and Stablein 1992; Frost and Taylor 1996).

Journal publication is not the only source of knowledge. Within the journal system, special issues have become an important means to open the community to new ideas and approaches, and to consolidate developments. Here peer review plays a lesser role. Annual reviews, handbook chapters, book chapters, and books all have a place in contributing to our knowledge of organization. While peer reviews do play a part in the developing of these outputs, their function has more to do with shaping and sharpening the knowledge being communicated than it is about filtering and eliminating work produced in the community. In a sense, while the journals (certainly the more prestigious ones) constrain what we read by their review processes, other outlets allow more work to be seen, often by a wider audience. This serves to float more ideas and information into the arena than might otherwise be seen. The burden in the shaping process lies more with the reader than is the case with strongly edited products, but the existence of both sources (those filtered and those shaped) makes for a rich array of stimulants to debate and further research.

When the community of scholars meets the modern university, problems ensue. Perhaps the most important is the clash of ends-oriented and means-oriented rationalities. For the community of scholars, knowledge is paramount. The bureaucratic university tends to focus on the measurable means, that is, publication quantity and quality, rather than the more diffuse end of contribution to knowledge. In the realm of ethics, concern for visible compliance to the means of ethics-review procedures can obscure the end of good research practice.

For the community of scholars, the common good is more important than the individuals who make a contribution. The university tends to individualize. Individual career success, dependent on regular publication, may be divorced from the community concern for the progress of knowledge, which may sometimes come from thoughtful, slowly developing work. As Jean points out, the community also depends on the energy and unrewarded commitment of individuals to take on the tasks of reviewers, editors, association officers, and so forth.

Of course, the community of scholars is more than an intellectual enterprise. The community is a real social group made up of real people living a real life. We don't wish to denigrate the individual scholars. Individual career success is necessary for community success. We feel that by keeping community and knowledge salient, we might more closely align individual and career success. When Jane tells us about tending her garden, we see a scholar who takes the personal and the community seriously.

Jane and Kevin implicitly complain that they didn't learn about the social side of the community of scholars in graduate school. Jane has begun to research it (Gersick, Bartunek, and Dutton 2000) and teach about it formally. Perhaps it is time for all of us to treat the concept of community more holistically. We have some ideas about what that means for the lives we lead. Because community is personal, interactions and judgments are intensely meaningful, especially for junior members of the community (Ashford 1996a). For example, when we read the editor's letter and reviewer comments, the "community of scholars" can become a pretty abstract notion, even when the feedback is intended to be positive! (Murnighan 1996.) The softer connotations of community and caring are not very visible. We must try to remain aware of the emotional impact we have on colleagues.

We will say more about the social side of the community of scholars in our closing comments to this book. At this juncture, we note the heavy price that scholars pay, particularly those starting their careers, as a result of encounters with their community that they experience as toxic. As ambitious researchers striving to advance knowledge through our efforts, we will surely experience our share of emotional pain as we spend endless hours trying to get a project launched or written up, as we realize that our studies haven't worked out as hoped, or we learn that our manuscript has been rejected. We know implicitly, or through our training, that there is no gain without some pain along the way; that some experiences when we do our research will produce anger, frustration, and disappointment; and that this is part of the normal life of a scholar. Such pain becomes toxic when the way it is delivered or received serves to markedly undermine our self-esteem, to cause us to lose hope, when we are left feeling isolated and disconnected from our colleagues (Frost 2003). We experience toxicity when others treat us with indifference, or give us feedback on our work that is careless of our feelings or is malicious. It comes from the systems that dehumanize our lived experience as academics and from leadership that needlessly politicizes the life of the community.

We share Jane's interest in the contributions of the appreciative inquiry tradition and positive organizational scholarship (Cameron, Dutton, and Quinn 2003). We are especially inspired by the work of Ludema, Wilmot, and Srivastva (1997) on organizational hope. In a massive review of the religious and secular literatures on hope, they identify four core qualities: "It is born in relationship; inspired by the conviction that the future is open and can be influenced; sustained through moral dialogue; and generative of positive affect and action" (1017). The research journey is essentially a journey of hope. Intellectually, we are persuaded that science is the social enterprise of a community of scholars. Our own experience and that of our colleagues (for example, as reported in Frost and Stablein 1992) confirms the importance of human relationship in advancing organizational scholarship. As an applied form of inquiry, we experience the community as a hopeful one, dedicated to viewing the future as open to positive change. As scholars with emancipatory leanings, we have found the community to usually be open to dialogue and minority voices. For the most part, our experience of the community has been an arena of positive affect and fondness. Any contribution that we have made owes much to our colleagues in this community of scholars. Hopefulness promotes the renewal of research journeys.

Swimming Against the Tide

Aligning Values and Work

I GREW UP IN New England, near the sea, and like everyone else there, I learned that swimming against the tide was exhausting, especially where the currents ran fast. Now, I am a professor, with left-wing values, working at a school and in academic fields that are not known for liberalism. I sometimes wonder whether I have forgotten that early lesson. I should know that it is going to be difficult, given who I am and when and where I have chosen to swim. But every time the constant struggle to align my values and my work exhausts me, I am surprised by my inability to make easy progress. Good New Englander that I am, I blame myself for not working hard enough or skillfully enough; if only I were better at this or that, I could get where I want to go with ease, like others seem to do. Sometimes I long for broader encouragement and appreciation. But as my more pragmatic husband tells me, "How can you expect to be appreciated, when what you're doing is a criticism of the status quo?" In this chapter, I explore some of the difficulties that are inevitable when swimming against the tide and discuss some strategies that seem to help.

Fortunately, half of the time, the tide turns, giving much-needed assistance. And there has been some fine company on this swim—fellow swimmers and a support boat of people who have generously offered sustenance, bad jokes, and emotional encouragement. Their names, and citations to their work, appear scattered throughout this chapter as advisors, students, coauthors, colleagues, friends, and family. They have given of their time and skills, illuminating problems I have been struggling to solve. Like any long-distance swimmer, I could not have continued without their company and support.

In telling this story of swimming against the tide, I am writing especially to those of you who—like me—have values that are not particularly well aligned with the values of your colleagues, university, or field. My personal values center on a concern about unfair inequalities—especially those associated with class, race, and gender. Although your values, work demands, job, and priorities may be different than mine, we all face some variant of a struggle to align who we are with what work demands of us. Perhaps some parts of my story will echo some parts of yours.

There is a theoretical framework that has helped me conceptualize and anticipate the difficulties I have encountered. The usefulness of this framework is not an accident: it was developed by two of my PhD students, Maureen Scully and Deb Meyerson. We share many of the same values, and I thought that when they became professors, they might well be faced with some of the same dilemmas I was facing. So, during the years they were students at Stanford, when I was dealing with tough decisions or obstacles, I would sometimes talk frankly with them about my goals and concerns. They would offer advice and later, we would analyze what seemed to work and what did not. These conversations were a comfort and a help to me, but Deb and Maureen put them to more scholarly use. They developed a theoretical framework, "Tempered Radicalism" (1995; see also Meyerson 2001), to describe what they had observed. A tempered radical is someone who attempts to balance his or her own values with the opposing demands of a less radical work context. This is a delicate balancing act. Too much conformity in order to succeed can compromise a tempered radical's values, leading to cooptation; too little conformity can result in the tempered radical being ostracized, marginalized, devalued, or excluded—leaving few resources that can be mobilized to work effectively for change. A tempered radical runs the constant risks of a co-opted kind of success or the failure that comes with marginalization, and from time to time, experiences both. If your values are more conservative than your work context, or different in some other way, you may face many of the same kinds of dilemmas as a tempered radical, even though the content of your values differ from mine.

I am a prototypical tempered radical, having vacillated between co-optation and marginalization, as well as experiencing occasional times when I could find a balance. In these balanced moments, at the risk of mixing my metaphors, swimming against the tide seemed to be a fine way to spend my life. I like working for something I believe in, even if or maybe especially if, it is a struggle to succeed. Most tempered radicals encounter the same ups and downs, but these experiences take a particular shape, depending on the context where a person works and the values he or she is committed to. Below, I briefly describe the context (school and academic field) where I work and the personal values that are central to this story.

The Context: The Graduate School of Business at Stanford University

Stanford University is a private school with a large endowment. Compared to other universities, it is relatively conservative, especially among its alumni / alumnae. Liberal political values thrive in the humanities departments and some of the social sciences, but in the rest of the university (especially the Hoover Institute and the business school where I work) very conservative ideologies predominate. In addition, like most business school faculty, my colleagues tend to produce teaching and research that, directly or indirectly, aims to help managers (like the MBA students we teach) improve the productivity and profitability of their organizations. This managerial orientation is congruent with conservative positions on many economic and social issues.

There is one fact about Stanford University that is critical for understanding my story. Stanford has also been relatively very slow to hire and promote women to tenure, ranking nineteenth out of a group of twenty-one top universities in percentage of women faculty (Strober et al. 1993). Stanford's business school has been especially slow to hire and promote women; of the top schools, during the last two decades, usually only Dartmouth has had fewer women on its business school faculty. Although the number of women at Stanford's business school has increased in recent years, other comparable schools have improved even more, leaving our relative standing unchanged. For a decade after I came to Stanford in 1977, there were only one or two women in any department in the business school. I was the first to get tenure, the first to become a full professor, the first to get an endowed chair. Even now, as I write this in 2001, there are only three full professors who are women, in a school of eighty-five tenured or tenure-track faculty. Minority faculty members in the business school are even scarcer. Today, African American faculty at Stanford's business school can still be counted on the fingers of one hand, and none has tenure. Mexican Americans are also scarce, as are other minorities. As this chapter will make clear, these aspects of my local working environment have daily relevance and have had a deep impact on the ways my personal values have been reflected in my research.

Why Not Pick an Environment Where Your Values Are Shared?

I know why I came to Stanford, but it is harder to figure out why I have stayed. A few years ago I had a long discussion with a humanities professor at Stanford who shares my political views. When we had finished talking, he sat back and, laughing, said, "What's a nice girl like you doing in a place like this" The reasons for my choice of Stanford, after graduate school in 1977, seem understandable, and may still be important. Stanford was certainly at-tractive: it was and is a fine university with many intellectual and financial resources; a bright and sometimes brilliant student body; and faculty who, on the whole, are deeply committed to their research. In addition, to be honest, there is the weather/beauty factor. California is warm and sunny; palm trees, the Golden Gate bridge, San Francisco, and magnificent sea cliffs seemed fair substitutes for the icy gray winters of New England. I might have been more comfortable if I had taken a first job in a psychology department (my PhD was in experimental social psychology). However, business schools valued the five years I had spent as a consultant and manager before graduate school. (They did not seem to have noticed that my clients were mostly fed-eral government agencies, such as the Peace Corps, VISTA, and OEO, in-volved in the "war on poverty.") In contrast, psychology departments seemed to think these years of my life were irrelevant. I wanted my whole life to "count," and when I was a prospective assistant professor, five years seemed a lot of living to discount.

In addition, my political beliefs seemed, at that time, to be a positive rea-son to be at a business school. The street protests and demonstrations that had been so common during the late sixties and early seventies had largely died down by the time I graduated with a PhD in 1977. Increasingly, it seemed to me, the policy changes that would affect inequality—income dis-tribution and discrimination—would have to take place off the streets, inside private-sector organizations and the government. By working in a business school, I hoped I could influence the next generation of organizational lead-ers to pay more attention to the needs of those who have less, both inside and outside their companies. So, the die was cast: I came to work in a con-servative business school. I would be training the future "captains of indus-try," working with people whose political values, for the most part, were quite unlike mine. I would be working, said one of my leftie friends at a goodbye party in the East, "In the belly of the beast."

I certainly wasn't the only political liberal at Stanford's business school, but I was, for almost a decade, the only woman or one of two women. Be-cause of that, I experienced many of the kinds of blatant as well as subtle discrimination that Rosabeth Kanter (1977) described in her research on the effects of solo status. The blatant gender problems I encountered then have dramatically decreased as female faculty members have become somewhat more common at Stanford's business school and in universities across the country; my male colleagues have gotten used to the presence of women faculty and many of them have gone out of their way to be supportive.[1]

1. Jeff Pfeffer, Jerry Porras, Rod Kramer, Bob Jaedicke, Jim Van Horne, David Kreps, Anat Admati, Pam Haunschild, Roberto Fernandez, Jim March, Hal Leavitt, Gene Webb—these are just a few of the people at the Stanford Business School who have gone out of their way to be helpful.

Nevertheless, gender issues—some subtle and a few not—continue to plague everyday life for women faculty at Stanford and elsewhere, in ways that some men and women are not aware of. The problems faced by racial minorities are even more acute. Class issues still have large effects on which students are accepted, which ones graduate, who gets faculty positions and promotions, and whose contributions are seen as valuable. It is also a class issue to consider those Stanford employees who are not students and faculty. Stanford's inequalities are a microcosm of those in the surrounding society.

For me, the daily experience of gender difficulties at work had a benign effect: it focused my diffuse concern with unjust inequalities on a concrete political goal—to find ways to alleviate the subtle as well as the more obvious aspects of discrimination, in this local setting, in my academic field nationally, and—through my research, teaching, and activism—in organizations, broadly defined.[2] My personal experiences of discrimination, as well as my years of working with antipoverty governmental programs, are relevant here because they impacted my research. These experiences enabled me to see some blind spots in prior scholarship—insights that I could translate into concepts and hypotheses. However, relying on my own experience for conceptual insight has also limited what I have achieved. Over time I have come to focus more on gender inequalities than on race and class, where my background has been a source of privilege. This is an issue I am working to resolve in my current research . . . but that is jumping ahead of the story I am telling here.

The problem is, and always has been, how to balance my personal value commitments with the demands of my career. I wanted to do work that would combat gender-, race-, and class-based inequalities. I also wanted to achieve success as an academic, earning tenure and doing fine research. And I wanted to have enough credibility within Stanford and within my profession nationally, so that my efforts for change would be effective. I had chosen to work within the system, not outside of it—a classic tempered radical position—and I was about to experience each of the dilemmas and difficulties Meyerson and Scully describe. This chapter tells the story of this balancing act. I'll begin with the last year of graduate school, when I chose the topic of my dissertation.

---

2. At the time I became an assistant professor, there were only a handful of prominent women scholars in the field of organizational behavior. For example, Jan Beyer, Karlene Roberts, Rosabeth Kanter, and Lotte Bailyn were fine researchers, committed to helping other women. Although the word "role model" is overused and makes most of us wince, I was very grateful to find older women who were living testimonials to the possibility of survival—with grace. I was surprised and delighted when each, in her own way, did so much to help me grow and adjust.

The Pretenure Years (1977–1984)

RESEARCH

As a graduate student in the social psychology PhD program at Harvard, I studied distributive justice and relative deprivation. At that time, most of the study participants in distributive justice, equity, and exchange research (indeed, in most psychological research) were middle-class college students, with little experience of relying on their pay to support themselves and possibly a family. I was surprised at the experimental results reported in the literature that suggested people who earned relatively little compared themselves as individuals to other similar individuals and were satisfied with their low wages, finding reasons that they, as individuals, did not deserve more. I thought that equity theories based on the reactions of these relatively privileged young people were probably unrepresentative of those who held lower-paid jobs or were disadvantaged by sex, race, or ethnicity. Why didn't disadvantaged people make group-to-group comparisons and feel discontent, because members of their group earned less than members of more privileged groups, rather than blaming themselves as individuals for their low wages? Tom Pettigrew, my dissertation advisor, introduced me to theories of relative deprivation, which gave me a theoretical base to explore these hypotheses. He and my other advisors, Shelley Taylor, Jim Jones, and Sandy Jencks, were supportive as I insisted that the participants in my study be lower-income assembly line workers, much to the puzzlement of other faculty and students in my department. This was going to be an experiment conducted with working-class adults, in a "real-life" field setting. Getting a company's permission to study assembly line workers was tough (I eventually was reduced to asking my father for help in gaining access to the company where he worked). It was also hard to find a research assistant willing to help me collect data during the graveyard shift in Roxbury, a dangerous area of Boston.

The study participants watched a documentary videotape portraying people who held a management job or a blue-collar job at a company much like their own (Martin 1982b). Participants were then randomly assigned to react to one of four pay plans, showing how much the people in the videotape earned. In these pay plans, the pay distribution was experimentally varied. The pay inequality between the management job and the blue-collar job was either large or small and the inequality within the blue-collar classification was either large (high variance) or small (low variance). The participants evaluated blue-collar pay rates to be just and fair in all conditions except one: where the inequality between labor and management was large and where the variance in pay within the blue-collar classification was small. In other words, even large labor-management inequalities did not cause discontent, so long as just a few blue-collar workers earned almost as much as the managers. Relative deprivation theory neatly anticipated these results (by predicting when comparisons to dissimilar managers rather than similar blue-collar workers would seem relevant to these workers). Nevertheless, I was surprised that these blue-collar workers were so willing to accept being paid so much less than managers.

I continued this line of work at Stanford, exploring this apparent tolerance of injustice in a series of experiments and theoretical review papers focusing on how equity and exchange theories were formulated in ways that underestimated discontent with between-group economic inequalities (such as labor versus management, blacks versus whites, men versus women), in part because most study participants were relatively privileged (for example, Martin 1981; Martin and Murray 1983). With a series of PhD student coauthors (Alan Murray and Bob Bies), I expanded and tested theories of justice, such as relative deprivation, that focused on large-scale, intergroup sources of discontent and predicted violent protests and revolutions (Martin and Murray 1984). I also studied gender inequality, and with Greg Northcraft (1982) I examined how pay inequalities and chances of promotion into managerial positions affected female secretaries' satisfaction with their own, low pay levels. With Phil Brickman and Alan Murray (1984), I found that female secretaries' discontent with (male) managerial pay levels did not predict their willingness to join in a protest against their low pay; they would join if and only if they thought the outcome might be positive. Pragmatism, rather than moral outrage, was determining protest behavior. These results, combined with other researchers' findings (for example, Pettigrew 1967; Crosby 1982) lead to a reconsideration of the ways feelings of injustice affected individual and collective behavior, on the streets and in organizations.

So, here I was in a business school, studying protests and revolutions, as well as causes of discontent among working-class employees. In contrast, most of my colleagues were doing research of more (apparent) direct relevance to the captains of industry who were our school's alumni/ae. In my research I was asking why people seemed to accept what seemed to me to be flagrantly unequal and unfair pay distributions. I was interested in finding out just what it would take before they would engage in collective action to improve their situations. Getting entry into companies to conduct this research, as you might expect, was time consuming and difficult. For example, I asked companies to let me study how discontented their secretaries were when they compared secretarial to managerial pay levels. Fortunately, some good-hearted and broad-minded executives were willing to give me entry. Others were not. Getting my colleagues to see the relevance of this work, in a business school context, was also a tough sell. Fortunately, most of my colleagues in my field had some sense of why this kind of work might be interesting. Although the focus of my interest, on lower-status employees' feelings of injustice, was unusual for a business school, the theories I was working with were in the mainstream of social psychology and my use of experimental methodology was also orthodox, an asset I would shortly come to appreciate.[3] The fact that some business schools (although not ours) had a strong commitment to labor economics or industrial relations also helped acceptance of my work.

My intellectual interests, however, were about to take a sharp—and unanticipated—turn. One of the delights of being at Stanford is the PhD students. They help you accomplish things you know you want to do, and they challenge and question you (so you don't do some unfortunate things that you might otherwise have done). Sometimes they bring entirely new interests into your academic life. In the late 1970s, Alan Wilkins wanted me to advise him on his PhD thesis, which focused on a novel topic, organizational culture. I told him I couldn't do it because I didn't know anything about the subject. Undeterred, he began to bring me articles about culture, mostly from anthropology, and leave them on the corner of my desk. He'd come back in a day or two, replacing old articles with new. I noticed that when I had a bit of time between classes, I would read something from the culture pile, rather than the stack of justice papers relevant to my research. Inferring my attitudes from my behavior, I eventually agreed to advise Alan on his thesis (although he seemed to teach me as much or more than I taught him).

I became fascinated with cultural theory and research. In retrospect, I wonder whether it was because I had begun to suspect that organizational cultures might provide one explanation for why workers seemed so willing to accept the status quo, while others challenged it. Caren Siehl, a doctoral student of unquenchable good spirits, was my collaborator in many of these first culture studies. With Caren, I wrote ("just for fun," I told myself) a paper that studied how John De Lorean (at that time, a vice president at General Motors) created a counterculture in his own division of the firm (Martin and Siehl 1983). The dominant culture of General Motors emphasized conformity, loyalty, and subservience to one's bosses. To counter this dominant culture, De Lorean modeled dress norms that deviated slightly but significantly from the conservative dress favored elsewhere in the company. He told stories and created rituals that reinforced the values he was trying to instill. His was a tempered radical's balancing act, deviating from the dominant culture just enough but not too much. I too was a deviant in writing this paper. It was odd, to say the least, for an experimental social psychologist to

3. If I had done postmodern or even qualitative work I doubt I would have been hired or gotten tenure at that time, or perhaps even now.

study stories and rituals. It was odder still that the methodology we used was qualitative.

By the time this paper was published, De Lorean had been asked to leave General Motors, had founded, and folded, his own sports car company, and had ended up in jail for drug use. Undeterred by this example of the dangers of deviance, I gathered an exceptionally bright and brave group of PhD students, including Caren, Mary Jo Hatch, Melanie Powers, Martha Feldman, Sim Sitkin, and Michael Boehm. Soon we were doing a raft of studies about the ways stories in organizations were used to generate commitment to a culture. We did experiments showing that stories (about a single instance, an "n" of one) were more convincing than solid statistics (based on an "n" of many) (for example, Martin 1982a; Martin and Powers 1983a and 1983b). We found that employees in a wide variety of organizations told common stories to explain what was unique about their organization. They didn't realize these same seven stories (with only the details changed) were told in virtually all organizations we studied—a phenomenon we called the "uniqueness paradox" (Martin Feldman et al. 1983). These stories focused on acquiescence and resistance to managerial attempts to control employees' values as well as their behavior; in these papers we noted, but did not take a critical approach, to these control issues—first signs of a growing conformity to a managerial ethos. At this point in my career, I was making good progress publishing research in both the cultural and the justice areas, but a critical focus congruent with my personal values was more evident in my justice research than in my cultural studies.

GENDER ON THE JOB

Bringing my personal values in line with my work was also difficult in the task domains outside of research. I was also doing the usual things an assistant professor does: working impossibly long hours, getting journal rejections, and teaching the usual load of MBA courses and working—constantly—with doctoral students. The one unusual aspect of my job was the fact that my sex and my political values made me different from other faculty members. I certainly wasn't the only political liberal at the business school, although I might have been the most leftist. However, I was, for a long time, one of very few women there. At the beginning of my time at Stanford, quite a few faculty members were simply unprepared for having female colleagues, and this resulted in some difficulties. I will describe the nature of these difficulties briefly, as they shaped my life and my research interests and gave a positive impetus, eventually, to moving my research interests closer to my personal values.

There were some blatant acts of discrimination, especially during the years I was an assistant professor, before other women joined the business school faculty. These are the easiest to describe, as the problem is evident. For example, a colleague invited all faculty interested in teaching abroad for a quarter to meet a visiting professor from Paris. I accepted with pleasure. When I arrived for the lunch, I walked toward the table where the (male) faculty members were seated with the visitor. My host stood up, greeted me warmly, and escorted me to a separate table, where my host's wife and the wife of the Parisian professor were seated. I was embarrassed and disappointed that I would not get a chance to meet the Parisian visiting professor, but my host was a senior faculty member. I took a deep breath, had polite small talk over lunch with the wives, and waited for a "teachable" moment to confront my host in private. That afternoon I knocked on his office door and asked him why this particular seating arrangement had been chosen. He said, "I wanted to be sure you were comfortable and thought you would have more in common with the women rather than the professors." I explained with some trepidation and a lot of self-control why it would have been better to seat me with the other professors. My host was well-meaning and sincere, I believe, but this was by no means an isolated incident. Another example, from a different context, highlights the importance of these kinds of incidents. Learning to teach MBAs was an essential part of a faculty job and learning to do it well was difficult for all of us. Women faculty, though, got an especially big dose of trouble. My first day of class, year after year, some MBAs would walk out as soon as they realized "Professor Martin" was female. Although such blatant discrimination, in relation to essential issues such as teaching and pay, was not uncommon in my first decade at Stanford, in recent years it has become rare, for all of the women on our faculty.

There is a second, more subtle kind of gender discrimination that still occurs, albeit with less frequency now that more women have joined the faculty ranks. Although these incidents may seem trivial, they undermine the professional legitimacy of women with a slow but constant—drip, drip, drip—reminder that a woman cannot be a professor. My mail would come addressed to all kinds of Martins, few of whom were named Joanne. "Professor Joseph Martin" was the most popular option. (Just last week Joseph/Joanne got another letter, so this problem has not disappeared.) Discouraged, I would turn from my mail and answer the phone, "Hello, this is Professor Martin." Sometimes, more than once, the caller would respond, "May I speak to Professor Martin please?" The library was no refuge; repeatedly, they wouldn't let me borrow books. When I went to find out what the problem was, it turned out they were convinced I was a secretary without borrowing privileges of my own. These may seem to be trivial slights, and, compared to violent forms of prejudice, they are. Nevertheless, incidents like these were constant reminders that my professional identity was simply inconceivable to some people.

These gender-related difficulties were demoralizing and tricky to handle. Should I label the problem when it wasn't evident to others, waiting for a teachable moment? Should I swallow my discomfort? My dissertation advisor (a prodigious scholar), Shelley Taylor, offered me comfort and solid advice ("When you get really angry, for mental health reasons, you should express that anger. However, it's better to kick a tampax machine than a senior colleague"). She also gave me a chance to coauthor a paper (1986) about "All the things your advisor never told you," which described ways to cope with some of the dilemmas that face assistant professors, including those who are women and who are minorities.

The other side of the coin was that I was welcomed by women, by minorities, and by some white men, from all over campus. All this helped, as did my contacts with the "one woman" in each of Stanford's departments. Sometimes this welcome, especially from large numbers of students, overwhelmed me. There was no way I could create a research publication record sufficient to get tenure and be responsive to the numbers of students who wanted contact with me. Some of these students had normal kinds of concerns, but the majority were coming to me for reasons associated with my sex and, later, my known concern for minority issues. When I held office hours, the line of students wound around the hallway corners and out into the terrace. My expertise, it was assumed, would include abortion and pregnancy counseling, sexual harassment advice, gender research, and the presumption (on the part of both men and women) that I could be trusted to provide comfort and sympathy for personal problems. I tried to hint, and even explain directly, that I was unqualified as a personal counselor. But still the line increased. Every minute doing these tasks takes time from research, and that is what ultimately counts at a place like Stanford, especially at tenure time. Tenure cases come in three categories: easy yes, relatively easy no, and borderline—difficult to decide. Discrimination enters primarily in the borderline cases, where the candidate's relationships with internal and external letter writers can enhance evaluations and where subjective judgments provide a place for unconscious prejudice to creep in. I knew that as a woman in a male environment, I couldn't afford to be a borderline case; my publication record had to be strong.

Other more formal demands on my time multiplied. Committees and theses needed "the woman's" point of view—as if one woman could represent all women. In no time at all, I was the faculty advisor for the Black MBA club, the faculty sponsor of the (at that time, undercover) gay and lesbian MBA organization, a faculty affiliate of the feminist studies program for undergraduates, and the only untenured member of the university president's affirmative action task force. All these requests took time, even if all I sometimes did was say "no" gently because there simply weren't enough hours in the day. I felt deeply torn when I had to say no to such requests, but I justified these refusals by hoping that if I earned tenure, I would do more good for women and minorities in the long run. And often, I said "yes" because there were few others to talk to about these issues, or because I did not want to be unkind. This kind of work demand affects many women and minorities (including me, still), and the costs are high, as gender researchers have shown:

1. This is what Joyce Fletcher (1999) has labeled "invisible work," because in jobs as varied as engineering and academics it is seldom rewarded. Indeed, in some kinds of environments, including my own, this kind of work is openly *de*valued ("Why are you hand-holding them? They are adults").

2. Solo status is a two-edged sword (Kanter 1977): visibility is easy to attain, but your failures are as visible as your successes. What's worse, a white male working in a white male world may have a bad day (or a bad week, month, decade), but if you are a solo (one of a kind, or one of very few) every misstep is attributed to your minority status ("Women just can't handle this kind of job"). This lends a disproportionate seriousness to any mistake ("I will ruin the chances of other women"), and it can also provide a source of support ("I can feel these others cheering for me, and if I can succeed, their chances will be enhanced").

3. Being one of a very few makes it difficult to get frank feedback; people tend to be unfairly critical or too easy on your work (Kanter 1977). It is like flying an airplane without instruments to tell you your altitude, tilt, direction, or speed.

4. For academics, lawyers, and consultants seeking partner status, as well as "fast-track" employees in corporations, chances for promotion are determined in the first few years of employment. For most women in academia, the tenure clock and the biological clock coincide. This is perhaps the single most important instance of institutionalized sexism in academia (Martin 1994). If a woman faculty member wants to bear children, she often has to do it pretenure. When the seven-year tenure clock was introduced, it was designed to protect faculty (some of whom were women) from being exploited in untenured positions, with no chance for review. Arguably, no one planned to construct a tenure process that put women who wanted to have children at a systematic disadvantage. But that is what the seven-year "up or out" tenure rule does, because by the time women get a PhD and then work seven years, their child-bearing years are coming to an end. And although this rule may not have been introduced to disadvantage women, its perpetuation without due consideration of gender differences in its implications does indeed seem

intentional. Roughly nine months after a fine celebration of my first promotion (after three years, to nontenured associate), I gave birth to a son. Some of the colleagues I most respected announced their approval in these terms:

"Well . . . you weren't productive enough before. Now, you'll never make it."

"How wonderful you are going to have a family! I am really pleased. Of course, now you'll never become famous enough to get tenure."

These remarks (in the first case, a well-meaning goad to publish from a friend) made me mad, and I set out to prove them wrong. This I tried to do, and it is especially clear in retrospect that it was the people in my support boat who made it possible for me to continue swimming against the tide. Doing it alone is simply not possible. Below are the types of support I am most grateful for.

1. An Understanding Partner

Easier said than done, I know. My husband did half of what Hochschild (1989) has called the "second shift," including diapers, laundry, and cleanup. This is rare. One day, when my child was very young, I sat in a faculty meeting and estimated who, among the married faculty present, had washed the socks he was wearing. My estimate: one, perhaps two, out of sixty. The male faculty at the business school were not attempting a second shift at night. Even though I was lucky enough to have a partner who did half the work at home, that still left me doing 50 percent, considerably more than the young men who were vying with me for tenure. My husband was similarly handicapped in his career, perhaps more so; at least when I left at 5:30 PM to pick up my son at the day care center, I was conforming to gender expectations, while he was not. Like most dual-career couples, we spent most evening and weekend hours doing housework and child care, while many of our peers were relaxing or getting more work done. This is a systematic disadvantage, invisible to most who are not in dual-career marriages. Dual-career couples are more plentiful now, even where I work. And it is important to note that, even when our dual-career approach was relatively rare, we had one important advantage, not available to all: we could afford to buy some help.

2. A "Dream" Department

Your real department probably has sources of support, even if you're an outlier in it. But if swimming against the tide is wearing you down, it helps to reach out to supportive colleagues in other universities, maybe even other countries. My remote "mail" mentors, most of whom were men, were amazingly generous with their time. Some read and commented on drafts, even drafts not close to their own approaches to research. Others made a place for me in edited books, special journal issues, and conference symposia. Some did research congruent with their values, showing me it could be done. In various ways, in person and through their work, all offered encouragement when the struggle seemed hopeless. I owe each of them a big debt.[4]

3. A Local, University-wide Network

I found the one woman or the one critical theorist or the one gender researcher in each department at Stanford.[5] It took time to get to know each other and to learn enough to understand each other's work, but it was well worth the investment. Who else could understand the unique pressures and rewards of working in this university? We gave each other emotional support, practical information, and political counsel.

4. Students

The students I have worked with have been a godsend. They provided intellectual stimulation, good company, and practical help on research projects. And sometimes they became long-term professional friends as well.

5. Get a Life

Remember why you are doing it all. In my case, combining full-time work with a young family was exhausting, but tickling my young son's belly and hearing him laugh was a great reentry from work to home. It's easy to slip into a routine of grim perseverance, where everything's a task, a chore, an item on a "to-do" list. That's bad enough at work—definitely not recommended at home.

The Verdict

I came up for tenure in the fall of 1984. I had hoped that my string of justice experiments, exploring mainstream theories of justice using mainstream experimental methods, would appeal to the social psychologists among my reviewers. Business school reviewers, however, I feared would criticize my justice research, saying, "What do studies of violent protests, secretaries, and blue-collar workers have to do with helping managers improve firm per-

4. Thanks are especially due to Peter Frost, John Van Maanen, Ed Schein, Jan Beyer, Karlene Roberts, Paul Lawrence, Paul Hirsch, Richard Hackman, Phil Brickman, Barry Staw, and Walter Nord.

5. Especially Myra Strober (an economist, and my first, and most helpful, female colleague at the business school, Myra moved to the education school), Jane Collier (anthropology), Deborah Rhode (law), Cecilia Ridgeway (sociology), Hazel Markus and Laura Carstenson (psychology), Barbara Babcock (law), Estelle Freedman (history), Sylvia Yanagisako (anthropology), and Diane Middlebrook (English).

formance?" I had hoped that these business school reviewers might be appeased by my cultural publications, which were clearly organizational, in focus. This meant that I had to publish enough justice work to satisfy the social psychologists who might discount the culture work, and enough culture work to satisfy the organizational researchers, who might find my justice experiments irrelevant or organizationally unrealistic. This dual publication strategy was probably not a bad idea, given that I had to have a solid list of publications to convince the business faculty to give tenure to a woman, for the first time. Fortunately, they did so unanimously, and a fine celebration was had. The next day I wore a t-shirt under my suit jacket. Written in masking tape on the back was one word, "Tenured." I showed it to only one person, my secretary.

The First "Five-Year" Plan: Aligning Values with Research (1985–1989)

In the year after tenure, with the help of friends whose research was more radical than my own, I did a critical assessment of my research to date. I concluded, reluctantly, that I had been co-opted. Co-optation is a danger that all tempered radicals constantly face, and I had succumbed to a significant extent. In my justice research, I was studying race, income, or sex inequality, often using clerical and blue-collar employees as participants, in accord with my values. However, my papers mentioned these facts only in a brief sentence or two in the methods section (and my motivating values not at all); the remainder of these papers discussed theories of justice in abstract terms.

Even worse, my studies of culture implicitly furthered managerial interests—a development that became clear to me from invaluable discussions with friends and from the frankly critical papers they wrote (see Calás and Smircich 1987; Stablein and Nord 1985).[6] In the early 1980s, most U.S. culture researchers (and quite a few elsewhere) tended to endorse a "value-engineering" view of culture that focused on leaders and top managers, arguing that they could and should try to create organization-wide consensus around their own values, for the purposes of increasing commitment, productivity, and profitability. Although my work had not explored links to productivity and profitability, I had assumed a managerial perspective and not challenged the desirability of encouraging apparent agreement with values chosen and articulated by top managers. I had not studied the views of lower-level employees, not explored the development of dissenting subcul-

6. My critical and feminist consciousness has been sharpened, repeatedly, by Deb Meyerson, Linda Smircich, Ralph Stablein, Gideon Kunda, and Marta Calás.

tures at lower levels of hierarchies, and not allowed for conflicts of interest between the advantaged and the disadvantaged.

I should have known better. In retrospect, it was clear I had let my desire for approval, and for tenure, lead me away from ideas that would be deemed unacceptable by those who would decide my tenure case. Today I remain convinced that if I had done work that was more radical, I would never have gotten tenure at Stanford. I regret that fact, but I wouldn't advise others to do what I did; each of us has to balance our values and our career options individually. After tenure, and after taking a hard critical look at my research, I was embarrassed by the extent to which my culture studies had become managerial. I decided to deeply rethink the cultural theories I had adopted without critical assessment, reading more broadly in the critical, feminist, and postmodern literatures.[7] I decided to begin a "Five-Year Plan" (yes, it was named after the optimistic centralized economic plans of communist regimes) to align my work more closely with my values. My goal was to make my research more radical every year for five years. This was a goal I would not have dared to approach pretenure, but post-tenure I was determined to use my research to swim against the tide.

JUSTICE RESEARCH

At just the right time, I was asked to write a review chapter, summarizing the results of all the justice studies that I had conducted to date. I titled that chapter, with a sigh of disappointment, "The Tolerance of Injustice" (1986a), because the cumulative results of my studies showed that even those who earned the least were generally content with income-distribution rules that put them in a disadvantaged position. Using my PhD seminar as a way to gather students interested in justice, I began a new kind of justice research. For example, Maureen Scully, Barbara Levitt, and I analyzed the speeches of revolutionary leaders such as Rosa Luxemburg and Mao Tse-tung, to see how they attempted to arouse the perception of injustice in their speeches and writings. Contrary to our expectations, these leaders did not spend much time painting a rosy, detailed picture of a just future; instead both successful and unsuccessful revolutionary leaders stressed the inequalities between the rich and the poor, detailing the injustices of everyday life familiar

---

7. My interest in postmodern and feminist theory was first stimulated by an interdisciplinary feminist faculty seminar, attended by many of my "one in every department" friends on campus. In addition, European conferences, such as SCOS (the Standing Conference on Organizational Symbolism), introduced me to postmodern, critical, and feminist approaches to organizational scholarship, such as that of Hugh Wilmott, Steve Linstead, Sylvia Gherardi, Antonio Strati, Pasquale Gagliardi, Mats Alvesson, Nils Brunsson, Kristian Kreiner, Majken Schultz, and Barbara Czarniawska. Without the help of these colleagues, I would still be mispronouncing Derrida and underestimating the far-reaching implications of this approach, although they would be the first to agree that I have much to learn in this regard.

to their audiences, in effect, damning the past and ignoring the future (Martin, Scully, and Levitt 1990).

I was delighted when my dissertation advisor, Tom Pettigrew, invited me to join him in writing a review of research focusing on African American reactions to racial inequalities in organizations (Pettigrew and Martin 1987). We tried to extrapolate from research to suggest strategies and structural changes that might foster the retention and advancement of these employees. This last study was different from my previous work in two ways. It focused on race, rather than sex or blue-collar work, as a source of disadvantage. Also, in addition to examining the reactions of the disadvantaged, this paper explored what organizations could do to improve the situation.

Taken as a group, these and other related justice studies were an effort to go beyond the tolerance of injustice to study ways that inequalities could be challenged or changed. Nevertheless, it was clear that even if conditions aroused strong perceptions of injustice, these attitudes alone did not consistently predict when and why the disadvantaged would be willing to act to change things. I had ironically ended up studying how people rationalized being disadvantaged, rather than how they might mobilize collectively and achieve change. From my political point of view, my justice research was close to an impasse.

CULTURE RESEARCH

In my cultural research, an increasingly radical orientation was easier to attain. As a first step, students Sim Sitkin, Michael Boehm, and I showed how difficult it was for even an extremely charismatic leader of a small entrepreneurial firm to create a culture, cast in his own image, and reflective of his own values (Martin, Sitkin, and Boehm 1985). The managerial literature of the time was trumpeting the crucial importance of managers doing exactly this. What we found was that, within months of a company's founding, employees began to form subcultures and develop differing patterns of shared values, quite unlike those of the leader. We asked employees to describe key events in the company's history and explain what those events meant to them. Whereas the leader saw himself as critical to each of the key events in the company's history, employees saw his role as less central and, often, told event histories that featured members of their own subculture as the heroes who "saved the day" in times of crisis. This study suggested that a leader's ability to create a culture that reflected his or her personal values may have been overestimated.

The findings of this study were a surprise to many; once again I was swimming against the tide. In the early 1980s, most cultural researchers in the United States were arguing that cultural change was a form of "value engineering," whereby top managers could articulate values that would, if reinforced consistently, come to be shared by employees throughout an organization. According to this view (we labeled it the "integration perspective"), organizational cultures are characterized by internal consistency, organization-wide consensus, and clarity. In contrast, Deb Meyerson and I (1986, 1987) showed how a variety of change processes had altered the culture of the Peace Corps in Africa, creating subcultural differences, exacerbating conflicts between the leadership and rank-and-file employees, and fostering ambiguity rather than clarity. For example, the volunteers who taught English found themselves sharing similar problems and exchanging effective teaching techniques; they developed a professional subculture that crossed national boundaries. An environmental "jolt," such as a change in the climate, could trigger cultural change. For example, a drought changed the content of some volunteers' tasks, from water-based sanitation and irrigation projects to teaching the planting and cooking of new kinds of famine-resistant grains. This longitudinal study showed that there was more to culture than the integration perspective could reveal.

This broader view of cultural theory was reflected in a volume I coedited with a set of colleagues, Peter Frost, Larry Moore, Meryl Louis, and Craig Lundberg (1985), who had helped these ideas develop. In a subsequent paper, coauthored with Caren Siehl (1990), we challenged the idea that lies at the core of popular interest in organizational culture: the seductive promise that an organizational culture viewed from the integration perspective (organization-wide value consensus, consistency across the manifestations of the culture, and clarity rather than ambiguity) can provide a key to improved firm performance (for example, productivity and profitability). We reviewed all the relevant studies on this topic and showed that the claim of a link between integration and firm performance was empirically unsupported. Although such claims continue to surface every year, they are virtually impossible to substantiate. Culture is important, not because it offers a key to profitability, but because it captures aspects of life in organizations—the lives of all organizational employees, not just managers—that are not fully reflected in other organizational theories.

At this time there was a growing body of critical cultural research, labeled the "differentiation perspective," which delineated differences among subcultures and focused on inconsistencies in the meanings attached to various cultural manifestations. For example, top management's espoused values might emphasize the need for egalitarianism, while lower-level employees might see great inequalities between themselves and their managers. The differentiation view allowed for conflict between subcultures (such as labor and management), which was why it became the favored view of scholars with a more critical perspective (for example, Rosen 1981; Van Maanen 1991; Young 1991; Alvesson 1993). Next, Deb Meyerson and I (1987, 1988) explored the ways that prior culture research had focused on what was clear and consistent, ignoring that which was ambiguous, paradoxical, ironic, and constantly in flux (for example, Feldman 1991; Kunda 1992; Weick 1991). We called this ambiguity-centered view of culture the "fragmentation perspective." It provided a needed supplement to the integration perspective that had characterized so much of the prior culture research, and it too created room for more critical and feminist approaches to cultural study.

The academic year 1989–90 was a sabbatical for me. My husband is an Australian, and he wanted to bring our young son to the neighborhood on the sea in Sydney where he grew up. The plan was that our son would go to his Dad's school, learn the Australian version of world history (referred to as "the truth" by my husband), and enjoy the pleasures of fishing and cricket. During this year, I wrote books and papers and, from time to time, enjoyed life on an Australian beach. Immersed in this multicultural experience, I decided to write a book, building a theory of culture that would draw on a large part of the research done to date, both in the United States and (to a lesser extent) abroad. In *Cultures in Organizations: Three Perspectives* (1992), I did a critical review of the growing body of cultural research, showing that most studies reflected only one of three possible (integration, differentiation, and fragmentation) theoretical perspectives.[8] I argued that any organizational culture would be better understood if it were studied from all three perspectives in turn. I applied these ideas in a study of a large multinational high-tech corporation, showing how a three-perspective study could reveal insights invisible from any single viewpoint. In addition, again with Peter Frost, Larry Moore, Meryl Louis, and Craig Lundberg (1991), I joined in editing a second volume of culture papers. The first part of this volume was based on the three-perspective framework, including case studies by a variety of authors, written from integration, differentiation, and fragmentation perspectives.

And so the Five-Year Plan came to an end. The collection of books and papers that I had written during this time critiqued the management-oriented, integration view of culture that I and so many others had (implicitly) accepted in the early 1980s. My new cultural studies drew on the work of critical theorists, attended to the views of lower-level employees, allowed for differences of opinion and perspective, and fostered the study of intergroup conflict and ambiguities. This was a theory of culture that went far beyond the simplistic, managerial assumptions of my early work, and I was pleased.

But, as with my justice research five years earlier, the success of this re-

---

8. Ed Schein commented, line by line, on a draft of this manuscript, an extraordinarily generous act given that, as a leader of the integration approach to the study of culture, he disagreed with much of it.

search program laid the groundwork for a deepening of my commitment to make my research more radical. My readings in culture had brought me in contact with postmodern organizational scholarship, which challenged the neopositivist methods and epistemology that I, like most U.S. social scientists, had adopted (for example, Alvesson and Deetz 1996; Cooper and Burrell 1988; Czarniawska-Joerges 1998). For years, in the evenings, I had struggled to follow the unfamiliar, esoteric, and convoluted phrasing favored by postmodern literary criticism, feminist theory, and philosophy. Prior to reading postmodernism, I had thought of empirical research as a way to test theories and arrive at, for lack of better words, the objective truth. The postmodernists challenged these fundamental assumptions, arguing that what passes for empirically based knowledge is more a subjective opinion, tempered by historical conditions, than it is an objective truth. Postmodern writing challenged everything I had thought I was doing, making me rethink my activities as a researcher from ground zero.

In an attempt to understand postmodern analysis by doing it, I used the postmodern technique of textual "deconstruction" to analyze a speech by the chief executive officer (CEO) of a large, well-known corporation (1990). When the CEO gave this speech, half of the audience (of Stanford MBAs) seemed pleased with his company's work-family policies, while the other half erupted in hisses of disapproval. He was describing all that his company was doing to "help" a pregnant employee maintain her connection to the company while it launched a new product and while she had her baby. My deconstruction of the CEO's speech contrasted the language he used to describe the product launch with the language he used to describe the birth. I analyzed how his speech would have had to change, had he been describing hospitalization for open-heart surgery rather than for a birth. This deconstruction revealed a series of surprisingly overt sexist assumptions underneath the CEO's bland, and seemingly kind language, making it clear why his speech had received such a strongly mixed reaction. I was amazed by the power of what deconstruction could reveal, even in my clumsy, neophyte's hands. This was work with radical potential.

The Second "Five-Year" Plan: The Activist Years (1989–1998)

YEARS OF LOCAL ACTIVISM

When I returned from sabbatical, I did a critical review of what I had accomplished, and not accomplished, during the first Five-Year Plan. (Introspection every five years seems, for now, the most I can manage.) I decided that I was more content now that my values were more aligned with my research, but that I still had a long way to go. I liked the goal of making my work more radical each year and decided to undertake a second Five-Year Plan. I was happily imagining where feminist theory and postmodernism might take my work! At the same time, there was an additional consideration, one that at first glance, may seem unconnected with the research focus of this chapter and this volume. After some more exposure to critical theorists (especially through Paul Adler's interest group at the Academy of Management, David Knights and his colleagues in the United Kingdom, and Mats Alvesson in Sweden), my life as a Stanford academic seemed too much of an ivory tower existence. "What kind of radical am I," I asked myself, "if I don't spend some of my time as an activist working locally for a cause I believe in?"

I decided therefore to add an activist agenda to this second Five-Year Plan. Perhaps because of my own experience as a gender pioneer (however ill-prepared I had initially been for this role), the causes I chose were women and minorities (class inequality once again neglected). I took a series of leadership positions, in the Academy of Management Board of Governors, on the Stanford University Advisory Board (an elected group of seven faculty who vote on all faculty hires and promotions), the Stanford Female Faculty Caucus, and on a variety of task forces, committees, and so on, both formal and informal, on campus and off. In each of these roles, I worked long and hard, trying to raise people's awareness of the subtle aspects of discrimination. I worked to combat the tendency to rate women and minorities with tougher and different standards than white men, especially in borderline cases where subjective judgments were most likely to be influential. This took an average of about twenty hours a week, in addition to my usual teaching and citizenship assignments.

I will not burden you with the details of these efforts. Suffice it to say that the hours invested were many, and the second Five-Year Plan became ten. The results of this activism were most often defeats (especially locally), and there were more small wins than great victories. During these years nontraditional faculty at Stanford of all kinds were seen by the administration, more literally than you might suppose, as "forces of darkness," seeking, for example, to weaken the university's commitment to scholarly excellence, rather than as members of a loyal opposition, seeking to bring new sources of strength into the academy. My experiences in this regard, I have learned, are much like those of activists fighting sex and race discrimination in other kinds of organizations, such as big corporations, the Catholic Church, and the military. Friends say there is value in fighting a good fight, even if you don't win, but these years of local activism left me exhausted. Would I have been smarter to spend those hours doing change-oriented research, which ultimately would reach more people?

POSTMODERN RESEARCH—A CONTRADICTION?

During these years of activism, I remained an active researcher. The next big intellectual step came when friends criticized the cultural research I had done (for example, Gagliardi 1991; Mumby 1994). They made me see, for example, that the three-perspective view of culture could be seen as a totalitarian metatheory that encompassed, and hence claimed to be superior to, all other cultural theories. Instead, these critics argued, I should have deconstructed the three-perspective theory, revealing its weaknesses. I did a bit of that in the last chapter of my 1992 book (much to the dismay of some readers who felt that I was destroying all that I had built), but I could have done much more. In a (1995a) article, I discussed reasons for the style and structure of the controversial postmodern chapter of my 1992 book and outlined how a more sustained postmodern approach might undermine my own claims to have found an empirically more solid and inclusive approach to studying culture. I was enthusiastic about integrating postmodernism more seriously in my research, and uncertain how to do it.

Invitations to contribute essays on culture to the *Blackwell Encyclopedic Dictionary of Organizational Behavior* and the *Handbook of Organizational Studies* (1996) presented a strong challenge to my budding postmodernism. Usually essays in handbooks and encyclopedias, contrary to postmodern arguments, describe the authors' views as truth, or tell an enlightenment tale of progress toward greater knowledge (for example, "Early mistaken ideas were corrected when a study proved that . . . "). In the *Encyclopedia* essays (1995b), I abandoned my postmodern aspirations, writing a straight description of the three-perspective theory of culture, citing supporting empirical evidence. In the *Handbook*, however, Peter Frost and I (1996) took an approach to writing a review article that was more consistent with postmodernism. We described the last two decades of culture research as a war between a series of competing camps (for example, integration versus differentiation, the qualitative versus quantitative methodologists, and so on). Rather than a tale of progress toward greater knowledge, we told a tale of intellectual warfare. Postmodernism helped us offer a view of scholarship that many of us have experienced, but few of us have written about. Some of these ideas, especially with regard to how to conduct and write up cultural research, were incorporated in my next, and last, book (*Organizational Culture: Mapping the Terrain*) about organizational culture (Martin 2002). I remain excited about exploring postmodernism, although I find myself unwilling to follow its implications fully, as I fear the action paralysis that might come if everything, even my personal value commitments, were to be deconstructed. This intellectual dilemma has attracted scholars in a variety of disciplines, and I plan to join them in trying to find a way to mix postmodern insights with political activism and, if possible, with empirically based theory development.

FROM JUSTICE TO GENDER

In these last few years, my interests in justice have been transformed. I have struggled to find ways to align my justice research with my values and with what I learned from my struggles as an activist working for change. With another talented PhD student, Joe Harder, I did an experiment (1994) that showed how organizations use egalitarian distributions of emotional rewards (such as praise or one-on-one time with a top executive, and so on) to draw attention away from unequal distributions of economic resources, such as pay. These results echoed the slogan of striking clerical workers who wanted "Bread, not Roses." I also wrote a review article that reframed the results of all my justice studies to date, showing how the results helped explain the ways organizations legitimized inequality (1993). Soon, however, I began to move my justice work toward a focus on gender inequality. No longer would gender inequality be discussed in a few sentences in the methods section of a paper; now gender would be the primary focus on my work. My first effort in this regard was an historical overview of the field of organizational behavior, entitled "The Organization of Exclusion." I showed how the dearth of women faculty, and the paucity of female authors in handbooks and textbooks, had resulted in gender-biased "knowledge" that ignored and distorted the experiences of women in organizations. In addition, as other feminist scholars have done, Kathy Knopoff and I took on one of the classics of our field, Weber's work on bureaucracy (1997). We showed (using deconstruction) how Weber's language excluded and demeaned women's voices and experiences, creating a theory of bureaucracy that enhanced and reified masculine power.

Moving from theory to the field, Deb Meyerson and I explored the experiences of seven of the eight highest-ranking female executives in a very large technology company. Each woman reported feeling extreme isolation and discouragement, as she was misunderstood, ignored, or demeaned by male colleagues who shared a different sense of what was important and a different set of beliefs about how people should treat each other. Because they had so little contact with each other, most of these highly successful women remained unaware that their problems were not unique. They blamed themselves individually for problems that were due to being a woman in a man's world. Most of these highly talented women decided to quit the corporation—an outcome that surprised and disappointed many of their male colleagues, who had seen the company invest so much in their success. First published as a series of teaching cases for MBAs (Martin and Meyerson 1997), this interview material was subsequently used to analyze the ways these high-ranking women were caught in a Foucauldian web of power relations that affected them differently than their male colleagues (1998).

I had grown tired of studying organizations that institutionalized practices that systematically disadvantaged women. I decided to seek out an organization whose values I admired and whose track record of hiring and promoting women was stellar. I chose The Body Shop, a cosmetics company based in England, with shops in forty-two countries. During the years Kathy Knopoff, Christine Beckman, and I studied its policies and practices, The Body Shop maintained its strong commitment to a sociopolitical agenda that included environmentally sensitive policies, a refusal to test products on animals, community service, and political activism in causes such as Amnesty International. Compared to other organizations of its size, particularly in Europe, The Body Shop had an unusual number of women, even in the top executive and middle-management ranks. Observing employees at work, interviewing them both on the shop floor and in pubs, after work, and filling bottles of "fuzzy peach shampoo," we tried to understand the workings of this idealistic company, struggling to maintain its value commitments in a harshly competitive marketplace. In many ways, this company's struggle to align its values with its work echoes my own.

The first of several papers to emerge from this large study (Martin, Knopoff, and Beckman 1998) focused on the ways the company fosters "bounded emotionality" (Putnam and Mumby 1993) rather than the impersonality and emotional control lauded by Weber, or the "emotional labor" (for example, Hochschild 1983) required of flight attendants and retail shop clerks. Papers now being written will ask whether the company's political agenda is sincere, or whether it is a hypocritically inexpensive way to market cosmetics. Another paper will explore whether the company's idealism can be exported to other countries. The Body Shop's value commitments were developed at headquarters in the south of England. As the company has expanded rapidly, it has encountered some cross-cultural difficulties. For example, The Body Shop's Amnesty International campaigns were not especially welcome in Singapore, and posters advertising condoms as an AIDS preventative aroused controversy in the Bible Belt of the United States and—closer to home—at the shopping center on Stanford University land. Papers such as these will address a question posed by Anita Roddick, founder of The Body Shop: Is it possible to do business differently, given the efficiency and growth demands of the capitalist marketplace? This series of papers will, I hope, live up to my promise to myself: to bring my work in the next few years ever closer to my own values, integrating ideas from feminist and critical theory, as well as postmodernism.

AND SO IT GOES

Writing this chapter, and explaining how these various research activities did or did not reflect my value commitments, has been an encouraging experience. On a good day, as I read about all this work I have done, I feel strengthened; maybe the shortfalls are not so great—certainly I did try. But this would not be an honest chapter, and it would not be a chapter that could actually help someone else who is trying to align his or her own values with work, unless I admitted what I often feel: it is a struggle to swim against the tide, and those of us who do it often feel unjustly devalued and marginalized. Is this because our values are not those of the mainstream? Or is it because our skills as communicators, teachers, and scholars fall short of what they could be? You never know. I say this, not to discourage others, but to say that getting tired, or feeling discouraged, is inevitable when the tide is running. This is why that support boat, full of friends, family, and colleagues who understand the struggle, is so essential. Moments of ease—when the tide turns in your favor, or even just when it pauses between rise and ebb— are all too rare.

By contrast, moments of ease, pleasant though they are when they happen, are not the only reward. Precisely because it hasn't been easy, I know that swimming against the tide has mattered to others. It is not that I am somehow representative of a larger group, or that I am part of some kind of well-defined social movement. My struggle to align my work with my values matters to the students and colleagues who face similar struggles and could use my support; some may derive encouragement just from the example of a fellow swimmer who hasn't given up. My struggle matters because it lends support to other researchers who, rather than seeking solely to serve the needs of our corporate sponsors and managerial alumni / ae, prefer to ask what other interests we might also serve. It might matter to university leaders whose first instinct is to preserve the status quo, when they could be building a better future. And it even matters to those who disagree with the values I struggle to support, because by providing a clearly articulated alternative I (and other tempered radicals like me, of all persuasions) force others to be clearer about what they are doing and why they are doing it. After such conversations, maybe we will all become a bit more open and inclusive. These are worthy goals, no matter how far, or how little, I have been personally able to achieve them—so far. And so, I think I will keep swimming against the tide for a while yet.

FRANCES J. MILLIKEN

Parallel Lives

Living the Drama of Tempered Radicalism

BEING ASKED to write a reaction to Joanne Martin's chapter for this book is quite an honor. I remember as a doctoral student seeing Joanne on the dais at more than one of those very large symposia at the Academy that everyone wants to get into, so much so that people end up standing in the hallways. I have always admired Joanne's work and I have also admired Joanne because she did not seem to be afraid to present what some people might consider to be radical ideas and frameworks. Perhaps she was afraid— but she did not look like she was.

When I read Joanne's chapter, it hit close to home. Until I read the article Deb Meyerson and Maureen Scully wrote on "tempered radicalism" (Meyerson and Scully 1995), I did not have a term to describe how I have felt throughout much of my career as a female professor of organizational behavior in a business school. I have more than once asked myself: "Why am I doing this?" Thus, when I read Joanne's writing about her life at Stanford, I felt as though I was living a "parallel life," not perfectly parallel but disturbingly so.

In thinking about writing this commentary, I realized that my reactions to Joanne's chapter have clearly been shaped by my experiences. So, I thought it might be useful to make the points of similarity and points of difference explicit as they clearly shape my perspective. Like Joanne, I am a woman teaching in a male-dominated business school. Like Joanne, I teach organizational behavior. Further, I teach it in a school that is filled with students who want to major in finance and work for investment banks and, thus, regard organizational behavior as a course they have to take but do not necessarily want to take.

Like Joanne, I have children and value my time with them enormously, something that often puts one at odds with the dominant ideology of some administrators of business schools in the United States.[1] Like Joanne, I have always had an interest in gender issues although I have not studied them directly. My interest in work-family issues and in diversity in teams, for example, reflects my interest in how organizations are adapting to the changing demography of their workers (for example, greater numbers of women, of single parents, of dual-career workers, of workers from diverse ethnic, racial, and religious backgrounds). And finally, like Joanne, I have always been attracted to theory and research that questions the "managerial imperative." I chose to get a PhD in organizational behavior because I was interested in how people find meaning in work. Thus, I agree with a statement like the one Joanne makes in her chapter about the study of organizational culture. She writes, "Culture is important, not because it offers a key to profitability, because it captures life in organizations—the lives of all organizational employees not just managers."

Unlike Joanne, I was fortunate early in my career to have been surrounded by women in my department. This made my life much easier than I think hers was. In fact, all of the women with whom I had the good fortune of working as I entered academia in the mid-1980s either already had, or have gone on to have, enormously successful careers. Included in this group are Jane Dutton, Janet Dukerich, Theresa Lant, Marlene Fiol, Ruth Raubitschek, and Jan Beyer. Thus, I had no shortage of women to look to as potential role models. In fact, I believe that having had the opportunity to work with this "critical mass" of women was a critical factor in shaping my career and that I owe all of them a debt of gratitude for being such professionally stimulating and personally supportive colleagues. I continue to be surrounded by wonderful female colleagues including Theresa Lant, Elizabeth Morrison, Caroline Bartel, Batia Wiesenfeld, Sally Blount, Kim Wade-Benzoni, and Amy Wrzesniewski, each of whom I admire.

So, it is with this set of experiences that I read Joanne's chapter and write this commentary.

One thought I had as I read Joanne's chapter was to wonder whether women and minority faculty members in business schools have a set of experiences that are not shared and, perhaps, not generally understood by their male, nonminority counterparts. There may be three interrelated ways in which the experiences of women and minority faculty members are different from the experiences of men or of people who are in the majority

---

1. On our annual Faculty Performance Appraisal, we are asked how many hours we spend in our office, as if this is a measure of how hard we work or of our commitment to the institution. I spend many hours at work even though I may not be physically in my office at work. I have chosen to work at home one or more days a week in order to see my children when they come home from school. In fact, I do my best writing at home where I am less likely to be interrupted.

group. First, we may have a different "lens" or perspective on organizations, which is, I believe, partially a product of our backgrounds and partially a result of our position in the organizational contexts to which we belong. Second, we are likely to have lower levels of power and, thus, may be more likely to be "tempered radicals." Third, women and minority faculty members may suffer from the problem of being a "token" or a member of a very small group.

The "lens" through which one looks at organizations is partially a function of one's own experiences in organizations. If women and minorities have a systematically different experience of organizations, then they are likely to have a different "lens" or perspective on organizations, a perspective that perhaps is borne, in part, out of our experiences as "outsiders" to the power elite. This leads me to wonder to what extent people's perceptions of their organizations vary systematically with the amount of power they have in the system. If one is a member of a demographic category that is in power, the opportunities provided to you by virtue of your membership in that category may be invisible to you. Perhaps people can only notice what they themselves do not have. Thus, individuals may be much more likely to notice the privileges that power affords when they are a member of a non-privileged class. This, though, sets up an unfortunate dynamic where those not in power complain to those in power about the lack of equity in the system and those in power cannot understand what the complaint is, given that it is an experience that they themselves have never had (Ragins, Townsend, and Mattis 1998). In fact, as Joanne points out, those in power may view those who raise concerns as "forces of darkness" who seek to weaken the institution rather than as "members of loyal opposition" who seek to build and strengthen the institution.

For us as organizational scholars, our perspective on the organizations we study is vitally important to our lives as researchers because it suggests that the research questions we are interested in may be different from those who do not share this "lens" on organizations. Thus, it seems quite plausible that women and minorities would be more likely, for example, to perceive organizations as political systems and to be more likely to be intrinsically interested in issues of procedural justice, networks, gender, diversity, and voice.

That organizational researchers have different perspectives on the critical problems and issues of organizations is critically important to the field because these differing points of view can lead us to a more complete understanding of organizations. Studying organizations from the "bottom up" (that is, from the point of view of lower-level members) rather than from the "top down" (that is, from the point of view of top-level managers), for example, may be quite critical to building our understanding of them.

Thinking about the idea that the organizational issues we see and study are shaped by our position in the organization led me to wonder whether women and members of other underrepresented groups in business schools might also be more likely to have a "drama of tempered radicalism" that they live in addition to the other dramas of their lives (work, family . . .). In other words, we may be more likely to perceive issues of procedural unfairness or problems with course content that ignores the reality of organizational life as we know it. If so, are we more often in the position of a tempered radical in the sense that we have to make a choice about what to do about our perception (for example, whether to speak up or take some sort of action)?

This is another place that power plays a role. Because women tend to not be at the top of hierarchies, they always have to decide whether to "sell" the issues that concern them up the hierarchy. As a person who has concerns about the nature of the organizational system and who is not in a powerful position in the organization, your range of options for coping with a system that you do not always agree with include: conformity, silence, gentle speech on a few select issues, and speaking up. Choosing to speak up, though, means that one potentially risks being labeled as a "troublemaker" or not a team player and losing credibility in the eyes of one's bosses and colleagues (Milliken, Morrison, and Hewlin 2002). In fact, I wonder whether it is possible to be a social activist (for example, a tempered radical who expresses her opinion often) and not be labeled. It is perhaps only natural for individuals in leadership roles to want to attach negative labels to those people whose ideas seem to threaten the legitimacy of the procedures and policies of the systems that they direct. Thus, whether one is a "force of darkness" when one raises gender equity issues or a "loyal organizational citizen" depends on who is doing the labeling.

It seems to me that whatever you choose to do when deciding whether to bring up a potentially controversial issue, there are potential negative consequences. Choosing not to speak up means that one has to live with not having tried to change the system. Choosing to speak up means potentially paying a heavy price for one's voice if one's concerns and ideas are not appreciated. How do you balance your desire to influence the system with the negative impact of trying to influence the system? In other words, how do you maintain your capacity to influence the system and avoid getting a negative label like "troublemaker" when you raise issues that concern you? How does one raise issues but not become marginalized? To some extent, we can look for advice in the research on issue selling (for example, Ashford et al. 1998; Dutton et al. 2001). Theoretically, if we follow the advice garnered from research on issue-selling attempts, we may be able to learn from others when it is wise to speak up and when it might be wise to be silent. One variable that was mentioned frequently by individuals surveyed, for example, was the favorability of the context. However, if we have strong beliefs, for example, in the importance of gender equity, then waiting until we perceive the context in our business school as favorable for the selling of gender equity issues may be too long a time to wait.

The question of when to speak up and when to be silent is a question with no easy answer. To quote Joanne, "A tempered radical runs the constant risks of a co-opted kind of success (achieved, perhaps, by being silent) or the failure that comes from marginalization (achieved, perhaps, by speaking too much), and from time to time, [the tempered radical] experiences both." Being a tempered radical can create great uncertainty and stress as an individual tries to figure out what the right thing to do in each particular instance might be. Thus, it takes time and energy to live a drama of "tempered radicalism" in addition to trying to manage one's career and personal life. It is also hard to feel like one is repeatedly "swimming against the tide."

How hard our experience is probably depends a lot on whether we go through it in relative isolation (for example, as a token) or in the company of others. Kanter (1977) has told us that the behavior of "tokens" is more visible and, thus, tends to be highly scrutinized. So, the simple fact of being in the minority, especially when one is a token, can lead to visibility and scrutiny. When one is a token, one's errors attract attention. Furthermore, "tokens" may have a hard time interpreting their experiences and may tend to blame themselves if they have problems. When we work in institutions in which there are many other women or minorities, we are fortunate in that we are able to talk with each other and come to understand that our experiences are shared. The importance of this ability to talk and share experiences cannot be underestimated, as Joanne's research on high-powered women in high-technology industries has demonstrated. As Joanne writes:

Each woman reported feeling extreme isolation and discouragement, as she was misunderstood, ignored, or demeaned by male colleagues who shared a different sense of what was important and a different set of beliefs about how people should treat each other. Because they had so little contact with each other, most of these highly successful women remained unaware that their problems were not unique. They blamed themselves individually for problems that were due to being a woman in a man's world.

If there is one piece of advice that I would give to women entering our field, it is to make sure that you have a support network of other women with whom you can share your experiences. If you are not as lucky as I am to have been surrounded by wonderful women in your department, then seek out a network of women from other departments in the business school or from other schools. This seems vital to me to deal effectively with the experience of feeling out of sync with one's institution, should that experience occur.

Although Joanne describes herself as "swimming against the tide" of the dominant elite of business schools and of "the managerial imperative," I would also point out that she is "swimming with the tide of her values." This suggests that all tempered radicals may actually be pulled by conflicting tides. So, people who find themselves occasionally out of step with their institutions have to recognize that to completely conform to the institutions would put them out of step with their own values. As Debra Meyerson writes about tempered radicals, "If they conform completely, they essentially silence a core part of their selves" (Meyerson 2001, 16).

Joanne dealt with many difficult issues during her climb up the ladder of the business school hierarchy, but she was not silent. In not being silent, she gave those of us who watched and admired her the courage to try to shape the environments in which we live into ones that we hope will be even more welcoming to the generation of women who will follow us onto the faculty of business schools.

CHRISTINE PEARSON

Clarity and Alignment

An Experiential Reflection on Values and Work

> The challenge is to be yourself in a world that is trying to make you like everyone else.
>
> Greeting card wisdom, author unknown

I MET DEB MEYERSON's concept of "tempered radicalism" with exuberance. As a caring and independent mentor, Joanne, no doubt, engendered this thinking in Deb, and now Deb's work was nurturing my resilience. Just as I was staking research choices, Deb's theory confirmed my inclination to buck the system and follow my own path. By naming my (self-) perceptions, she had, in an almost paradoxical way, legitimized me. Now, as I read Joanne's reflections, I can't help wondering whether many of us, in fact, see ourselves as tempered radicals. Does our shared status make us less "radical" than we see ourselves? Don't many of us believe that we strive to be inside-outside, savvy change agents balancing one foot on the boat and one on the dock, regardless of the play of the tide? So, to provoke initial reflection on Joanne's chapter, I invite you to consider to what extent a personal struggle in aligning our values with those of our colleagues, our university, or our field is exceptional? As we build our academic careers on traditions centuries old while yearning to discover the possibilities of tomorrow, isn't that a juncture that attracts tempered radicals?

As Joanne suggests in this chapter, whether our attempts to buck the system are met with success or failure, at the end of the day, strength and comfort reside in knowing that we are clear about what we have done and why we have done it. The closer we are to authenticity, the easier the trek through the muck. The better we see what we are aiming for, what we are willing to forfeit, and where we will draw the line (rather than adjust or retreat), the less frightening and distracting the muddy waters.

So how can we become insightful about the essence of our work and our values and their tenuous integration? Insights rest right below the surface, waiting to be tapped by simply setting them free. As Joanne contends, it is a struggle to align our values with our work, and there is much to be gained (by heart and mind) in surfacing the nature of that alignment, as well as points of misalignment. Toward that end, rather than suggesting that you outline the merits of your choices, write journal entries, or compose pro-and-con lists, I urge you to uncover your own personal framework playfully.

To stimulate your thinking about Joanne's insights and to apply them to your personal context, how about a return to childhood expressiveness? Creating a collage has the potential to help you unveil personal truths, reveal hidden values and their parameters, and have fun in doing so. If you're game, turn on your favorite instrumental CD, gather vibrant colors of your youth (whether crayons, pens, or poster paint), collect a broad assortment of image-filled magazines (a vivid escape from the aesthetic dreariness of most of our readings, to be sure), and let your preconscious right-brain self set the course. Flip through the magazines without focused thought, allowing yourself to be drawn to images of what you value and why. If you are in the spirit, the images will speak to you. Tear out those that do, then glue them to a generous banner of paper. Make it your own Ouija board. Let your intuition have full reign. To complete the activity, you may want to draw inferences, associations, and conflicts with crayon, ink, or paint—but try to avoid words themselves—the richness here lies in imagery. The sensemaking and insight come with the action: you may find that "you don't know what you think until you see what you've pasted."

I have used this technique three times. Most recently, I did so in desperation to keep bobbing despite the undertow of injustice and related career challenges. The product was both a lifeline and a compass setting. As I collected and arranged images, the strengths and fit of my choices were reconfirmed, despite short-term agonies. I watched my emotional path unfold. The contrast across the banner was sharp as the pain that had been inflicted on me took the forms first of darkly shaded gargoyles and then bizarre, vibrantly colored comic book villains, but with a couple of local faces. As images unfolded to the right of the paper, the values that I had held found their places—light and serenity were reflected in my choices of palm trees, roses, beaches, family gatherings, and group fun. The product reassured me: there was such good to hold onto.

Earlier in my career, I used collages as means to sort through the swirl of values that I was experiencing, first as a doctoral student and then in my first academic position. Getting images on paper helped me to differentiate and integrate what mattered most to me, as compared to values driven primarily by academic norms. As a doctoral student, my collage took on three distinct layers of poster board, each engulfed in and clipped through the other—the outer, public shell of me was women dressed for success, armed with books and briefcases, baby in one hand and test tube in the other, ready to take on whatever the academic or business worlds could hurl; the mucky and vulnerable middle board held question marks and vanishing roadways; and to the solid core sheet were glued images of stability and fundamental values, of family, friends, and the rewards of earnest effort, images that had long provided assurance. In this emergent collage form, it was humorously reassuring to discover that I was a peanut M&M.

In the process of creating a collage, you may expose some surprises as you gain insight into your values and the essence of your work. Regarding this tricky integration, you may uncover potential avenues to convergence as well as prospective underlying muck. It's likely, too, that parameters by which you segregate what you will do from what you won't and *why* will become clearer to you. Enjoy the discovery!

Ethics in Research

It's Not About the Paperwork!

Joanne, Christine, and Frances encourage us to reflect on our own ethical stance vis-à-vis the research that we do. Clearly both the subjects we choose to research and the research processes and practices that we engage in must relate in some way to our values and ethics. Recent corporate scandals and crises have stimulated a debate on the nature of personal ethical stances of employees, managers, and board members to business and society. *Time* magazine (2002/2003) Person of the Year was awarded to the trio of whistle-blowers from Enron, the FBI, and WorldCom. These issues have been linked to a demand for examination of business education (for example, Barker 2003). Others have raised the connection with current corporate governance practices, including a call for responsiveness to a wider set of constituencies that reach beyond the representatives of stock owners.

These are significant research issues. But it is important to hold onto the reflexive significance of these events. Ethics in the workplace is not just an issue "out there" in the big, bad business offices of Houston or Washington DC. We face our own ethical dilemmas in the academic workplace. We believe it is timely to reexamine our personal ethical choices as researchers.

There are two key research realms where our choices are operationalized. The first is in our choice of a research agenda. The scarcest resource for research work is time. Therefore where we choose to put our research energy is critical. There is only so much time and energy for research. Sure, there is a place for opportunistic research and taking the easy path, but if we always follow the hot topic we will be spent without honoring our core values. Joanne explicitly links her values with her research agenda using five-year plans. Christine asks us to allow our values to speak to us more intuitively.

Because we belong to a community of scholars rather than a collection of individual researchers, ethics has a social dimension, as well. Brief and

Cortina (2000) draw our attention to the Academy of Management's commitment to the public interest. Brief (2000) documents the failure of our journals to represent this broader public interest. Performance is the dominant dependent variable. Even when studying employee morale, it is from a performance point of view. Perrow (1986, 131) put it clearly when he suggested the following organizational effectiveness survey items, asking the question:

Is this the kind of organization where you can:

- Have pleasant chats with others about things that interest you?
- Daydream or relax from time to time without being bothered?
- Use the organization's facilities for your own personal needs (the telephone, typists, office supplies, machine shop, personnel department, auto maintenance shop, travel facilities, etc.)?
- Hide your mistakes and advertise your successes?
- Pick up interesting tidbits about the world by working here, or be more interesting at social gatherings because of what you do here or learn here?
- Make use of tediously acquired skills and knowledge so that you have some sense that what you're doing is meaningful and related to your abilities?

(Perrow 1977, 102)

So thoroughly have researchers adopted the premises of management that it would be heretical to consider the above questions as valid measures of organizational effectiveness. But why not?

(Perrow 1986, 131)

Brief and Cortina (2000) argue that as Academy members we have an ethical responsibility to consider the public good in the research questions we ask. This may involve studying the less privileged or from the perspective of the less privileged. It may involve researching the impact of organizations on nonmanagerial stakeholders. We must not succumb to the temptation to become a study for management rather than the study of management. We note that the American Psychological Association, American Sociological Association, and other professional organizations make similar commitments.

We are not suggesting that only researching the less privileged serves the public good. Better corporate governance, better decision making, better HR practices, and so on all positively impact the public good. However, we do suggest that the less powerful participants in society are underrepresented on the field's research agenda. In his role as editor of the *Academy of Management Review* Art Brief has made the challenge to broaden our research agenda explicit. He emphasizes the established purpose of the journal to "challenge conventional wisdom concerning all aspects of organization and their role in society." Consistently, "the journal is open to a variety of perspectives including those that seek to improve the effectiveness of, *as well as those critical of management and organizations*" (Brief 2003, 7, his emphasis). That is, *AMR* can recognize better the social impact of management and organizations; therefore its authors, when appropriate may wish to address the public policy applications of their scholarship.

He also promises a series of special issues as a medium for meeting the challenge, such as the special topic forum on stigma. In recent years the Academy of Management has shown responsiveness to a broader range of ethical responses in our research by extending formal status to the Gender, Diversity, and Organization, Organization and the Environment, and Critical Management Studies groups.

The second core domain for ethical decision making is in doing the research. It is here that paperwork has come to overwhelm ethical decision making. Recent years have seen the bureaucratization of ethical behavior in university research: the development of formal peer review, institutional rules and regulations, and standard application forms. Canada has recently instituted a universal, national code of conduct for research with human subjects. This approach has both the strengths and weaknesses of bureaucracy. On the plus side, undoubtedly, the amount of grossly unethical research behavior has been reduced. But, there are negative effects, as well.

The main weakness we identify is the classic means-ends inversion identified by Merton. There is a danger that compliance with ethical regulations may distract our attention from the research activity itself and create a sense that we have met our ethical obligations once permission has been granted. It can be too easy to breathe a sigh of relief and conclude, "that's done." It is harder to maintain our attention and respect the rights and needs of our research participants, especially the less powerful.

It is difficult to keep research ethics on the A list. But it is important to do so. We are reminded of the Tylenol scare. Johnson and Johnson did the right thing. The managers at J&J had just rededicated themselves to the Credo. It made the issue of ethical behavior salient for them. We need to find ways to do the same for our organizations and for our work.

We have our codes of ethics. But are they living documents? We must admit we had to look for the Academy of Management ethics statement. We don't have it imprinted on our hearts and minds. In fact, we could not easily find it on the Academy Web site. We struggle to devote more than a few hours to research ethics in our research methods courses. We need to engage in the meaning of our ethical rules regularly, so as to keep them alive and vibrant and something we as researchers can buy into.

Joanne puts it simply, "Doing it alone is simply not possible." As colleagues, we must support each other in our ethical dilemmas. As mentors, we need to indoctrinate our students and junior colleagues in the importance of these issues. As reviewers and editors, we need to legitimate discussion of ethical norms and practices. As researchers, we must attend to the ethics of our daily practice, not just the paperwork.

Puddle Jumping as a Career Strategy

EARLY IN MY academic life some of my elders feared I was going to have "career problems" unless I adopted a more orthodox approach to scholarship. Among the many unsolicited admonitions I received about cleaning up my scholarly act, one was particularly memorable. The place was Monterrey, California. The year was 1984, several months before I defended my dissertation. The occasion was a conference whose purpose I can no longer remember, although I must have delivered a paper based on my dissertation. Otherwise, Ed Schein, who managed MIT's fund for student travel, would not have granted me money to attend and I could not have paid for the travel without his assistance. After the conference, on the way to the airport in a shuttle bus, I found myself seated beside a distinguished, senior scholar. In a fatherly manner, he leaned toward me, peered over his glasses, told me he enjoyed my paper and advised me to give up ethnography and establish a solid stream of research that built on itself. If I didn't do the first, he warned, I'd have trouble getting papers published. If I didn't do the second, scholars would see me as a dilettante and my career would suffer. At the time, I considered giving him a piece of my mind but held my tongue. Today, I thank God for that momentary lapse into restraint, because in retrospect I feel obliged to be more charitable to my would-be mentor. Although I never considered taking his advice, I can now admit that his diagnosis was correct, although his prognosis was somewhat hasty.

Many of my contemporaries talk with justifiable pride about having had streams of research. As the senior scholar in my story anticipated more than fifteen years ago, the most I can say for myself is that I have managed to dig a series of research puddles. Some have been deeper and wider than others, but in the end they constitute an aggregate much like the collages my oldest son made in kindergarten. My desire to build on prior studies has always been weak. I prefer to get in, get out, and do something else. I have never adopted, much less worked out, a consistent theory to which I could attach my hopes or identity. So if, as the editors of this book suggest, research careers are journeys, then mine has been one of wanderlust.

At some point I decided to carry a few maps that have remained with me since the beginning. But aside from setting the broad direction in which I wanted to go, I have never made a decision about my scholarly itinerary that didn't amount to the equivalent of choosing which town to go to next. I have usually chosen to do studies because I wanted to visit somewhere I hadn't been or because I wanted to show that some route was navigable. Just as often, happenstance was my compass.

This, of course, raises the issue of how I make sense of what I've done, and this essay is an act of such sensemaking. I will start by recounting how I came to do several studies. If nothing else, this will explain why I've played in puddles rather than streams. I will then articulate a handful of convictions that I think have shaped my approach to research. If there is any coherence to what I have done, it probably rests on these proclivities. My objective is to show that even a series of haphazard moves can have meaning, and that you can do reasonably well as a researcher without following anybody else's script including, I might add, my own.

Substantive Interests, Personal Agendas, and Luck

Despite what I usually say in the introductions to my papers, all of my studies have begun as attempts to wrestle with topics that I found personally compelling. I have never done a study to test or develop a theory, and only once was I interested—even secondarily—in exploring a new method. I have never aspired to extend a body of research. This is not because I find such goals objectionable. On the contrary, I respect this kind of work and admire it in others. The problem is that I have never had the foresight or patience that such work demands. I am too concrete to theorize in the absence of specifics and I am better at seeing patterns than posing hypotheses, although I have published several papers with hypotheses. I have also learned that if a research agenda does not speak to me, it has the proverbial snowball's chance of holding my attention long enough for completion. The life expectancies of research programs have always threatened to be greater than the duration of my interest and on numerous occasions they have made good on their threat. As evidence I could offer my hard disk: an electronic graveyard for data that might have become books and papers, had I only been able to persevere beyond an initial analysis.

Over the years I have accumulated a handful of relatively stable interests that are broadly substantive and nearly intellectual. These are the more or less public motifs that cut across my papers: the study of work and employment, an interest in science and technology, a concern for the dignity of labor, discomfort with corporations, and a questioning of organization studies' relationship to management. These themes have set the direction of my wandering and have defined the territories where I dug puddles. The reasons why I did specific studies are more personal and usually reflect a confluence of happenstance with an idiosyncratic agenda. Unlike my substantive interests, these reasons never show themselves in print, just as they don't appear in most other scholars' work, but I know they are what sustains my attention long enough to see a study through. A history of starts that ended in limbo have taught me that I should never begin a study unless the interplay of interests, idiosyncrasies, and happenstance is, like Goldilocks' porridge, "just right." To show how I decide what's "just right," let me explain how I embarked on three, substantively different studies. If nothing else, the differences validate the incoherence that my senior colleague warned me about so many years before on that bus ride in Monterrey.

FUNERAL WORK

My career began where most scholars' end: in a funeral home. I began studying funeral directing during my first year as a graduate student at MIT during John Van Maanen's introductory course in organization studies. John required students to do fieldwork. To prepare us for the ordeal, he taught us ethnosemantic techniques a la James Spradley (1979), a linguistic approach to ethnography that appealed to me as a former English major. Since MIT also required doctoral students to write a second-year research paper, I thought I'd kill two birds with one stone: I'd do the project for John and, in the process, do enough research to satisfy the second-year requirement. Three years later the study resulted in two papers: one published in *Urban Life* (now the *Journal of Contemporary Ethnography*) and the other in the *Administrative Science Quarterly* (Barley 1983a, 1983b).

Although I presented these papers as intentional investigations of organizational and occupational culture using the concepts of semiotics, neither organizational culture nor semiotics was on my mind when I began. In 1979 I had heard of neither. For better or worse, finding a theory after doing a study is a habit that I have indulged throughout my career. I justify it by arguing that theories found or developed later are closer to the data and make for better accounts.

A student at Yale once publicly deconstructed me, claiming that my decision to study funeral directing indicated that I was deeply troubled by Thanatos. Although I've never known what to make of that charge, I will admit that funeral work had the lure of the macabre. What is certainly true is that I was not and have never been interested in funeral homes as organizations. I was not interested in funeral directors as entrepreneurs or as small businessmen. I chose funeral directing because it spoke to my interest in what other people do for a living and, more specifically, because I thought it would teach me how to arrange a funeral, an issue that was heavy on my mind at the time. I also sensed it would be a good place to study symbols, thereby satisfying Van Maanen's requirements, but who knows what my subconscious was up to.

Given that I graduated from a doctoral program in organization studies, my choice to study work rather than organizations may seem skewed. You might argue that I did so because Van Maanen, who is also an ethnographer of work, was my mentor and actively supported my proclivity, which is true. You might also argue that I was granted more freedom than most students either enjoy or deserve. This is true as well. MIT's Organization Studies faculty encouraged students to follow their interests wherever they might lead, so long as we behaved like good empiricists. You might even make the intellectual case that I thought organization studies should be grounded in studies of work because work is what organizations organize. I have recently made such a case in print (Barley and Kunda 2001), but offering such an account of my agenda in 1979 would require too much retrospective construction. In 1979 I could not have articulated such a perspective because I didn't know enough organizational theory to have had the thought. The real reason I turned to studying other people's work had no intellectual merit at all. I was drawn to the ethnography of work because it gave (and still gives) me a chance to learn how to do different things—to be a voyeuristic jack-of-all-trades. In other words, that distinguished scholar hit the nail on the head back in Monterrey in 1984: studying work allowed me to be a dilettante, albeit not the sort he had in mind.

By the time I entered MIT, I had a varied history of employment. At fifteen, I took a job cleaning road kill off the highways of Virginia. From there I went on to sell shoes, lay gas lines, run a backhoe, work in a pathology lab, wash dishes, wait tables, do landscaping, teach junior high school, do counseling in residence halls, and supervise custodians. In the process, I discovered that even people who do menial jobs are proud of their work, that what they do is usually more interesting, more complicated, and more dignified than most people suspect, and that despite making the world go round, most people get little respect for what they do. I gravitated to the ethnography of work because it allowed me to write about the intricacies and dignities of other people's worlds, while granting me a license to peer into their lives. In short, studying work seemed like fun with a mission. It also meant I didn't have to deal with managers or with issues about which MBAs fantasize.

As I've already alluded, I chose funeral directing in part because my father was ill and at the time I thought he was dying. I thought that if I learned about funerals before I had to plan one, I'd be better prepared. As it turned out, my father recovered and lived another decade. I chose the specific funeral home I investigated because it was located a block from where I lived: a sample of convenience if there ever was one.

The paper I wrote for my second-year requirement bore little resemblance to the papers I ultimately published. At best, it was a facsimile of an ethnography of work in the tradition of Everett C. Hughes, Anselm Strauss, and Howard Becker (who have long been my intellectual heroes). I submitted the paper to *Urban Life* and was soundly rejected. So I put the paper in a file drawer and for two years pondered what to do with it. Most of my subsequent papers have had similar time-outs.

In the meantime, I took a course on metaphor from Don Schon and began reading linguistic anthropology, structural linguistics, and eventually semiotics (but then, as now, very little organizational theory). I slowly realized I could use the data I had collected to illustrate how semiotics can be used to study occupational cultures. I wrote a long paper detailing the code structures of funeral work. Peter Manning, who was visiting MIT at the time, had an interest in semiotics and served as my mentor. He advised me to break the paper into two parts. The first, I successfully published in *Urban Life*. The second, I submitted on a lark to the *Administrative Science Quarterly*. In 1982 *ASQ* put out a call for papers on organizational culture. I decided I had nothing to lose by submitting a paper on funeral directing that illustrated the utility of semiotic analysis. In three days I put a front and back end on a section of the longer paper that I had already written and then submitted it, thinking that I would surely be rejected. To my surprise (and the even greater surprise of the faculty), the paper was accepted. This taught me an important lesson about publishing: nothing ventured, nothing gained.

MEDICAL IMAGING

Arriving at a dissertation on medical imaging was no less haphazard. Just as I entered MIT with no intention of becoming an ethnographer (I went thinking that Ed Schein would teach me to be an organizational consultant), I also had no intention of studying technology. But the longer I was at MIT, the more my childhood interest in science and technology reemerged and I discovered yet another path by which research can substitute for doing the real thing. In high school, I was Mr. Science. I was the president of the science club. My science fair projects went to state and national competitions. As a senior, I envisioned myself majoring in biology and becoming a physician, if not a molecular biologist. For a variety of reasons, most of which are too embarrassing to admit in print, I abandoned my scientific aspirations during college for literature and the social sciences. Being surrounded by scientists and engineers at MIT apparently stimulated latent scientific urges.

By then, however, it was too late to become a scientist or an engineer, and even if it wasn't, I still didn't want to take chemistry or advanced calculus. So I thought, "If I can't be a scientist or a doctor or an engineer, why not study them"?

I reached this decision slowly, and Tom Allen provided the necessary serendipity. In 1982 I was working as Tom's teaching assistant in his course on managing research and development. Tom assigned his students Mertonian sociology of science to read. I became interested in the sociology of science and began reading it avidly, finding yet another way to avoid organization theory. At one point, I remember saying to Tom that I had uncovered plenty of research on science and scientific work, but almost nothing on engineers and even less on technology. To this he replied with a characteristically succinct global statement, "There is no sociology of technology worth talking about." (This was before Trevor Pinch and his colleagues framed the "social construction of technology" paradigm [see Bijker, Hughes, and Pinch 1987].) Since Tom was not a sociologist, I was skeptical of his sweeping claim, but further attempts to discover a literature led me to admit that even though he was an engineer, he was right. Tom's comment was for me the functional equivalent of the advice that Dustin Hoffman received in the early scenes of *The Graduate*. If there were no sociology of technology, then whatever I did in this area would be a contribution, no matter how poorly I might do it. This is when I learned another lesson that has influenced how I choose research topics. If you pick a topic of reasonable importance in which few others are interested, then it's harder to fail. When no one else knows much about something, they can't critique you with much credibility. Studies of technology and work were precisely the nearly null set I desired.

I began to read what I could on the impact of technology on work. After discarding the futurist and managerial literatures, which largely consisted of ungrounded opinions, I discovered that most real research on technology and work had been done by sociologists in the 1950s and by MIS people. In both cases, however, researchers tended to focus on blue-collar or clerical work. Gradually, it dawned on me that I had found an even emptier set: research on how technology alters the work of professional and technical workers.

At this point I cast around for computer technologies that were influencing how professionals did their jobs. Computer Assisted Design (CAD) was a relatively new development in engineering and architecture. I spent some time investigating the possibilities of studying CAD systems and learned two sobering facts. The first was that I had no clue what engineers did and that to learn enough engineering for me to comprehend what engineers were doing with CAD systems seemed like too much work. Second, I discovered that even though architects were talking about CAD, few used it and those who did were automating the work of drafters, on which there was already an emerging literature. So I turned to medicine, an area where I was more knowledgeable because I had minored in biology and had worked in a pathology lab.

My initial thought was to examine how artificial intelligence was altering medical diagnosis. I quickly learned, however, that despite the hype surrounding AI in medicine, no program was being used outside of the experimental setting in which it was built. In the process of stalking AI programs, I interviewed an expert in medical informatics. He told me that anyone who wanted to see how computers were changing medicine should study radiology because that's where "it was happening." At first I was disillusioned. CT scanners didn't look like my notion of a computer and they seemed far less sexy than artificial intelligence. But as my alternatives narrowed, I managed to convince myself that the suggestion made sense. Not only did I know something about anatomy and pathology, but if I did radiology I could at least hang out in a hospital!

Although I began studying medical imaging with the idea that I would examine how CT scanners and ultrasound were affecting the work of radiologists and radiological technologists, as in the funeral study I had no plan for making sense of what I found. I simply had faith that if I gathered data with enough points of comparison, something valuable would emerge. I completed my fieldwork before I discovered Giddens's (1976, 1984) theory of structuration, which eventually enabled me to tell a sufficiently sophisticated story about how CT scanning had evolved in the two hospitals to place a paper in *ASQ* (Barley 1986). It took another three years before I ran across Siegfried Nadel's (1957) theory of roles, with which I was able to frame differences between older and newer technologies in a way that led to my second *ASQ* paper on medical imaging (Barley 1990a).

MANAGERIAL IDEOLOGIES

While I was at MIT, the Organization Studies Group found itself at the center of emerging academic interest in organizational cultures. There was excitement about a new, more symbolic, approach to studying organizational life. For a while it seemed to some of us that anthropology might actually influence how organizational theorists studied organizations. Although the doctoral students at MIT may not have known much about organization theory, we did know how to do fieldwork. In time, however, it became clear that organizational culture had become more of a management fad than an intellectual revolution. Even scholarly work soon began to speak to managerial interests with—at least to my ear—overtones of social control. Resentment of this change initially led me to write a paper showing that despite what academics like to believe, practitioners had more of an impact on how academics conceptualized organizational culture than the reverse (Barley, Meyer, and Gash 1988). Being able to prove empirically what I saw as a sellout disillusioned me even more about the field's general pandering to the interests of managers. I thought that organizational culture had been co-opted and turned into a tool for normative control. Gideon Kunda, who shared an office with me at MIT, reached much the same conclusion in the course of doing his dissertation on a company known for its intentional promulgation of a crafted culture (Kunda 1992).

In 1989 Kunda visited Cornell University, where I was teaching. During a conversation over coffee, he argued that organizational theory has always been about control. What seemed to differ from one period to the next was whether fashionable theories advocated rational or normative control. Both of us had come to organization theory with a proclivity for seeing organizations as social problems. We were also, by then, both interested in distancing ourselves from the study of organizational culture, at least as it was commonly framed, so we vowed to write a historical paper that would make our case. Thus, began the research project that ultimately became "Design and Devotion" (Barley and Kunda 1992). The research was rooted in our desire to level a critique at the field as a whole.

"Design and Devotion" was written over three years during which we initially read and reread texts in managerial and organizational theory published as early as the mid-1800s. We also read histories of managerial and economic thought. Within the first year we were convinced that ideologies of rational and normative control did indeed oscillate, but we couldn't explain why. Without an explanation, the odds of publishing a paper in a highly visible journal were low, and why bother protesting if you aren't going to be read? We sat on the paper hoping to concoct an explanation for why the oscillations occurred when they did. In the meantime, I began reading long-wave theory with the intent of developing lectures on long waves for my course on science and engineering in industry. For reasons I can't explain, one day I noticed that the estimated timings of the upswings and downswings of long waves seemed to coincide roughly with the eras when we believed significant shifts in managerial discourse had occurred. Thus, the germ of our theoretical account for oscillations between rational and normative ideologies of control emerged serendipitously. With this insight in hand we gradually devised a consistent argument for the timing of ideological surges and began to gather data to dispute alternative explanations (in particular, that changes in managerial rhetoric were reactions to periods of labor unrest).

I could offer similar accounts for why I have pursued every other research project throughout my career. The specifics of each story would differ, but all would be tales of how interests, agendas, and happenstance blended at some point to motivate me sufficiently to embark on a project. My intent in offering these accounts is to illustrate why I have done what I have done and why my research career may appear to be more scattered than most. Although substantive interests do link some of my studies, most of the coherence in my work is a matter of style, which springs from a set of proclivities and convictions that form my sense of self as a scholar.

Disciplinary Eclecticism

I have long had difficulty pledging my attention to a single field. Even in high school, when I was primarily oriented to the sciences, I found more real joy in literature, history, philosophy, and government. I went to college thinking I would major in biology and minor in English but ended up doing precisely the reverse, and even then I couldn't keep myself from taking large numbers of courses in philosophy, sociology, and psychology. This caused trouble in my English classes where I routinely wrote sociological and psychological rather than literary interpretations of texts that my professors preferred. I went from English into a master's program in Student Personnel Administration heavily weighted toward counseling and developmental psychology, where I started reading organization theory on the side. By the time I found myself in a graduate program in organization studies, staying within the accepted boundaries of a field seemed too confining.

On this score, MIT was a fortuitous choice. The organization studies faculty had little faith and even less interest in the field's mainstream. They did not expect students to be interested either. In fact, mainstream organization theory was so invisible at MIT that as doctoral students we eventually felt we had to hold our own seminars to learn what outsiders considered to be the field's core. Instead of mandating an elaborate curriculum, the faculty provided two overview courses and then encouraged students to follow their own interests. Instead of management theory, we read anthropology, sociology, psychology, and, in my case, linguistics, semiotics, and philosophy. Although I was never explicitly taught it, I learned at MIT that innovations occur when scholars bring together ideas from disparate places in ways that allow us to see old problems in new ways. This type of scholarship seemed to be more fun than becoming an expert at seeing new data in old ways (which is the logic of hypothesis testing within an established line of research).

I attribute most of my success in being published to my willingness to plunder ideas from disciplines that other organizational theorists rarely raid. Anthropology and linguistics have served me particularly well. My exposure to anthropology began with Van Maanen's decision to teach ethnosemantics, the branch of anthropology dedicated to mapping how members of a culture classify plants, animals, and other objects salient to their experience. Exposure to ethnosemantics took me deeper into linguistic anthropology and to the work of Benjamin Lee Whorf (1956) and Edward Sapir (1921) who argued that language encodes how members of a culture think about their world. I moved from reading linguistic anthropology to linguistics itself and then to semiotics, the study of codes. As I have already explained, semiotics provided the tools I needed to make sense of the culture of funeral directing. Familiarity with linguistics also proved crucial in developing the syntactical and semantic indicators that Deborah Gash, Gordon Meyer, and I used to show that practitioners had more strongly influenced academic discourse on organizational culture than the reverse.

Linguistics is not the only field from which I have borrowed. The notion of long waves that Kunda and I used to explain oscillations in managerial ideology came from reading European economic theories of technological revolutions (Mensch 1979; van Duijn 1983; Clark, Freeman, and Soete 1984; Coombs 1984). The history of technology provided the data and ideas necessary for "What Can We Learn from the History of Technology?" (Barley 1998). Cultural anthropology provided the concepts of polychronic and monochronic time (Hall 1969), which allowed me to analyze data on how computational technologies altered the temporal experiences of radiologists and radiological technologists (Barley 1988).

At this point you might ask why I have been so willing to contribute to a literature (organization studies) that I eschew as a primary source of ideas. The disparity disappears, if you accept that organization studies is not a discipline but rather a substantive area for research. Organizations are important social phenomena. They have monumental consequences for individuals and societies. In fact, I do not believe that we can understand contemporary life without understanding how organizations shape our realities. Nevertheless, as important as organizations may be, they remain but one facet of society and, as such, are an area for substantive application. Because organization studies is a substantive area, I believe that it has not yet yielded (and that it is unlikely to ever yield) a consistent, paradigmatic framework for analyzing social life. Organizational researchers must turn to the theories and modes of analysis of the disciplines (economics, sociology, anthropology, psychology) for frameworks to help us make sense of the empirical patterns we observe. Confining oneself solely to organization theory leaves one little choice but to predicate research on historical antecedence (so and so did this) or untheorized contingencies (they studied manufacturing, we are studying services).

After two decades of raiding other fields, I can offer several observations on using other disciplines as a source of ideas. First, you can never predict when you will use a pilfered concept. Sometimes, as was the case when I was writing about the temporal structures of radiology departments (Barley 1988) and the roles of ESA scientists (Zabusky and Barley 1997), you encounter the concepts before you have the data for which they appear relevant. In other instances, the data sit waiting (sometimes for years) until you chance on an idea that allows an elegant interpretation, as was true with my use of semiotics, structuration, long waves, and commodification.

A second observation follows: a proclivity for disciplinary eclecticism requires acts of faith. Because it is impossible to decide what concepts will prove relevant for a particular piece of research ahead of time, all you can do is compile a store of ideas with the hope that sooner or later some will prove useful. Interestingly, the strategy of collecting disparate ideas with the hope that they may prove relevant for future innovation seems similar to the way Hargadon and Sutton (1997) claim that designers work.

Bridging Camps

Just as I have disregarded the substantive boundaries of the field, so I have chaffed at being too closely identified with a specific methodology, epistemology, or ideology. My preference has been to slink back and forth across the lines that define the field's politics.

QUALITATIVE VERSUS QUANTITATIVE RESEARCH

The line for which I have the least patience is the one so frequently and passionately drawn between qualitative and quantitative research. My impatience with debates over the relative superiority of qualitative and quantitative methods began in graduate school. Qualitative research flourished at MIT, but it was by no means universally viewed as legitimate. Students heard, and not always in muted tones, the same arguments that rage in the field over the relative advantages and disadvantages of numbers and words. All of us know the litany. Qualitative research is more attuned to interpretations, it remains closer to the data, and it is well suited for exploratory research. Quantitative research is more rigorous, more suitable for drawing generalizations, and less dependent on the skills of the researcher.

Both camps have a point. Because I worked closely with faculty who stood on either side of the line, I concluded, perhaps out of self-preservation, that each style has advantages as well as blind spots. To align oneself, a priori, with either is, therefore, irrational. Like craft workers, researchers are better off choosing the most appropriate tools for the job or the tools with which they are most handy. Because of this conviction, I have dug some of my research puddles exclusively with qualitative tools and others with quantitative tools. In yet other studies I have mixed methods. Over the years, I have developed rules of thumb about when to use one approach, the other, or both.

As unsophisticated as it may sound, I believe qualitative methods are better for determining "what happens" and that quantitative methods are better for showing "that something happened." Said differently, because qualitative data invite wallowing in behavior, events, and interpretations, they facilitate discovery and pattern finding. In contrast, quantitative methods require you to have a pattern, model, or framework in mind: to count effectively you first have to know what's worth counting. These respective strengths indicate how one can fruitfully combine the two techniques in a single study. Participant-observation, textual analysis, and other qualitative methods enable researchers to identify regularities in interpretations, actions, and interactions as well as instances of behavior, talk, or writing that can serve as indicators of the regularities. Quantitative data can then be used to show the existence of and stability or change in the patterns to which qualitative analysis points.

This was my approach to mixing qualitative and quantitative data in my first paper on medical imaging (Barley 1986). I relied on observations of interactions between radiologists and technologists to identify scripted behaviors that characterized different time periods in two radiology departments' histories. To show that the scripts differed in the two departments, I then coded the interactions that appeared in my field notes and subjected the codes to regression analysis to confirm that periods of structuring occurred.

Quantitative data are also better suited for ruling out alternative explanations. They enable one to judge the consistency or inconsistency of an explanation across cases, a task for which contrary cases and counterfactuals are ill suited. Kunda and I turned to quantitative data for this reason: to rule out labor unrest as a consistent explanation for shifts between ideologies of rational and normative control (Barley and Kunda 1992). Quantitative data are also requisite for showing the existence of trends. Debby Knight and I used quantitative data on stress articles to show that stress talk in the popular literature lagged research interest in the topic, and that nursing journals were more likely to discuss stress than were journals written for physicians (Barley and Knight 1992).

Conversely, I rely more heavily on qualitative data when the objective is to portray how a group of individuals understand their world (an emic agenda) and how their activities are structured (an etic agenda). The comparative work that Bonnie Nelsen and I published on EMT's (Nelsen and Barley 1997) and the paper that I published with Stacia Zabusky on technicians' careers (Zabusky and Barley 1996) are examples of an emic use of qualitative data.

Despite these advantages, there are dangers in mixing qualitative and quantitative methods that I did not anticipate early in my career. First, those who are committed to dismissing qualitative research can use your work to argue that mixed-methods papers succeed because of their quantitative data. On more occasions that I care to count, I have been told that my work on CT scanners was exemplary because, unlike most qualitative researchers, I "did more than tell a story." When I hear such comments, I worry that I have done qualitative research a disservice insofar as my papers are used as models to instruct graduate students on how to do a "good ethnography" because of their quantitative data. A second danger in mixing methods is that people may focus on the paper's analytic style rather than its substance. I encountered this with my research on CT scanners and on rhetorics of organizational culture. Commentators sometimes focus on my methods but fail to mention the paper's message, which was the purpose for doing the research in the first place. When I hear such comments I think the field needs to continually remind itself that doing research is ultimately about substance, not tools.

CONSTRUCTIONISM VERSUS REALISM

Drawing battle lines between qualitative and quantitative research sometimes masks a deeper and equally misguided schism: the war between constructionists and realists. Over the last decade, it has become fashionable in organization studies to claim allegiance to a pure ontology. On one side are those who claim that organizational realities are socially constructed, a claim, which in its most extreme form, implies "relative" and "ephemeral." On the other side are those who argue that social life has an objective reality akin to the natural world. These alternate views of social reality are as old as philosophy itself and have diffused into organization studies from sociology and anthropology, where realists and constructionists have elevated ontological debate to a cottage industry. My conviction is that taking a strong stance on ontological matters may be good for one's career. It certainly provides one with a community. But too much ontology saps energy away from empiricism and may, in fact, substitute for serious research.

On these issues I was strongly influenced by the Chicago School sociologists of the first half of the twentieth century who adopted a pragmatic stance toward ontology, in both senses of the term (for accounts of the Chicago School, see Faris 1967; and Lewis and Smith 1980). It seems to me that because social worlds are, by definition, products of human action and interpretation, it is impossible to argue against social constructionism. But to say that something is socially constructed is not equivalent to saying that it has no facticity. As W. I. Thomas put it, "When people believe things to be real, they are real in their consequences" (Thomas and Thomas 1928, 572). In this regard, technology is particularly instructive. There can be no doubt that technologies are socially constructed: They are designed, adopted, diffused, and used by humans. Consequently, technologies almost always encode beliefs about the way the world works, and often, the way it should work. But to propose that because technologies are social products, they pose no material constraints or affordances, demands an act of ideological blindness. To prove the folly of such a stance one need only attempt to do without electricity for a day. Although perhaps different in degree, the mixture of the interpretive and the material that characterizes the use of a technology is no different in kind than the mix of interpretation and facticity that marks all social life. This I take to be the primary point of Anthony Giddens's (1984) theory of structuration and Bourdieu's (1980) theory of practice.

Since graduate school I have therefore resisted aligning myself with either side of the ontological debate just as I have refused to fight in the methodology wars. My approach has been to find a middle ground: to document how and why people interpret their worlds in the way they do and then to show how these interpretations have effects that go beyond what was intended or foreseen. As a result my papers tend to mix interpretations and descriptions of interpretations with data on trends and structural explanations.

The approach carries costs. One is that colleagues may insist on allocating your work to one of the camps you hope to transcend. I am frequently said to be a social constructionist (and sometimes a subjectivist), in part, because I do ethnography and, in part, because readers have only read the papers I have written with an emic agenda. At other times I have been embraced or maligned as a realist and a materialist on the basis of papers that take a more etic stance and that locate causality in the economy or the material properties of technology.

BEING CRITICAL OR MAINSTREAM

Over the last decade a new distinction has emerged in organization studies to create even more boundaries and identities. On one side are scholars whose research is intentionally critical not only of organizations and management but of organization studies itself. On the other side are a much larger group of researchers who accept the role that organizations play in society, who embrace organization studies as it is typically practiced, and who pursue research from either a scientific or utilitarian perspective. Members of the first group have generally drawn the line. Members of the second group are often unaware of their membership. The first group frequently calls the second group, the "mainstream," and which is said to be "unreflective." Critical researchers usually distinguish themselves from the mainstream in terms of methods, ontology, and epistemology. In general, they are more accepting of qualitative research, social constructionism, phenomenology, postmodernism, and other French philosophies. These differences are, however, epiphenomenal: they are correlates of a deeper distinction, which is social and political. Critical researchers tend to be dissatisfied with the status quo and dedicate their research to identifying, if not eliminating, the inequities of organizational life. The critical wing views organizations as loci of social problems ranging from gender discrimination to unequal distributions of power and control.

Being strongly influenced by the counterculture of the 1960s and 1970s, my sympathies have long lay with the critical agenda. My initial interest in organization studies was strongly shaped by my attraction to an earlier generation of scholars who criticized organizational life: for instance, Chick Perrow, David Silverman, Egon Bittner, Alvin Gouldner, Kenneth Boulding, and John Van Maanen. In fact, I like to think that some portion of my research has also been critical in its intent and tone (Barley, Meyer, and Gash 1988; Barley and Kunda 1992, 2001; Stern and Barley 1996). Nevertheless, my stance on the emerging critical wing of organization studies is one of ambivalence, especially with respect to tactics and strategy.

Accompanying the trend for scholars to identify themselves as "critical" has been a tendency not only to define one's work in opposition to the mainstream but to distance oneself from the mainstream altogether. The urge to build and legitimate a distinctive critical identity has led to founding journals dedicated to critical studies (for example, *Dragon, Organization*) and to forming professional societies to promote the critical turn (the Standing Conference on Organizational Symbolism, Critical Management Studies). Although I understand the benefits of affiliation and legitimation, there is danger in turning inward. Although being part of a safe community makes it easier to say whatever one wants, it increases the odds of speaking only to like-minded others. If a researcher's agenda is social change, it seems to me that nothing could be more defeating than self-marginalization. This is why I have chosen to work my variant of a critical agenda within the mainstream.

Early on I set myself the goal of publishing in journals, in particular the *Administrative Science Quarterly*, read by the majority of the field. I resisted publishing in less widely read journals that were more sympathetic either to my message or my methods. I believe that unless you can communicate with the center, there is no hope of effecting change on issues that one holds dear, of influencing how members of the field think, or of broadening the type of research that the field considers legitimate.

There are, of course, costs to adopting such a strategy. For instance, to play in the center, one has to accept some of the center's rules to be granted admission to the game. These include choosing one's language carefully; softening—if not disguising—one's indignation; adopting methods, forms of discourse, and styles of reasoning that are more widely held to be legitimate;

and stomaching reviewers' comments even if you don't agree with them and then making changes that enable your paper to be published. Taking this stance may also increase the effort required to publish one's work. Liminality is another cost. Being neither fully mainstream nor fully critical can leave one feeling like a perpetual outsider. In the worst-case scenario, writing critically for the mainstream may invite the charge of having sold out.

Nevertheless, for me, the benefits of speaking to the mainstream have outweighed the costs. As I look over my career, I am certain that I have had opportunities that would not have become available had I chosen not to speak to mainstream organization studies. Perhaps the most significant was the opportunity to edit the *Administrative Science Quarterly*. Although editors have much less power over what a journal publishes than many scholars believe, editors can encourage submissions on specific topics from scholarly communities that do not normally see the journal as an outlet. As editor of *ASQ*, I hope I was able to make qualitative and critical researchers feel more comfortable submitting their papers to *ASQ* for publication. What I know for sure is that I would have never become editor of the journal had I not chosen to publish in the mainstream and, particularly, in *ASQ* itself.

Another important consequence of my decision to play within the mainstream came in 1996 when Bob Sutton and I founded the Center for Work, Technology, and Organization at Stanford's School of Engineering. The credibility that we had managed to develop in the field at large undoubtedly influenced the Engineering School's decision to allocate resources and new faculty lines to establish a research program focused on qualitative studies of work and technology. Finally, by choosing to work within the mainstream, I have gradually acquired visibility that has brought opportunities to serve on committees that advise policymakers on workforce issues. In short, I firmly believe that straddling the boundary between mainstream and critical studies while writing primarily for the former, increases the odds not only of disseminating important critiques but of gaining access to positions from which it is possible to make a difference in the field and on social issues. This, for me at least, is worth whatever compromises I may have made.

WALTER R. NORD

Comments on "Puddle Jumping as a Career Strategy"

TWO THEMES ARE implicit in "Puddle Jumping as a Career Strategy" by Steve Barley that seem important in accounting for his successful career: they are passion and craft. In commenting on his paper I suggest that those of us who attempt to guide others in developing their career strategies ought to give these themes more emphasis than we ordinarily do. In addition, we might consider redesigning doctoral programs to place greater emphasis on them.[1]

Barley's review of his career is engaging, thought provoking, and informative. I hope many people will read it. In my comments, I attempt to cull some themes from it, assess them using my own experiences, and suggest that these themes can be informative in considering academic career strategies more generally. In particular, I suggest that we can improve the career process if we overcome certain illusions about careers and what is needed to do good work in organization studies—illusions (although he did not call them that) that Steve was able to avoid by allowing his passions and sense of craft to guide him.

Early on, in reflecting on the worlds of the advisors and the advisees, Steve highlighted tensions in advice giving about academic careers. This portion of Steve's paper was especially interesting to me because I too have served (less successfully than I wished) as "elder," advising doctoral students about their careers. Unfortunately, like many of those who advised Steve, the guidance I offered was based on my image of conventional practice.

In retrospect, I fear that this advice suffered from my neglecting the positive contribution personal passions make to good scholarship. For example,

1. The helpful comments of Ann Nord and Michele Walpole on earlier versions of this paper are greatly appreciated.

a few years ago, I recall advising female graduate students who wanted to focus on women's issues to try to develop a theoretical orientation rather than
pursue a research trajectory that seemed to promise a less obvious "academic" contribution. Later on my friends Linda Smircich and Joanne Martin convinced me that this well-intended advice was probably not good and
I would have done better had I attempted to work with the students' mind-
sets rather than the illusions I had of what yields academic success. Using
Culbert's definition—mind-sets are "distinctive viewpoints, needs, agendas
that determine how an individual views and engages categories of events"
(1996, 330).

In view of my own career and my less than successful past advice giving,
as I was reading the first few of paragraphs of Steve's piece, the words of one
of my favorite songs by Joni Mitchell that Judy Collins made famous years
ago, "Both Sides Now," kept going through my mind. The song goes as follows:

Verse 1

Bows and flows of angel hair and ice cream castles in the air
And feather canyons everywhere, I've looked at clouds that way.
But now they only block the sun, they rain and snow on everyone.
So many things I would have done but clouds got in my way.

Chorus

I've looked at clouds from both sides now,
From up and down, and still somehow
It's clouds illusions I recall.
I really don't know clouds at all.

Verse 3

Tears and fears and feeling proud to say "I love you" right out loud,
Dreams and schemes and circus crowds, I've looked at life that way.
But now old friends are acting strange, they shake their heads; they say I've
    changed.
Something's lost but something's gained in living every day.

Chorus

Repeat

The word "illusions" and the theme of both sides indicating appearances
changing over time are key here, because when advising on careers I was using my images of the path to a successful academic career. However, as I
have aged and reflected on my own career, I think I am closer to seeing
"both sides now" and recognizing that the career image I was using as a
template may have been an illusion based on my reading of the published

work of successful scholars and an image of what some have called the "received view." I fear that such an account may privilege the cognitive dimension and neglect aspects of the human side that helped the scholars do their good work. Perhaps most importantly, it bypasses any passions that may have energized their work.

In retrospect I should have known better, because most of what others and I consider to be my own best work was highly driven by my passion for the subject matter at the time. For example, I remember when I was doing my early work on Marx (Nord 1974) I was impatient to get out of bed at 5 AM to work on the project. By contrast, like Steve, I have a number of incomplete projects that have resided in vertical (not circular) files for years because I lost interest in completing them.

Why, if passions played a large part in my own work, did I not advise others to follow their own passions? Probably, there are a couple of reasons for this. First, I was wary about encouraging other people to take what seemed to be high-risk avenues. Second, my focus was on how they might make themselves look best with respect to gaining an entry-level position. Third, in my own training, passions were never emphasized as a legitimating reason for intellectual/research work. In short, I was offering others an illusion of the path to success, rather, as my friend Sam Culbert (1996) would advise me, working within their mind-sets.

The illusions theme helped me understand more deeply what Steve might be saying. Specifically, Steve had been able to resist being controlled by many of the notions that Weick (2001) might suggest as mentors we use to "make sense" of our field (for example, qualitative versus quantitative research, critical versus mainstream, and so on). To do the type of work that he personally valued, Steve fought off illusions that people like us (colleagues and mentors) permit to govern our actions. Governed by these perceptions, in addition to overlooking the role of passions, we may ignore some other important matters, specifically, in Steve's case, the importance of being a good craftsperson. This craft dimension is the second theme I read into his paper that helps us to understand how Steve, despite refusing to follow conventional wisdom, was able to make such valuable contributions as he has.

It appears that sense of craft permitted Steve to do high-quality work by following his passions, free from the tradition-imposed straitjackets that constrain others. MIT faculty played a big role here by supporting both passion and dedication to craft. In Steve's words they "encouraged students to follow their interests wherever they might lead as long as they behaved like good empiricists." I speculate that these commitments to craft guided so heavily by his passions helped him to do such excellent work.

If one studies Steve's previous work, his strong commitment to craft is evident. For example, one of the very few methods sections that I have ever read that I can, to this day, almost write from memory is the one in his paper on CT scanners (Barley 1986). What made this section so memorable for me is the care reflected in the extraordinary time and effort he put into data collection.

Recall that in this study Steve compared the radiology departments of two hospitals. To collect data, his observation at both hospitals began about four months before the scanners began to operate. Detailing his methodology he wrote:

> Throughout the study, I gathered data by attending individual examinations in their entirety. The occurrence and timing of events were recorded chronologically during the course of each examination . . . to create behavioral records for every procedure observed. Conversation between participants was either taped or written in shorthand devised for the purpose of documenting setting-specific argots. In addition to behavioral records, I also sought and recorded participant's interpretations of events at the time that they occurred or shortly thereafter.
>
> Over the course of the study, approximately 400 complete radiological examinations including 96 CT scans were observed. With the exception of a six-week hiatus during the Christmas holidays, data were collected at the two sites on alternate working days for the period of one year. (85)

Thus, while in the current essay Steve described his decision to study the topic as being haphazard, just as his decision to become an ethnographer was (although personally meaningful), there was nothing haphazard about his approach and his commitments to collecting high-quality data.

In short, in his work Steve has combined passion with dedication to excellent craftsmanship. In actualizing this pattern, he struggled successfully against being controlled by the socially constructed "guidelines" about how we academics "make sense" of our experience or punctuate our professional world. In addition to not allowing himself to be limited by his elders' dire predictions of "career problems" from his unorthodoxy, we see how the commitments helped Steve resist the traps set by some of the prevailing apparent dichotomies that dominate our field such as "critical" versus "mainstream" and qualitative versus quantitative. Indeed, one of the things I have admired most about his radiology study is how he combined what appeared to be qualitative data with quantitative analysis (for example, analysis on linear and quadratic trends) to gain insights.

Obviously, Steve took risks; being "outside the dots" one's peers and academic mentors use to construct their understandings could leave one anomic and without a useful framework to work within (not to mention without a PhD). Similarly, one's passions could lead to chaos. These things did not happen to Steve, so it is useful to ponder the "why not?" question.

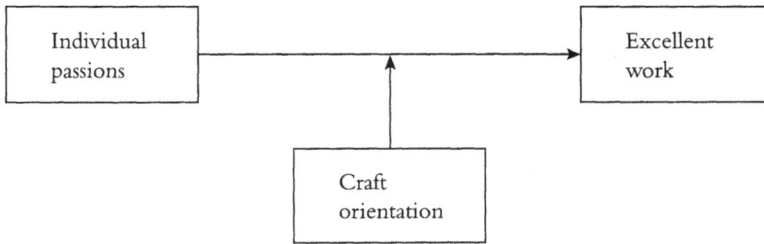

FIGURE I. Some highlights of the process underlying Barley's work.

Using the themes I have noted above, the answer to the "why not?" question seems reasonably clear. What helped Steve to pursue his passions in intellectually valuable ways was that throughout his career they were guided by his sense of craft. Steve chose his methods because they helped him explore what he was interested in. He valued good data, with "good" being defined in terms of the particular research objective that his passions dictated, rather than some abstract notion such as ratio data. In Figure I, I attempt to capture the highlights of the process I see underlying Steve's efforts.

Clearly, Figure I is not the whole story and perhaps some of the arrows should point both ways. More than likely it omits many possibly important contributors to his excellent work, such as individual talents, propensities to take risks, luck, and so forth. However, it does feature some concepts that are useful for explaining what worked for Barley and that to date seem not to have been emphasized sufficiently in analysis of career strategies in our field. Importantly, however, it suggests that passions and craft may work in combination.

Reflection

Reflecting on Steve's description of his intellectual journey we see that he relied on his passions for energy, inspiration, and direction and then moved forward guided by his ingrained sense of quality craftwork and avoiding the distractions of the illusions that many of us use to make sense of our progression and to try to advise others.

Because I respect Steve and his work so highly and I wish our field had more people like him in it, based on the foregoing I offer the following addendum, in which I take the hazardous step of trying to derive a framework that others might consider in developing doctoral students.

Addendum

For years now, members of our department at the University of South Florida have been trying to get our dean's support for a PhD program in organization studies. Serendipitously, at about the time I was completing the first draft of this paper, we met with our dean in this regard. In the conversation I asked him, "What specifically, from your perspective, do we need to do to get your support?" He responded that he wanted to see what the product would be. While writing the second draft of these comments, the dean's request for an image of the product was in the back of my mind.

As I came to the sentence in the above where I indicated that I think our field would be far better if it had more Steve Barleys, I began to think about using Steve as an image of our product for our dean. Accordingly, I began thinking about how to design doctoral programs that would foster development of such people.

Given what I abstracted in Figure 1, I began to think that perhaps Steve had inadvertently provided guidance about what a good doctoral program might be like. Two important components (the passions that motivate and the sense of craft that helps to guide the passions into quality work) are crucial. Providing this sense of craft might be what we as faculty can help give to our students. We might also encourage them to articulate their passions, although I doubt that as a faculty we are prepared to engender the passions and probably should not do so even if we could. At the very least, however, we should do our best not to stifle their passions. Perhaps we can help them overcome the socialization that occurs in much of the educational process that leads them to repress their passions.

Moreover, we might constantly keep the craft goal active not only in how we advise students but also in how we design PhD programs. For example, we might employ the "craft test" to decide what becomes part of the program and what does not. The craft test is straightforward. It consists of one question for any proposed addition to the program: "Does it [the proposed addition] contribute to developing the sense of craft?"

This simple test screens potential additions to the program. I do not know the specifics of what might be added to or deleted from current programs, but I expect that if faculties applied the test in their local settings, they could find ways to provide such experiences and to avoid building in passion-dampening requirements. One possible step would be to discuss the craft dimension when we critique published work in seminars; a second would be to think about colleagues on our campus in terms of their "craftspersonship" and encourage our students to work with those, almost regardless of their academic area, whom we judge as strong on this feature. I suspect that often, such enculturation could be furthered by promoting contact with faculty from disciplines outside the College of Business. For example, in my own career, although I was in the Psychology Department, much of my appreciation for the culture of scholarship was gained by my fortuitous study of sociology with scholars such as Robert Hamblin and Alvin Gouldner (see Nord 1993).

Of course some things, for practical reasons, might not be subjected to the craft test, but exceptions should be few and have substantial justification. Undoubtedly we could and should insist that our students become familiar with the key components of the past and present literature of organization studies, whatever we define them to be. Further, we would need to be sure graduates have some recognized subject to teach, so they can get an academic job, but of course teaching itself should be viewed as a craft. Relying on the general approach of passion guided by craft orientation, with these caveats, we might design programs that do better than our current ones to help others to achieve great success as Steve has, by using passions to direct their journeys and to guide them by the discipline of craft.

Returning to the message of the Joni Mitchell's song, I conclude, I have looked at careers in organization studies from both sides now and I seriously entertain the possibility that I really don't know them at all. However, if I am aware that it may be the illusions that I recall—perhaps I can do more good or at least do less harm. I might even be able to offer an orientation that helps produce more stimulating and productive colleagues. Steve's path still seems risky but from his career its potential benefits are clear. I need to be careful not to let my own propensities for low risk interfere with others for whom greater risk is comfortable. Perhaps in advising them, the best I can do is to share my perceptions and present them as perceptions, making clear the illusionary quality they may have.

Although I do not know a simple way to manage the passion problem, I have several thoughts. Perhaps the most difficult and important thing we mentors can do in this regard is to manage our own egos so as to avoid following the temptation to try to make those we try to teach become as much like us as we can make them. To manage our egos, we may need to "let go" in some respects. Perhaps the orientation for such letting go resembles that of the prototypical Rogerian psychotherapist. Following this orientation we would accept that not everyone has our values and passions. However, we would also recognize that strongly developed passions may be a major stimulus for doing good work, and that we may be well advised to look for their passions and to encourage them to own and articulate them and to express them in their work. In doing so, not only may we help them to do better work but also, at the same time, we may learn from them.

LESLIE A. PERLOW

Puddles, Principles, and Passion

The rain has stopped, leaving everything fresh and inviting. So Ernst, a young blue crocodile, and his big green brother, Sol, search for things to collect in their shiny pails. Conventional Sol plans to fill his pail with rocks and seashells, feathers and string. Ernst is more imaginative and would like to collect colorful, slippery puddles. "You can't collect them"! Sol scoffs. But Ernst finds a way to put more of the world into his pail than Sol ever thought possible.

So writes Elisa Kleven in her children's story book, *The Puddle Pail*.

Our field, much like Sol, scoffs at the idea of collecting puddles. It cannot be done. It will amount to nothing worthwhile. Yet, like Ernst, Stephen Barley has found a way and, indeed, has become a preeminent scholar in our field.

Ever since my first days in graduate school at MIT, I have routinely been pointed to Steve and his work for guidance. He is always held up as a model, as someone who knows how to structure and present his theoretical framing, the analysis of his ethnographic data, and the discussion and implications of his findings. I long ago lost count of the number of times I read his doctoral dissertation. I had it checked out of the library for months as I tried desperately to figure out how to make sense of the huge quantity of data I too had amassed.

So it was with great respect and curiosity that I read about Steve's career strategy. And I found great reassurance in what I read. Maybe it is because we both engage in qualitative, inductive data collection, or we trained at MIT, or we share the same mentors. Whatever the reason, much like Steve, I too have found myself wandering from various pursuits of passion in a nonlinear and often unconventional way. And I too have frequently found my path to be the subject of intense questioning and criticism.

Yet, what Steve's chapter—and his career on which it's based—suggest is that maybe there is nothing wrong with that path. Indeed, maybe it is an alternative approach to building a career, not a worse one. After all, it is not that Steve advocates no principles. Rather, his chapter is deeply rooted in principles—principles that ensure research quality in both method and content. He describes his obsessive empiricism demonstrated through his amassing of large quantities of quality data and his conducting of comparative analysis. He also writes of his desire to bridge camps of qualitative and quantitative researchers as well as the deeper schism between constructivists and realists. And he is clear that despite his eclectic and critical interests, he has made sure to publish in widely read and highly regarded journals.

Still, principles and passion, without a clear direction, have generally not been considered sufficient motivation for conducting research in our field. Indeed, despite the groundwork Steve has laid for a nonlinear career progression based on passion, many tell me what Steve heard back on the shuttle bus in 1984—what it takes to get tenure is having an identity associated with your name. For many, the problems start with writing the dissertation proposal. And for those who are lucky enough to find faculty who will support them in getting past that hurdle, there is the job market to contend with and the constant questioning of the research stream one is building. And that interrogation only intensifies throughout the promotion process as constructions develop about a person's position within our field.

Yet, when research is guided by principles, and driven by passion, is that not ideal? Why does it matter if one purposefully engages in the systematic development of a stream of research that builds on itself and ensures publication? It begs two questions: What are we trying to accomplish as a field? And how can young scholars most effectively contribute?

Institutional Terrain

The stories in this book are set against particular backgrounds. Each author draws your attention to significant contexts of their particular experiences. Here we draw your attention to features of the broader background that most of the stories share. In doing so, we hope to help readers identify the changing institutional terrain you traverse in making your own research journey and telling your own story. The terrain of the scholar's journey has shifted. We know that these changes mean that the younger scholar and the non-Anglo scholar will face different signposts and different crossroads.

Attempting to provide a broader context for the interpretation of the stories has been a humbling experience. Each time we've tried to draw boundaries around the field of inquiry, to describe periods or schools of thought, we found our attempts wanting. We simply have not been able to account for the diversity of intellectual activity that has brought us to where we are today. We have discovered for ourselves what Jones (2002), following Derrida and discussing the reception of Foucault's oeuvre in organization studies, describes as "the problems of reading and interpretation, which are our one in the same time problems of decision, of marking out heritages and dividing them up." Thus, we acknowledge the partiality and the subjectivity of this particular history.

For, history it is. The most important contextual factor for this set of stories is the history of organizational studies (analysis, behavior, development, science, theory, and so on). Today, beginning scholars enter an established field of enquiry. It has not always been so. One of the first travel atlases that attempted to map the field, the *Handbook of Organizations*, was published in 1965. The editor, James March, referred to the "immaculate conception of organization studies" (xii) in describing the genesis of the field with "a history but not a pedigree" (ix). He continues, "The field as a more or less identifiable cluster of research interests within a number of social sciences dates for most purposes from a group of books written between 1937 and 1943—Barnard, Roethlisberger & Dickson, and Simon" (xiii). A bit later, he adds, "This Handbook reflects the vigour of the field and its tendency to become better defined. It could not have been written 15 years ago; certainly it will not survive another 15" (xv). All of the chapter contributors to this book began their PhD education within that fifteen-year "use-by" estimate. One of our contributors, Karl Weick, contributed a chapter to the *Handbook*.

Within each of the established social science disciplines a study of organizations grew. Industrial/organizational psychology is a healthy subset of psychology (Dunnette 1990). Organizational sociology is perhaps the most vibrant sector of sociology. Organizational economics is thriving. However, Pfeffer (1997, 9–18) notes that organizational political science has all but disappeared and the organizational has become less important and too applied for the psychology and sociology disciplines. The intellectual ferment around the study of organizations intersected with institutional change to shift the bulk of organizational studies to the business schools.

From the late 1950s, business schools faced the challenge of transforming business education into an academically respectable program. The pressures were made explicit by the Ford Foundation (Gordon and Howell 1959) and the Carnegie Foundation (Pierson et al. 1959) studies of university business education. As put by Pierson, "Implicit in the conception of business education set forth in this study is the prime role which should be accorded research. The need is not for just any kind of research, as that rather elastic term is often defined, but for research which meets high scientific standards and is aimed at problems of general significance" (Pierson et al. 1959, xv). In response, business schools hired from the disciplines: psychology, sociology (for example, James Thompson, the founder of *Administrative Science Quarterly*), political science, economics, and so on. These scholars worked hard to successfully raise standards, build research programs, and develop hefty publication records. Certainly from the sixties through the eighties much of what went on in American business schools was oriented toward earning the respect of the nonbusiness faculties. The rest of the university lagged in its recognition of these efforts and achievements. Even within the business school, self-esteem has been an issue. For example, in hiring, there was a continuing reliance on discipline-trained staff. It took a graduate student revolt in 1981 to get Northwestern faculty to consider job candidates with business school PhDs, that is, to challenge the unspoken belief in the superiority of discipline-trained PhDs.

As business schools became more research oriented, both the number of doctoral programs and the number of total graduates increased. In 1956, about twenty-five schools awarded 158 doctorates across all the business school areas (Pierson et al. 1959, 297). By way of contrast, there are now one hundred seventeen institutions in America offering doctoral programs in business (AACSB 2001a). Collectively, 1,290 doctoral degrees were awarded in 1997–98 (AACSB 2001b). The University of Pennsylvania (home of the Wharton School) had 188 students enrolled in doctoral study in 2001 (AACSB 2003a). Gradually, these business school doctorates have come to fill most faculty slots in the business schools. The available university jobs for these graduates has expanded and contracted and expanded again. In the seventies and early eighties there were a lot of jobs. But in the later eighties and nineties, students, not faculty, became the critical constraint (Near 1996, 476). Now job vacancies are becoming plentiful again. Demand for business school academics should exceed supply for at least a decade (AACSB 2003b).

By the mideighties, an American Assembly of Collegiate Schools of Business (AACSB) report (Porter and McKibbin 1988) documented the success of the American business school and criticized their complacent self-satisfaction. However, just as the business school was finding that its tenure and promotions recommendations were being accepted at university level and disparaging comments began to abate, a new challenge emerged in the form of the 1988 *Business Week* rating of MBA programs. The business community was concerned, not about research quantity and quality, but rather about teaching quality and the relevance of research and curriculum. The attention of the business school shifted from critics internal to the university toward the external constituencies of potential students, corporate recruiters, and executive education consumers (Miles 1996). New faculty faced pressures to simultaneously publish at top journals, teach effectively to tough student audiences, and relate well in executive classrooms. Walsh (1996) summarizes the job description:

It seems to me that we are exhorted to conduct theoretically and methodologically rigorous research that bears practical relevance to undergird our teaching and consulting. We are asked to embrace the latest in pedagogical technology to serve a range of domestic and international students from undergraduates to MBA students to Ph.D. students and to executives of all ages and responsibilities. In the end, we are to help society meet the challenge of postindustrial work in our new global village. Our job does not end there, however. We are also encouraged to take the time to educate our presidents and provosts about the place of the business school in the university (and in society), while also contributing our management expertise to the training and development of a variety of local administrators as they come to grips with the human resource management challenges posed by operating in this new world. And, of course, many of us are trying to earn tenure under these expectations, just when tenured positions are becoming more precious thanks to outsourcing and technology—enhanced faculty downsizing. (482)

We will have more to say about these mounting pressures on researchers later.

Meanwhile on the other side of the Atlantic, organizational studies developed, for the most part, outside business schools and away from the traditional elite universities. As in the United States, psychology was the first mover. In Britain, the most common label was "industrial psychology" until the 1950s when "occupational psychology" became more common (Hollway 1991). Industrial sociology produced Joanne Woodward and Andrew Pettigrew. More psychoanalytic in orientation was The Tavistock Institute, publishers of the journal *Human Relations*. It originated in servicing the needs of the military during World War II. It is not university-based. The final ingredient in the early development of organizational studies in the United Kingdom was the extraordinarily productive Aston group working with Derek Pugh in the 1960s.

The first business schools (London and Manchester) were formed in 1965. Many more followed. Even Oxford and Cambridge now have business schools. Organization studies shifted to the business schools. Derek Pugh moved to London Business School. Tom Lupton shifted from being Liverpool's professor of industrial sociology to Manchester Business School's professor of organizational behavior.

The 1970s were strongly influenced by Silverman's (1970) *Theory of Organizations*, which introduced a phenomenology-based critique of systems theory and positivism (Clegg 1996). Burrell (1996) and Reed (1996) describe the shift from functionalism in the sixties to paradigms in the eighties to postmodernist European social theory in the nineties. More so than in the United States, critical approaches to organization studies have been considered legitimate in the U.K. business school.

If nothing else, over the years, the research community has grown in size. The Academy of Management, the primary professional association for organizational researchers (at least those employed in the American business school) has more than thirteen thousand members. The number of journals, both general and specialized, has exploded. Keeping track of all developments in scholarship is now impossible.

What does this mean for the reader? We do think deciding on your heritage matters. Beyond that, we're not sure. We do know that change will march on, that the background against which you make your choices as a scholar will be different to that described here. The journeys reported in this book crossed a terrain of growth and opportunity. Growth in sheer size will not be as dramatic. However, we see plenty of opportunity ahead for intellectual innovation and contribution.

A Renaissance Self

Prompting Personal and Professional
Revitalization

Renewing Research Practice: Scholars' Journeys

On the next page is a photo I shot in 1970, of a fellow workman and his reflection. I have for many years thought of it as an alter-ego photo of myself.
I revisit it periodically to trigger reflections and to stimulate imaginings of
my own possibilities for the future. The top half or "actual" part of the double image is obvious enough—even if I was a bit melodramatic in printing
it in high contrast. It is an image of a person pushing a wheelbarrow in some
nondescript factory somewhere (central Florida, actually). It is a fairly representative photo of the time and place, and not a bad piece of photowork in
its own right. Yet, it is the bottom half or "virtual" part of the image that
captures the eye and the imagination. That reflection image balances so pre-
cariously on the boundary between the real and the surreal that it gives me
pause, holds my attention, and helps evoke my own reflections on various
aspects of my personal and professional self.

When I let my imagination run a bit, I sometimes envision the upper image as "me now" and the lower, reflected image as "me tomorrow" or "the
possible me." What I like most is that the future image is somewhat more ill
defined, more unclear, more full of unrealized possibility, but still so obviously related to and connected with the top image of the present me. I do
not necessarily think of the future image as some target to reach in goal-ori-
ented fashion (as I am not a very linear person), but rather as some possibilities to be realized in some form—sometimes with intention, sometimes by
pursuing opportunities, sometimes through serendipity. I find myself looking to define that image in some way that just seems promising. This photo
hangs in my office as a triptych, with the entire image as a centerpiece and
the actual and virtual images framed individually above and below the centerpiece so I can study each one separately.

In any event, this photo is one of a number of means I use to help me focus on my own renewal, to keep myself consciously aware that a renaissance self requires a little reflective guidance to give a simultaneous sense of stable continuity and continuous change. I use other ways, too, of course, including reading, talking, teaching, traveling, music, musing, and so on, but the aesthetic avenue has always been important to me, and my main medium of artistic expression has been photography since I was fifteen. So I use it to assist in my occasional rejuvenations.

Now, I don't want to sound too pretentious (or too weird) about this process. I am quite confident that I share aspects of reflection and renewal processes with many people, although perhaps my ways of surfacing them might be different in form from some other people in the field of organization study. As is probably evident by now, I am a closet artist, and I make room for art and aesthetics in my personal life. An artistic eye is an avenue for seeing differently. And, to me, "seeing differently" is essential for contributing to theory and research; therefore, I also have tried to find ways of including an artistic view in my professional life, too.

So, what does revitalization look like to me? Do I periodically change my stripes and do something completely different? No, not really. Like most people I don't actually reinvent myself. In general, I revitalize myself by engaging in variations on my themes. That is why periodically I like to revisit "Double Image, Many Reflections," with its image of a reflected image and its double entendre title. It prompts me to reflect on ways that I might vary the theme of what I am doing, sometimes fairly dramatically, but usually in a way that keeps me connected to my main theme: figuring out how people make sense of their organizational experience.

A Little Backdrop

In their initial brief for this volume the editors described their intent as "trying to capture the tacit wisdom of active researchers on their personal journeys." First of all, that charge seems a little grandiose for me. (I am not so sure about this wisdom thing.) Nonetheless, I am an inveterate reflector on my personal and professional lives. Besides, I once cowrote an obscure chapter on tacit knowledge (Gioia and Ford 1996) that treated tacit knowledge as "knowing without knowing how you know," so what better way to try to manifest what I supposedly know in ways that (I hope) might be useful to others? Before engaging in that exercise, however, allow me to offer a couple prefacing personal tidbits that form some of the shaping backdrop for my career and for my approach to revitalization.

First tidbit: I was fascinated from a young age with space flight so I chose engineering as my first professional identity. I won some sort of physics competition in high school by writing about an ion engine that would propel us to the far planets. Science fiction, really, but it was a fascinating little paper that taught me the value of an engaging idea. Wish I still had that paper. It helped me get into engineering school. Ultimately, though, engineering turned out to be relatively uninspiring in its day-to-day pursuits (too many boring calculations). Nonetheless, my engineering education was instrumental in putting me in the right place at the right time for the big adventure in my life. I signed on with Boeing Aerospace, subcontracted to NASA, and worked at Cape Kennedy as a member of the Apollo/Saturn teams that launched the first missions to the moon. I sometimes think my subsequent life has been one long hope for topping that experience and recognizing that I never will. Yet, both the romanticism and the aspirations of the enterprise still constitute the subtext of much of what I do today.

Second tidbit: I love fast cars. Always have. Because of a small accident of location in being raised near Sebring, Florida (host of the annual twelve-hour sports car race), and because of my Italian heritage, I have had a life-long passion for the Ferrari racing team. It is the kind of irrational enthusiasm that continuously makes me realize the value of passion as a motivator of my activities and also helps me understand my affinity for other people with passion—passion about almost anything, even if I don't understand the source of the passion (like sailing). My early love for fast cars led to a dream of working for Ferrari as a racing engineer, even though I don't speak Italian. The impracticalities of that dream finally caught up with me, so I went to work for Ford instead, with the same intention—unfortunately, just as Ford pulled the plug on their racing program. By some convoluted path I then ended up as the company's vehicle recall coordinator, a move that found me initially in charge of the Pinto fires case, with which I am now often associated, sometimes infamously.

The Pinto was Ford's entry into the then burgeoning small-car market. It was alleged to have a faulty gas tank that could lead to explosions during low-speed (twenty-five mph), rear-end collisions. To make a long and unpleasant story short, I was a member of the decision-making group that missed an early opportunity to recall the defective car. That misstep became the first in a long line of dubious company decisions that resulted in the Pinto case eventually becoming an embarrassment to Ford and a staple in the teaching of business ethics and corporate social responsibility ever since.

In truth, the experience at Ford probably has affected my professional life more than the experience at Cape Kennedy, even if it wasn't as romantic. Certainly, the experience of managing—and arguably, mismanaging—the Pinto problem taught me much of what I think I know about cognitive schemas, decision making, leadership, and the practical problematics of corporate ethics. It was an exciting, but sobering experience that showed me how organizations really work. The Pinto case has a way of staying alive with me, for a couple of reasons. First, its precedent-setting character as the first case in which a *corporation* was charged with homicide makes it interesting, not only to historians but also to educators and researchers in our field. Second, the fact that I felt the questionable urge to write about my experience with it some years ago has made me the target of some interest, as well. The thing just doesn't go away. I still get calls from people who only recently have stumbled onto the article in the *Journal of Business Ethics* (1992) who "just want to talk to me," including a few who want to upbraid me not only for my role in the case, but also because they think I have tried to rationalize my actions with some esoteric academic explanations. Professionally, I am resigned to being forever associated with the damned thing, but that is not necessarily bad. Keeps me thinking.

Themes in My Revitalization Schemes

In my research life, I am a grounded theorist. I pick peoples' brains for a living, trying to figure out how they make sense of their organizational experience. I then write descriptive, analytical narratives that try to capture what I think they know. Those narratives are usually written around salient themes that represent their experience to other interested readers. When I received the invitation from Peter and Ralph to write this essay, I found myself in the unusual position of having to pick my own brains to articulate how I go about keeping myself fresh. Using some arcane self-analytical processes, here's how I think I do it . . .

I. I Stay Grounded (In My Own Experience)

LINKING MY SELF TO MY ORGANIZATION

How did I end up in academia? First, I simply was intrigued by the thought of living the academic life. That thought got magnified, complicated, and transformed as a result of my experience at Ford. Yes, I wanted out of the pressure cooker with sometime responsibility for life-and-death decisions. After a while, that sort of business became too weighty for my soul. But, my goodness, did I come to see organizations as incredibly complex, difficult-to-manage, take-on-a-life-of-their-own, living entities. Early in my working career, it became eminently clear (and also scary) to me that organizations, more so than individuals, were going to be the main players in any viable view of the future. I therefore concluded that it was important to put good minds to work studying organizations to make them more humane and more effective. In a bit of auto-flattery, I declared myself one of the good minds and went back to school.

I realized early on that learning about organizations was a way to learn about myself because I saw that much of my adult self was defined by organizations. Consequently, one of my long-linked themes is relating my research life to my personal life. Simply put, I am intrigued with myself and I understand myself better as I study and learn about organizations. No organization is more salient or more important to me than the one in which I currently live, so that helps to explain why I sometimes study my own university.

Connecting to My Past. This little fascination with myself, and especially myself-in-organizations, has helped define my theory and research stream for more than twenty years. That stream is sourced in questions that relate the self to organizations. The question "How do I work cognitively?" spawned a series of papers in the mideighties on attribution processes, cognitive schemas, and especially scripts. "How do I live the social and organizational work life?" led to a series of pieces in the late eighties and early nineties on symbolism and sensemaking. "Who am I—and more grandly, who is an organization—and how do I (they) change?" have driven my work since the nineties on identity, image, and change. And those questions are turning my attention now to questions relating organizational identity to organizational learning. Notable to me among these pieces is a series of studies that I call the "university studies," which are good examples of how I focus on my own organization to learn something (the pieces in *SMJ*, *Org Science*, and *ASQ*). A simple flow diagram of my career topic trajectory, then, looks like this:

Attribution → Schemas → Scripts → Symbolism → Sensemaking →
Identity → Image → Organizational Learning

There is no magic in that diagram. Anybody with a few years in academia and a knack for retrospective construction (some might say revisionist history) could produce something similar—as we often are forced to do when we must make sense of our careers for the benefit of tenure or promotion committees. If you look at those transitions, however, you can notice several things. First, all the topics connect to questions about me as a person living in an organization; second, there are a lot of them (topics, that is); third, they are all related. Each of those features keeps me interested. Together they keep me passionate.

II. I Get Lost, I Get Found

GETTING LOST

Given the comments in the above section, I want to avoid the impression that I have everything figured out according to some grand-design strategy.

I don't. In all honesty, sometimes this whole thing is a monumental struggle. I spend a lot of time lost. Intellectually, I mean. In fact, the subhead title is a frequent utterance of mine. I get lost. I think you need to get lost before you can get found. Staying found all the time leads to repetition, and there is little opportunity for renewal in that. So, I get lost. And when I'm lost I go exploring—for something interesting to work on. And then I get found. Simple. But difficult.

Most often I find myself not too far from home. Periods in my backyard wilderness usually mean that I am on the verge of another transition. So, even in the middle of my muddle, I feel a sense that something beneficial awaits my discovery or invention. In terms of my streams of work, this process means that even if my studies are not logical, incremental steps in the fulfillment of some master research program, they usually tend to relate to the prior work in some discernable way (like the actual and virtual images in the introductory photo).

Most of us learn to fear being lost. I certainly did. But I no longer feel that way. Now, I try to embrace getting lost. Actually, in some faintly perverse way, I welcome the intellectual and emotional ride, as well as the touch of minor desperation, that comes with getting lost and not knowing quite which way to go next. I like the way Don Henley captured some of this sense of disconnect and confusion, albeit somewhat less positively, in writing The Eagles' song "Desperado":

> Don't your feet get cold in the winter time?
> The sky won't snow and the sun won't shine.
> It's hard to tell the nighttime from the day.
> You're losin' all your highs and lows.
> Ain't it funny how the feelin' goes away?

I like my highs and lows, and one of the things I fear most, professionally, is having the feeling for the work go away, so I find myself not resisting getting lost. I don't recommend it for everyone, but so long as you have a confidence in getting found, lostness opens up a lot of unconsidered possibilities.

MY MULTIPLE IDENTITIES

Here is another reason why I tend to get found after I have gotten lost: I am afflicted with a benevolent multiple-identity syndrome. In addition to the usual complement of personal identities (husband, father, photographer, racing enthusiast, and so on), I also harbor many different professional identities because of the varied range of stuff I have done in print. At any given moment, I am a cognitive theorist to some, a strategic change researcher to others, Pinto fires co-conspirator to yet others, multiparadigm philosopher to the esoteric crowd, sensible writer to practitioners and consultants, incorrigible interpretivist to the methodologists, and teacher/educator to many, ad nauseam. The fact that I live comfortably within so many professional selves tells you something about how I keep the renaissance going. How could I fail to revisit and regenerate myself on frequent occasion, what with so many different voices calling for attention? All of those identities need to be accommodated and fed, you see. Sometimes they need to be maintained simultaneously, but something interesting always is happening in one or more of those domains that brings me out of any intellectual funk. So if I am lost in one, I can get found in another.

My Multiple Lenses.   Another aspect of this tolerance for getting lost is the intent to develop multiple ways of seeing. Professionally speaking, it is this orientation that led to the "Multiparadigm Perspectives on Theory Building" piece in *AMR* (1990) with Evelyn Pitre. Having done the piece, I was publicly obliged not only to think of myself as Mr. Multiparadigm but also to put on the mantle and live that identity, as well. That produced a great appreciation for alternative ways of seeing—as well as an expanded tolerance in reviewing work that approached study differently than I did. Public declarations of position are what we do via our publication process, but some declarations have more personal effects than others. This one changed my orientation toward the field, as well as my appreciation for its diversity more than any other I have done.

Historically speaking, however, I was already long-steeped in appreciation for alternative ways of seeing. I came of age intellectually in the sixties. Now, I know the sixties have been subjected to a lot of rewritten history, but the times really were revolutionary and, therefore, formative in so many ways—technically, politically, socially, and so on. In sensemaking terms, many taken-for-granted beliefs became precarious and up for grabs. Debate, challenge, and exposure to alternative belief systems and different experiences were in the fabric of my university years. There were so many ways to see so many things. Out of this milieu I discovered the nature of the social world, even though the Dr. Jekyll part of me was living the straight-laced academic life of a budding engineer. I came to see that the social world was first and foremost a consensually constructed world, subject to social circle, context, states of consciousness, and the vagaries of individual and collective sensation, perception, and interpretation. What an intriguing mess!

The larger point, however, was the realization that the social world was *profoundly* unlike the physical world I had been studying in engineering. I recognize that we are too often cavalier with the use of the word "profound," but I mean it literally here; this recognition was personal-world-altering, and its consequences have reverberated into my future. The recognition of the essential differences between the physical and social worlds was a shot between the eyes for me. Immediately and subsequently, it made little sense to use the techniques of the physical sciences to understand key social processes—a conclusion that set me adrift and got me lost for a long time. Of most import, I recognized that the really big questions—those dealing with *meaning*—were practically immune to exploration by way of the scientific method that had become so venerated in my normal realm.

III. I Try to Live the Renaissance Life

Some of the above might come across as patently idiosyncratic. I hope not, because I see patterns in my experience that are more generally applicable, at least as caveats, for others. Here are some things I try to keep in the front of my consciousness as ways of revitalization—ways that I am confident could be common to many of us.

DOING SOMETHING I FIND MEANINGFUL

I keep a hand-lettered sign on the back of my office door, so that I see it when I exit. It asks, "Does this path have a heart?" The line is from Carlos Castaneda's *Teachings of Don Juan*, and it at least serves to prompt the key question on a regular basis, even if I too often answer that I am caught in yet another activity trap, the outcome of which is not all that likely to make a difference. Still, it is a reminder to focus on doing things that matter. On a somewhat less grand scale, I also try to remind myself of the Pareto time principle: the folk recognition that we seem to spend a frustrating 80 percent of our time on things that generate 20 percent of the results, and 20 percent of our time on things that miraculously seem to generate 80 percent of the results. The message is not only to manage time well but also to concentrate on the stuff that matters. In addition, I try to keep my eye out for "cracks in time," those crucial, sometimes almost imperceptible, but pivotal moments when attention and action will make a difference. The concept of a crack in time has become central to my own life and has wended its way into my teaching. My students come away from any class I teach with an appreciation for recognizing and acting on turning-point moments of opportunity.

Providing Opportunities for Younger Scholars.   I attach some gravitas to the concept of mentoring so I don't use the term lightly. Nonetheless, I find that as I get older and more experienced, I am more comfortable with people referring to me as a mentor. I take it as a magnificent compliment and I try to honor the notion by giving the most considered advice I can. The act of suggesting ideas and career courses to younger people helps me to live again vicariously in a different way. Actually, staying young and fresh is something of an artifact of living the academic life. As my major professor once noted:

academia is a strange environment; every year we get a year older, but the students always stay the same age. Tough to grow old mentally in such a context.

I consider PhD students the life force of the theory/research enterprise. Truth is, I depend on them to rescue me from my intellectual fogs and to energize me. I like to follow *them* around for a while just to see how they see our field. For that reason I seldom ask PhD students to do their research directly on my ideas. That stance makes for a lot of new work but usually leads me off in some different direction, too. Cam Ford is a good example, with his forays into the study of creativity, an area in which he is now a recognized scholar.

More recently, I have been working with Kevin Corley, and he too is a good example. I asked Kevin to join Majken Schultz and me on the paper about the adaptive instability of organizational identity that was published in *AMR* in 2000. Majken and I had been fiddling with that paper for a while and we both knew it was based on a good idea, but we were both stuck as to how to make it sing. I thought we needed a fresh perspective, not to mention a swift kick in the butt to get over our thinker's block, so we invited Kevin into the project. He got wholly hooked on the idea and ran with it, devoting himself to fleshing out the key process model that we had only articulated with some old-fashioned hand-waving. With his help, we got a good idea over a hurdle. For his part, Kevin got to see a top-level publishing process, warts and all, including learning how to work collaboratively with two strong-minded coauthors and how to communicate with editors and reviewers. Now, he is dragging me, not quite kicking and screaming (but close), into the study of organizational learning, an area we both characterize as a "morass," but both recognize as fascinating and promising. Feels like a little rebirth coming.

Trying to Make (or Make Up) Some Sense What It's All About.   I take to heart the old wisdom, "Nothing is important and everything is important." I try not to work under the illusion that my work is destined to change the world in some dramatic way or that if I were not here the larger world would miss me (my family and friends obviously excepted). From that viewpoint, nothing I do is very important, which in one sense could be discouraging, but also is quite freeing. Yet, I also recognize that *everything* I do is important, from reading a colleague's paper, to grading the same exam question for the fortieth time. The trick is to continuously construct my work as important on *some* level. Importance can be decided on so many planes, ranging from a great idea, to a publication in a top-tier journal, to advising a twenty-year-old, to simply sitting with a friend who is having difficulty.

Living the Aesthetic Life.   It might tell you something about my orientation toward renewal to let you know that my idealistic heroes are Leonardo da Vinci and Michelangelo. I suppose it is no accident that there is a connection between my chosen title for this essay and the fact that both of these guys lived, and perhaps defined, the Renaissance (or the *Rinascimento*, as Tommaso Fabbri sometimes reminds me, because the rebirth began in Italy). It is not so much that both were geniuses, but that they both were completely immersed in the aesthetic life and also lived the "compleat" life. Every day was an opportunity to create, and both of them did so in many different arenas. I like that orientation. That is why I stay engaged with photography, work with wood, redesign my house myself, write in many different domains, and more generally work at living a balanced life. That also is why my main way of viewing my manuscripts is to see them as little works of art, as odd as you might think that characterization. Words, to me, are an artistic medium, and I like to work in that medium every day.

My brother (a professional artist and a really good one) invokes a useful question as a standard of judgment: How do I assess the quality of my day? I have adopted and adapted that standard. At the beginning of the day I ask, What will make this day a good day? At the end of the day I ask, How was the quality of this day? If the answer to that latter question too often comes up as "uninspiring," then I look to change the way I approach my work. Fortunately, things in academia have their own rhythms, so things change anyway. My own professional life has become somewhat seasonal. In the fall semester I am Mr. MBA instructor to a high-maintenance bunch that garners most of my attention and time. In the spring I am Mr. PhD professor and writer. In the summer I am Mr. Traveler. I find the seasons of the year to be rejuvenating and I also find the seasonal professional life to be rejuvenating.

Trying to Top Myself.   As I noted near the beginning of this essay, I once worked on the Apollo / Saturn lunar launch teams at Kennedy Space Center. I was an engineering apprentice for Boeing Aerospace on the Apollo 11 and 12 missions. Those were heady times. All of us on the support teams knew, just *knew*, that we were working on something big, something important, something that was an incredible challenge—and oh so romantic: to try to land a person on the moon. It was exhilarating! I have never been a part of anything so big, so team-oriented, so public, so energizing, or so successful. Everything else I have ever done pales by comparison. Consequently, I have found myself feeling that I have already worked on the most significant project in my life, that even if I might want to top that experience, I probably never will.

That, of course, is wrongheaded thinking. The challenge is in trying to top yourself in your now-chosen work. Sometimes making comparisons with your previous work can be enlightening; sometimes it can be misleading. Am I a better photographer than I was at age twenty-three (when I shot the photo that introduces this essay), for instance? I know I had a good eye then and I know I was a wizard in the darkroom. I should be better now. Am I? I am not sure. The work is so different now. But I keep trying to shoot or create the perfect image. Am I a better scholar than I was when I started this career? I know I had a sharp mind then and I knew I could express good ideas in writing. I should be better now. Am I? Not sure, the work is so different now. But I keep trying to create good research and engaging papers. The larger point is simply that I have a kind of idealism that leads me to want to try to top myself in work I consider important. I *know* that there is self-deception involved in a lot of it, but I love fooling myself, sometimes startling myself with new images and ideas. Keeps me engaged. Keeps me revitalized.

Developing a new way of seeing, a new insight (I call it a "shazzam!") is a major pursuit for me. It is one of my ways of contributing. In fact, in our field, I consider different ways of seeing to be *the* main way of contributing.

IV. I Take Umbrage

Most of us recognize that a good debate is energizing, and I love participating in the debates great and small that pepper organization study. Some of those debates are on the grand scale of ontology and epistemology; others simply involve trying to convince editors and reviewers that you are on to something good. On either level, I draw energy from fighting the good fight.

Questioning the Received Wisdom.   Early in her career, Barbara Gray once submitted a nicely executed case study to a top journal. For her trouble, she received a terse, one-line review: "This is a case study. We do not publish case studies." Ooooh! She was discouraged. *I* was incensed. The implied arrogance about "proper" ways of knowing was truly offensive and motivated me to do my bit to help make this field more open.

This little signal event happened while I was still early in my academic career, too, and it was an eye-opener. I had engineering training and I had engineering experience at Boeing and Ford. Furthermore, despite my undergraduate revelations that the physical and social worlds were markedly different, I had nonetheless been trained in engineering-like approaches to organizational research in my doctoral program. When I was honest with myself, however, I had to admit that trying to understand organizations in engineering-like terms did not seem to get me far enough in answering the questions that interested me. So, I got lost for a long while and went exploring. I discovered that there was a whole realm of possible ways of knowing in the social sciences (thank you, Gareth Morgan, 1983), and it led to the only major identity transformation in my academic career. In the mideighties I changed my basic orientation from "functionalist" to "interpretivist." Interpretivism adopts more subjectivist assumptions than functionalism and focuses on the ways that people construct meaning and make sense of their experience. Those assumptions seemed to fit my beliefs about the nature of human experience better, so I shed my engineering-inspired researcher identity and put on the new interpretivist mantle. My work in *The Thinking Organization* (1986) is my first professional statement of that transformation.

Ever since, in my (usually) nonconfrontational way, I have been trying to do high-quality conceptual and empirical work in this genre that questions the typically received wisdom that functionalism should remain our dominant way of knowing. (And it remains the dominant way of training our PhD students. My informal, if conservative estimate is that 80 percent of our training is still devoted to functionalist, quantitative approaches.) One small aspect of this effort is that I am on a personal campaign to try to get the field to downplay the use of physical science metaphors and models. Although it is always easy to find or invent some analogy between physical science and social science phenomena, we need to construct more theory and design more research in ways that acknowledge the fundamental differences between the two.

Sparring with Reviewers.   On a much smaller scale, I enjoy debating with reviewers. As a result of my interpretivist orientation, I find myself in constant head-butting contests with reviewers over the character and structure of papers. I will first admit that I tend to write unusual papers—ones that often do not fit reviewers' notions of what a theory or research paper "should" look like (which repeatedly reminds me of Ram Dass's refreshing and enlightening, yet amusing protest: "I am tired of being should upon").

My most telling experience along these lines was the original submission of the "Sensemaking/sensegiving" paper in *Strategic Management Journal* (Gioia and Chittipeddi 1991). Now, you must understand that this paper was a strange bird for *SMJ*, although I always thought it was just the kind of study needed to enlarge the then narrow scope of that journal. First of all, it was a case study; *SMJ* was, shall we say, not inclined to publish case studies. Secondly, it was an interpretive/grounded theory study. To my knowledge, *SMJ* had never published a grounded theory study. One of the distinguishing features of a purist grounded theory study is that the emergent theory is grounded in the data and, therefore, properly presented, logically appears *after* the data, near the end of the paper. Well, of course, that form does not constitute a "normal" paper, so one of the reviewers called us on it.

In our replies to reviewer comments we very carefully explained the ontological, epistemological, and methodological rationales for our approach and presentation (engaging in a common process for me that I call "educating the reviewers"). The reviewer wrote back that she or he understood and appreciated our explanation. But . . . would we please nonetheless put the theory up front, as per usual practice? (This informative incident always reminded me of a famous episode from the TV show M*A*S*H, in which a sergeant toting an automatic weapon brings a buddy with a concussion into the MASH [Mobile Army Surgical Hospital] unit and demands immediate care for his comrade. The doctors and nurses are actively engaged in triage, trying to decide which of many cases is the most serious and, therefore, should receive medical attention first. Hawkeye Pierce, the key doctor, nevertheless takes a moment to explain the principles of triage very carefully to the sergeant, and that according to those principles, his buddy rightly should not be placed at the head of the queue. The sergeant then nods his head knowingly and says that he completely understands the rationale offered; he then points his weapon at Hawkeye and tells him to attend to his buddy, or else.) I felt quite a lot like Hawkeye Pierce as I dealt with the apparently well-intentioned reviewer who figuratively nodded his or her head, said he or she understood, and then proceeded to use the power of the reviewer's position to force me to do his or her will. Nonetheless, this story has (for me) a happy ending. I devised a way to meet the wishes of the reviewer while still upholding my principles, by noting in the introduction the usual form of a grounded theory research report, but summarizing the theory up front while carefully explaining that the theory actually emerged from the findings that follow. I have used this form ever since in similar work. I still consider the SMJ paper my "blow against the empire," and it is that sort of experience that keeps me engaged in the good fight.

The story surrounding the sensemaking/sensegiving paper reminds me that I once (too early in my career) conducted workshops on "Responding to Reviewer Comments." The tenor of those workshops was that reviewers were the enemy, an adversary to be overcome or at least outflanked. Rick Mowday once brought me up short by simply asking whether it had occurred to me that reviewers could help improve a manuscript. Well, aaah, no, ummm, it really hadn't. Well, they can and they do, but sometimes via circuitous routes and unintended means. ("I know, because I are one.") Truth is, I like reviewers; I actually enjoy the opportunity to communicate with them over conceptual and presentational issues. I imagine the reply-to-reviewer letter to be a strange, stilted, but sometimes effective way to hold a professional conversation.

V. I Stay Connected to the "Real" World

I am a hopeless idealist. I once visited my former major professor, Bill Hodge, after some years away. While I was in his office, he received a call from another professor I had known, John Lee. Hodge said, "Guess who is in my office." The voice on the other end of the line said, "How in hell could I guess that, Bill? How about a hint." Hodge said, "Who is the most idealistic person you know?" And Lee said, "Denny Gioia can't be in your office, can he?" Well, I was and I am. But, I actually am not just any old idealist; I consider myself a practical idealist. I just hate the phrase "It's all academic," which has a certain connotation that an idea is so removed from everyday experience that it just doesn't matter very much. Relevance matters, so I usually try to work on ideas that might make a difference in practice.

Admittedly, I stir around in the academic ether on occasion, but not all that often. Strangely, I do not often draw my inspiration from organization theorists. I more often find it in popular literature and periodicals, or coming out of the mouths of the informants in my research projects, or from some comment blurted out in an executive program. And yes, I like to keep my hand in executive programs. Executives might be a tough audience to impress, but they are enthusiastically looking for a good idea that they can translate to their experience. I try to give them that, but I also keep my ears up and listen for the idea that might reenergize me.

Even in my writing I try to make space for pieces aimed at high-level practitioner journals and I have placed a number of articles in outlets like *The Academy of Management Executive, Sloan Management Review*, and *Organization Dynamics*. These pieces have the added advantage of being fun to write, and I am always looking for opportunities to write something in a lively fashion. I am not a fan of academese, so writing for an audience that won't sit still for boring writing is a breath of fresh air in an otherwise stuffy room.

Tacit Wisdom Surfaced: Some Parting Shots

Despite the many preceding observations and suggestions, there are a few other comments that did not fit so neatly into my thematic structure. So, if you are still on the lookout for hints to trigger your own ways of revitalizing yourself, here are a few that I try to live by.

Play to Your Strengths. I'm verbal. Words and arguments come easily to me. I'm OK at statistics, but just OK. I sometimes refer to statistics as "stamystics" because I oftentimes find myself mystified as to what the sophisticated techniques are doing and wonder whether they are masking or circumventing the close-to-the-bone feeling I want to experience in discovering how people make sense. This all might seem quite inconsistent with my training as an engineer, but sometimes you have to own up that you mysteriously have forgotten how to count. I think I have, but I get along nicely, thank you. I try to hone the things I do well.

Go for Cognitive Stickiness. I like to dig deep into organizational understanding and action, but as a cognitive theorist I find myself painfully aware of just how limited I am as an information processor (I am, however, by my own assessment, quite a marvelous sense-maker despite my shortcomings, but that is a different story). My awareness of my cognitive limitations helps me empathize with the poor reader trying to understand the point(s) I am trying to make in a given article. For that reason I work hard at trying to distill findings to their essences and to communicate them in simple, compelling ways. Although I once distained it, I have developed a great appreciation for "sound-bite" research reporting. Sound-bite journalism has received a well-deserved rap for "dumbing down" the complexity of the news, but a well-constructed sound bite has a certain memorability about it—what I like to call a "cognitive stickiness" that allows readers to remember the most important points you are trying to make. That's another reason I like quotes and song lyrics and cartoons and photographs as media of expression—because they capture the essence of an observation in memorable form.

I wish we could find ways to import more varied forms of communication into our field. Our reliance on the classic journal-reporting format makes us seem oh-so-stodgy when we are studying phenomena that are oh-so-dynamic. There is a place for sound-bite scholarship; very often that place is in article titles. The old wisdom (attributed to Alan Meyer) is true: "You don't want just to be published; you want to be read." But there is an important extension to that wisdom: *You don't want just to be read; you want to be remembered.* This is another little campaign of mine that helps keep me going.

Persist. I think I hold two world's records in organizational scholarship: longest time to publication for a manuscript (eight years—don't ask) and most rejections before publication (seven). This is not merely a testimonial to persistence (never give up on a paper you believe in—never, never, never, never, to paraphrase some famous Englishman), but also a reflection of my firm intention never to write something unless I believe the ideas deserve to see the light of day.

To Thine Own Self Be True. I don't believe in absolute truths in social life. Honestly, I am frequently baffled about what people mean when they talk about being "objective" or "finding truth" in organization study. I hope they are just turns of phrase, but I suspect that many who use them, believe them. Pretty vexing. I am the sort who believes that most of the stuff that matters is a social construction—much of which we construct as true. In a similar vein, I don't believe in a stable personal or organizational identity—although we tend to construct identity as stable by choosing enduring labels. For that reason, I am never quite sure what the phrase "to thine own self be true" means. Nonetheless, I work constantly at trying to be true to my currently constructed self. And yes, I recognize that this last sentence could be construed either as making no sense or as being paradoxical. I take it as the latter. I am my own paradox and I like it that way. I take it as important to understand your own constructions as a way of knowing yourself. That makes it a lot easier to revitalize yourself.

Finis

My initial working title for this essay was "Reinventing Myself," but I decided early on that was neither an apt nor an accurate description of what I am usually trying to do. What I see myself doing is continuously reenergizing, rejuvenating, renewing, revitalizing, reawakening, reinvigorating, refreshing, rekindling, and reviving myself, either by design or happenstance, which is why I chose "A Renaissance Self" as the title. Yes, I change. In some ways I have changed dramatically from my early years. (I remember the young engineer who wished that emotion would simply disappear from organizational life—would just "drop out of the equation," as I once remember putting it quite tellingly. Fat chance!) Yet, there has been a notable continuity and connection to my past and to my values in each of my many transitions.

For me, the introductory photo captures that continuity and change, that similarity and difference, as well as that sense of present state and possible future, all in a photographic stroke that freezes these multiple juxtapositions. Thus frozen, I can consider where I am, as suggested visually by the top image, and where I might go, as suggested by the more elusive reflected image. And then I look to my values and my experiential heuristics to guide me. I have tried to convey some of those values and heuristics in a way that might suggest useful parallels for you and your own revitalization. Perhaps the most important point of all, however, is that a personal or professional renaissance doesn't just happen. It needs to be shepherded along. I have developed and fostered my own guides. I hope my small stab at articulating them helps to prompt insight into your own.

Acknowledgments

I want to acknowledge a number of people encountered on my long, strange trip (with apologies to the Grateful Dead)—many for different reasons, and some who might not know how much I appreciate their presence or their influence.

I would like to acknowledge these people for just being good people, good colleagues, and good friends: Jean Bartunek, Dan Brass, Steven Cohen, Jim Dean, Janet Dukerich, Jane Dutton, Kim Elsbach, Tommaso Fabbri, Steve Fulghum Jr., Jim Farr, Marlene Fiol, Peter Frost, Mary Ann Glynn, Karen Golden-Biddle, Barbara Gray, Mary Jo Hatch, Anne Huff, Linda Johanson, Gerry Johnson, Chris Johnstone, Patty Johnstone, Martin Kilduff, Kristian Kreiner, Theresa Lant, Dorrie Lisle, Chuck Manz, Frances Milliken, Gareth Morgan, Joe Porac, Thoralf Qvale, Rhonda Reger, Susan Schor, Majken Schultz, Zur Shapira, Linda Smircich, Ken Smith, Jim Thomas, Linda Trevino, Jim Walsh, Karl Weick, and Dave Whetten.

People who helped me when I was younger: Bill Anthony, Ralph Berres, Steve Fulghum Sr., Hazel Haley, Bill Hodge, and Hank Sims.

My doctoral student colleagues: Mike Brown, Kumar Chittipeddi, Shawn Clark, Kevin Corley, Anne Donnellon, Jim Fairbank, Cam Ford, Alfredo Jaccoud, Dave Ketchen, Joe Labianca, Clint Longenecker, Ajay Mehra, Rajiv Nag, Evelyn Pitre, Peter Poole, Gary Weaver, and Stephanie Welcomer (I am proud to say I have published with all these good people).

PHILIP H. MIRVIS

Questions Matter

WHEN ASKED on her deathbed for the answers to life's mysteries, Gertrude Stein rejoined, "What are the questions?" Denny Gioia's reflective look at his life and scholarship illustrates how questions matter in revitalization. As a young thinker, he was fired by, "How do I think?" But while Narcissus looked in that mirror and narrowed on his self-image, Gioia found instead open spaces for discovery.

His conceptual interests—from attribution to scripts to sensemaking to image and onward—evolved by asking ever-deeper questions of himself and about his experiences in organizations. This reminds us that the admonition to know thyself speaks to a process, not a state, of being and circles into and from one's doings.

Our first look at his being is the "double-image" that Gioia created as a photographer and mounted it as a triptych. It is like a talisman or phylactery—a reminder to pay attention to life and to one's self. This is not, as he worried, so weird: think vacation photos, personal photos of, say, wonders of the world, or shots of the kids; or Dilbert cartoons, $14.99 motivational posters, even "real" art; all of these forms of decoration reflect who we are, or say we are, or wish to be, and can also urge periodic looks into the mirror. What's engaging here is that the picture *is*—if a bit small in reproduction. So squint.

It's also a sort of Rorschach test, or more so, one of those "thematic apperception" pictures where you look into it and say what's happening and thereby reveal what's happening inside you. The "bottom-half"—a reflection of the top but not so clearly formed—is what Denny calls his "future me." It speaks to him of to-be-realized possibilities and portends a hoped-for mix of intention and serendipity. He recognizes himself as a work in progress. What is constant connects to his main scholarly theme: figuring out how people make sense of their organizational experience.

Worth asking as your concepts and identity progress: What is your main theme? Who is your future-me?

As Denny and his scholarship matured, so did his questions. "How do I live in social and organizational life?" And "Who am I and how do I change?" Psychologist Howard Gardner's engaging study of *Leading Minds* makes the point that leaders lead through their "identity" stories. They talk about who they are, and what sense they make of themselves, and thereby help others whom they lead to form their own identities. This may begin with a candid look at the self. But it carries on into leadership when the look is forward, not just reflective, and when it sees unrealized possibilities, when it looks for better questions, and most especially when, as Gardner expresses it, "personal experiences . . . are transplanted to a larger canvas."

Denny's transplanting comes from "linking myself to my organization." Doing so, he asks, "Who are organizations and how do they change?" This led me to pay attention to the "upper-half" of the pictured image. Here is a "person pushing a wheelbarrow in some nondescript factory somewhere." But when the Mexican painter Diego Rivera saw a nondescript auto factory, he envisioned and then painted the massive and moving mural "Detroit Industry" that evoked both the beauty and the horror of the assembly line and Henry Ford's bossing system. Rivera's large canvas made such sense of organizational experience that Ford ordered the mural whitewashed. Ford's wife had it spared—as a legacy to the times and in honor of its artistry.

On a personal note, I saw that mural in 1977 and wrote an essay on the "art of assessment" that compared what Rivera revealed about work versus, say, prevailing theories about work design and their assessment through quantitative methods. Plainly Rivera was, in Gioia's terminology, "seeing differently."

Where do you go to look? Denny advises "getting lost." In one meaning, this is about giving up favored notions. Add to this curiosity, skill at mapping, and some gumption and courage. Too much? Consider mainstream academic advice to find your niche, flog it till tenure, and then, er, be free. In Gioia's lexicon, getting lost is getting free.

That said, identity is carried along the journey. Consider some of Denny's baggage.

Engineer. Picasso could draw very well, as could many lesser lights whose art might suggest otherwise. The engineer cum organization scholar needs to be good at developing logical maps of phenomena, calibrating the angles, and getting the dynamics tidied up such that sensemaking in organizations looks sensible. One suggestion is to first get the picture right before you get it in other ways.

Photographer.   Photography may be representational art, but composition, light, magic in the darkroom, and so on, all change the effect. Hockney even used photos to paint. Gioia uses multiple paradigms to change the effect.

Player.   The fast cars, Italian paeans, and all mean that there is more than a craftsman and aesthete at work here. Maccoby's character study of *The Gamesman* seems to apply to Denny: "I try and top myself." "Everything is important." "I take umbrage." On paper the renaissance self-referencing and self-labeling as Mr. This or Mr. That can sound pretty egoistic. In practice, however, it is leavened by a candid look at his role in the Pinto tragedy and those periodic looks in the mirror. And, in any case, self-assertion makes for an animated and productive academic life. You want to pretend that playing-to-win isn't a factor in success in academe?

Then there is Leonardo da Vinci as a role model. When I pictured Denny with his ion rocket model, I remembered Leonardo's airplane designs and my own clumsy attempts to write backward in a mirror. As role models go, da Vinci embodies technique extraordinary, an interest in reality and effects, and the eye of an aesthete. But a mentor? Not notably. Here Denny might look like Caravaggio: inventive stylist and great painter, but also a teacher to Orazio Gentileschi and his now celebrated daughter Artemisia. Denny's warmth shines through his mentoring and in the work of his students.

The move from the physical to social world yielded "profound" shifts in perspective for Gioia. Knowing one's self is part of seeing differently. Knowing the other is another part. This is yet another meaning of getting lost— getting lost in something and in some others. Look again at the upper-half of your talisman and ask, "What do I want to get lost in?"

MICHAEL G. PRATT

Reflections on a Renaissance Scholar

HAVE I DEFENDED my proposal yet? Have I completed my dissertation? How full is my pipeline? Am I in a good position for tenure? When should I attempt to go up for full?

In this goal-driven profession, it may appear that only full professors have the luxury to ponder and muse about such topics as "renewal" and "revitalization." This chapter offers an alternative to such thinking. Perhaps constant renewal is not a luxury, but a necessity. As Denny notes, it is good to get lost, to wander one's theoretical "backyards," to remember one's past lives, to take artistic photographs, and to embrace different facets of who we are. Granted, there are some times when such reflection seems easier than others. For example, transition points in one's career—and in one's life more generally— seem to involve "built-in" times for such contemplation. However, it may be necessary to renew one's self more often than that. Framed in terms of fast cars (in honor of Denny's passion)—*in the race that is one's career (and one's life), it is important to take frequent pit stops.* But unlike traditional pit stops, renewal in one's career may involve questions beyond *when* and *if* to return to a race. Career pit stops may evoke such queries as: "Do I really want to drive around in these circles, or should I take another path?" "With whom will I drive along (or invite into my car as a passenger)?" "What does it mean to 'win,' and am I willing to do what it takes (for example, drive fast enough) to get there?" Such respites can even challenge us to ask, "Can I change the rules of this race?"

Since you are reading this book, you may be at a point in your career when you need or want to refocus and reenergize. For me, having the opportunity to review Denny's chapter was well timed. Having just recently emerged from the tenure gauntlet (from assistant to associate), and having recently become a father, both my professional and personal "lives" seem very different than they were a year ago. As a result, it is a good time for me to reflect. And Denny has given me (and perhaps you) much to think about.

Like Denny, I "pick people's brains for a living." As such, I find truths—and reveal who I am—in the questions that I ask others. In that spirit, I invite you to revisit Denny's chapter as you consider the questions listed below.

1. What do you see when you look at Denny's photo? What is your current self or selves? What is your ideal self or selves? What is the reflective surface you are looking into? Is the surface your colleagues? . . . your written work? . . . your family? . . . others?

2. When you read this chapter—do you see yourself in it? For me, I resonated with Denny's artistic streak (though I work with pens, not cameras), and with his love of space flight. My research interests (for example, identity and sensemaking) and methodologies (for example, qualitative work) are similar to Denny's—so I resonated with these parts as well. What resonated with you? Do you see yourself as a closet artist or scientist? What traits or behaviors are necessary to renew, refocus, and thrive in academia?

3. It has been said that most writing is somewhat autobiographical. In Denny's case, how he framed "who he is" is very similar to the research questions that he asks. To what degree is your research, and your research questions, autobiographical? Are you trying to find out something about yourself in the work that you do?

4. One of the things that really intrigued me about Denny's life is his work on both the Apollo / Saturn teams and the Pinto fire cases. Are there analogies to these experiences in academia (for example, community work of international importance)? If so, what are they? If not, why not (for example, the scope of our activities, the absence of life-or-death decisions)? If you had these monumental life experiences—would you find them motivating or demotivating?

5. I loved the idea of being comfortable with "getting lost." How comfortable are you with "getting lost"? Do dissertation defenses, tenure reviews, and other milestones in academia make it difficult to be comfortable in this state? Is "staying lost" for a while a privilege of tenure—or is it necessary to achieve it (or neither)?

6 (a) As we see from his chapter, Denny has had many "lives" and currently has many "selves." How then can we be true to our "own self" as he suggests? Which "self" should we be true to? In what ways does it help and hurt to have had multiple past lives, and multiple current selves (not to mention, many possible future selves)?

6 (b) Denny also talked about the appeal of academia after working at Ford. I wonder if people who come to academia from other professions are differently motivated because they are more fully aware of the lives they *do not* want to lead. (As a side note, do you know what it is about engineering that seems

to propel people into organizational theory? I know several people who have made this switch. Does the reverse happen?) If this is your second or third (or more) "life"—what about academia is appealing? If it is your "first," what motivates you? I agree with Denny that persistence is critical to success in this profession. What keeps you going—even in the face of rejection and other challenges?

7. In academia, we often talk about "streams of research" whereby one engages in very programmatic research—one study leads directly to the next. Is this the model offered here? Like my own research, I see Denny's as more of a constellation—different points in the same part of the sky that we can connect together in meaningful ways. Is your own research more like a "stream" or "constellation"? Is there a better metaphor for how our own work fits together?

8. The "positive illusion" that Denny clings to is that he is always trying to top himself (and his experience on the Apollo/Saturn teams). What positive illusions do you have that keep you going? Can you thrive in this profession (or anywhere) if you are not an idealist?

9. Denny talks about how energizing relationships are—with doctoral students, with reviewers, executives, and the like. What are your energizing relationships? How do your connections help to define who you are?

10. I would find writing an autobiographical chapter both humbling and daunting. If you had to write your own research autobiography, what would you include? As important, what might you leave out?

America-centrism

Everyone outside the United States knows that study of organizations is dominated by American universities, textbooks, and journals (Inkson 1988; Chanlat 1996, Clegg, Linstead, and Sewell 2000; Huff and Pearse 1999; Mills and Hatfield 1999; Wong-MingJi and Mir 1997). This book is no exception. All but Barbara are U.S.-educated. All but Barbara and Anne Huff are employed in the United States. Peter is South African and works in Canada, but his doctoral education was in the United States. Ralph is American-born and -educated, but works in New Zealand. The international diversity of our experience makes us sensitive to this issue.

We wonder about the degree to which the American experience of academia has come to be seen as the desirable template for all organizational researchers. There is no doubt that the majority of university positions are in American universities. There is no doubt that the majority of journal articles are published by Americans. Historically, America did not move first, but it did move faster in pursuing business education at the university level.

Historically, business education at the university level has a short history, but it is not exclusively an American history. From the late 1800s there was discussion about the need for advanced business education and a number of educational innovations throughout Europe and United States (Barnes 1989, 1–10). In 1881, both the Ecole des Hautes Etudes Commerciales (HEC) and Wharton Business School were founded. The University of California (Berkeley) and the University of Chicago instituted undergraduate programs in 1898. Postgraduate education in business was first introduced by the Tuck School at Dartmouth University in 1900, and later by Harvard Business School in 1908 (Van Fleet and Wren 1982). In Germany, Cologne in 1901 and Berlin in 1906 opened independent business schools, in part, modeled on Wharton. Mannheim, Munich, Konigsberg, and Nuremberg soon followed. There is some evidence that the Berlin school and the Harvard Business School were linked via the friendship of the economists Ignaz Jastrow in Berlin and Frank Taussig at Harvard. However, Barnes reports, "From 1908 onwards, business education in Europe lagged behind and the United States forged ahead. By 1908 there were 13 business schools in the United States; by 1914 there were 31; by 1920 there were 65 and by 1951 there were 166 (if departments or colleges teaching business at university level are included)" (Barnes 1989, 6). The apparent success of American management (Servan-Schreiber 1967/1969) and American management education did not go unnoticed. The British consciously imported the American business school model through the formation of the London and Manchester Business Schools in 1965. Many British universities built business schools on the U.S. model, for example, at Warwick where George Bain took the lead (Pettigrew 1998). By 1980 there were fourteen business schools in Great Britain (Locke 1989), and thirty-one by 1988 (Barry 1989) (business schools at polytechnics would further add to that total). Today, even the red-brick universities have built business schools.

Australia brought Richard Cyert over in 1970 to consult on the development of management education there (Barry, Dowling, and Tonks 1995). The concrete outcome was the formation of the Australian Graduate School of Management in 1977. A second national business school was started at Melbourne following the Ralph Commission of 1980. Today, almost every Australian university features a business school (Byrt 1989).

Recent expansion has been undertaken by American business schools themselves. For example, in the 1990s Northwestern's Kellogg Graduate School of Management developed alliances with Recanti GSB in Tel Aviv, Koblenz, Hong Kong University of Science and Technology, and Beijing University. Wharton and Kellogg created the Indian School of Business in Heyderabad in 2001.

With the adoption of the American model came American demarcations of research fields including departments of organizational behavior. American-trained staff was recruited. Faculty visited American institutions and returned with new ideas about research culture, research writing, and research outlets (Pettigrew 1998). Good students were encouraged to study in the United States.

Why did others turn to the U.S. model? Locke (1996) argues that it was a massive attribution error. The world wrongly attributed American economic success to its management education.

A conspiracy-theory alternative explanation is available, as well (Clegg, Linstead, and Sewell 2000). The Ford Foundation hosted Sir Keith Joseph at Harvard Business School in 1957, setting in place a string of events that led to the formation of the London Business School and Manchester Business

School. In 1973, the Ford Foundation funding helped establish the European Institute for Advanced Studies in Management with links to the London Business School and European governments. The American government funded many Fulbright scholarships for visits to and from foreign universities.

At least part of the emphasis on the American model is unintentional. Since the 1980s, there has been a call by government funders for greater accountability from the universities. In the United Kingdom, this has led to a series of national, standardized comparisons of all universities on research quality (Willmott 1995). Good research has been operationalized as publication in top international journals. Top international journals are American, thus refocusing research activity away from books and toward work that meets the American standard. Similar comparisons are being made in Australia and New Zealand.

The American standard in organization studies is the journal article. Another reflection of the dominance of the American model is the relative disregard of books. Clawson and Zussman (1998, 8) discuss the book culture and the article culture of American sociology. They note how little these two sociologies interact. Thus books rated as influential by the editorial board of *Contemporary Sociology*, a journal of book reviews, barely overlap with journal citation ratings of influence (Cronin et al. 1993). Perhaps the importance of North American contributions to organizations studies is due to the confounding of nationality and book authorship. Perhaps American organizational scholars do not read books.

Walter Nord (2003), in his editor's remarks as the new book review editor at the *Academy of Management Review*, argues that we should start reading. He writes:

Specifically, among other things, books call attention to the context of a subject—something that is often lost in demand upon editors of academic journals to conserve space. Second, books facilitate publication of in-depth ethnographies such as the study the Challenger disaster (Vaughn 1996). Third, books are sources of deep and broad theoretical treatments, such as March & Simon (1958) and Thompson (1967). Fourth, books can help to open the doors to fields that are relevant to us but have been bypassed. Kuhn (1970) *The Structure of Scientific Revolutions* is paradigmatic in this respect (Nord 2003, 155).

It may be that encouraging Europeans and others to write in prestigious American journals does not serve the field well. As Mary Jo and Sally remind us, Barbara's books are a case in point.

At the same time that the American model continues to colonize business education worldwide, American management educators perceived a need to internationalize. There has been some success. For example, about 30 percent of the (American) Academy of Management membership is international. At least some of these members are non-American-trained and include vociferous critics of the American hegemony of organizational study, for example, Clegg, Linstead, and Sewell (2000). The American Academy recognized the *Handbook of Organizations Studies* with its strong international contributions as the Terry Book Award winner. The formation of the Critical Management Studies Interest Group represents, in part, recognition of an ongoing stream of organizational scholarship that has been marginal and minimal in America, but more central overseas. The alliance with the Iberoamerican Academy of Management is a more radical move toward internationalization as it embraces contributions in a language other than English.

The interplay of American dominance and internationalization is complex. Clegg, Linstead, and Sewell (2000) remind us that the American tradition can absorb the foreign and make it its own, as in the case of Elton Mayo (an Australian) and the human relations movement. The efforts to reflect the local in the national versions of American textbooks may amount to no more than the inclusion of local case studies. Local voices and local issues are further marginalized by their absence. For example, "the best-selling text *Organization Theory in Australia* by Robins and Barnwell (1998) does not cite a single Australian academic journal" (Clegg, Linstead, and Sewell 2000, 108), or mention the problems of the dispossessed Aboriginal peoples. At the same time, there can be no pure, indigenous organizational studies unsullied by the American tradition.

Clegg, Linstead, and Sewell (2000) insist that there is room for resistance to American imperialism. They offer the analogy of feminist scholarship as an example. Chanlat (1996) describes the movement from uncritical adoption of the American way to the translation of American scholarship into French to critique and to development of indigenous organizational studies à la Québecoise.

We believe that postcolonial scholarship has something to add to the understanding of these issues. We look forward to the application of these ideas to organizations studies (Prasad 2003). It is important that the American standard, which has been so successful, does not become a barrier to other modes of potentially successful scholarship. We suggest that looking to overseas scholarship may provide another avenue for individual renewal and the ongoing renewal of organization studies.

My Mother's Daughter

I WAS BORN IN 1948 in Bialystok, Poland (yes, I used to eat bialy bagels for breakfast), as a fifth child to my forty-one-year-old mother and fifty-year-old father. When I was three, my sister died and I was left with three older brothers. They are the best brothers one can imagine—I am indeed blessed with them, although I always longed for a sister and have invariably been attracted to women five or six years older than myself.

In my mother's version (since then I have learned that there are always many versions around), the most important events in her life were as follows. After having graduated from high school in 1925, she wanted to study accounting. But accounting was not taught at Mickiewicz University in Vilnius, where they lived. She would have to go to Warsaw School of Economics, a move that my grandmother, then a widow, strongly opposed. Longing to escape from my grandmother's despotism, my mother fell in love with my father (the choice turned out to be one between the devil and the deep sea). They married over the protests of my grandmother, who at that point would rather have seen her daughter go to Warsaw than to the altar. But it was too late.

After that came the Second World War, and the repatriation of the Poles living in Lithuania to the newly created Poland (Bialystok is only two hundred kilometers from Vilnius, and my parents hoped to go back very soon). I only know these events from my brothers' reminiscences, though. I remember that my mother did work as an accountant, but for a very short time. She showed the signs of rheumatoid arthritis that developed very fast and soon she could not walk anymore. She remained at home, refusing to be taken out. Later on, she developed a kidney cancer that spread. She died of a brain tumor when I was twenty-one.

What with her illnesses and her bitter marriage, my mother's was the unhappiest life I have ever encountered. My brothers comfort me, claiming that her first forty years were not unhappy at all, and I have mother's smiling pictures to corroborate this. She died in 1969, and her wishes for me were very clear: I was to be a journalist, travel all around the world, remain unmarried, and speak many languages. Much as I loved her, I was very keen on thwarting every one of her wishes—then.

Education was given the highest value in our family, and it was my mother who championed this value. She persuaded my father to complete his education (here, at least, all stories concur) and, once in the "new" Poland, he worked as a department head in the county administration. I was very pleased with his workplace, as it had a well-equipped library of which I was the main client. The bored librarian allowed me to take out five books at a time, in contrast to the city librarian who used to quiz me on the contents of the borrowed book if I returned it after just one day.

Two teachers were very important to me during my school years. Edward Grygo was my teacher of Polish literature. He was an ardent communist, and he had irritating manners and numerous enemies, thanks to both his politics and his bearing. He taught me everything I know about language. Maria Blicharska was a retired English teacher and my private tutor, as my mother was determined that I start learning languages. (I took Latin at school because my mother believed that it would help me to learn any other language afterward.) Ms. Blicharska came from a noble family, was gentle mannered, and she was an anticommunist. My two teachers knew one another and detested each other; they never mentioned it in my presence.

Graduating from high school (where I had buried my dreams of becoming an actress, albeit it was a quiet burial) I knew two things: that I wanted to write, and that I wanted to write about things that occupy most people for most of their lives. (If one were to believe Hollywood movies, it is lovemaking; if one looks around, it is work.) I thought that I may as well study to become a journalist, but at that time journalism was a postgraduate education. The choice was then between psychology and sociology, but the entrance examination was biology for psychology and history for sociology. I could never get any dates straight, so the decision was obvious.

The year was 1965, and the majority of full professors in psychology were women, many of them with an international reputation. The majority of the students (sixty of sixty-six in my class) were also women. We thought it was boring; we couldn't even have proper dance evenings. We thought that those old biddies who knew psychology so well and did qualitative studies were uninspiring. We loved young men who had been to the States, talked to us on a first-name basis, and knew how to use the statistics package.

One of the last oral exams I had to take was given by one of the "old biddies," a woman probably not older than sixty, a true lady who wore lace collars, rouged her cheeks, and pinned her hair up. As I considered her practically senile, I thought that memorizing the dates of births and deaths of important people plus some names of main schools would be more than enough. She asked me, in a quiet, pleasant voice, to compare philosophical assumptions of two schools in psychology. I remember thinking that the deep color brought to my cheeks by shame exceeded her rouge. I remember her gentle eyes fixed on some point above my head, as if she was afraid to look at me and show how little she thought about my protestations about "not being prepared for this angle." She let me go after I had recited some dates and names, and I could not stop wondering, what had led me to misjudge her so thoroughly? I thought that it was my prejudice against age, as other answers were not yet in my repertoire.

When I wrote my master's thesis and graduated in 1970, the majority of full professors were men. The women had retired, and I did not think much about the reasons for this change in proportions. Politics entered my world for the first time in 1968, when we occupied the University in protest against the system and in solidarity with the French students. The French were fighting in the name of the opposite ideology, but it did not matter much. I am not ironic—it truly did not matter, as they and we were both fighting against an oppressive system, no matter which color. But soon after, during the subsequent expulsion of the Poles of Jewish descent from the country, and during the workers' revolt, it had become abundantly clear that colors do matter in politics. It has also become clear to me that being a journalist in a party-ruled system had its complications that I had not taken into account previously (neither had my mother, an ardent anticommunist). It is not that I was particularly naive, I think. Most people in my generation grew up between two fanaticisms—as we now call it, one black, one red, one represented by our parents, and one by our teachers or bosses or the media. Many of us decided to join one of them, but equally many, perhaps most, reacted by developing an allergy to politics. The University, a place where the police beat up our dean when he tried to prevent them from entering the building that we occupied, seemed to be an island of freedom from the two oppressions.

I was offered an assistantship by two professors. I chose social psychology, but the professor who had the chair in industrial psychology convinced his colleague that his new group needed me more. I was both flattered and irritated that they decided my fate behind my back, but with time I appreciated their decision.

I soon discovered that it was not at all easy to write a dissertation in what we started to call organization psychology using the experimental design that felt "natural" to me. To distract myself, I started to participate in the activities of the Young Researchers' Group at the neighboring Department of

Education. We went to summer camps and interviewed people in the countryside about their use of the Culture Houses that were founded all over the country. This was my first encounter with anthropological methods, although I did not think about them in those terms. But those visits in the country households felt very exotic to me. I became close friends with many people in education and later, together with my two friends Jurek Szmagalski and Wojtek Nocun, created what we called the "New Horizons Cooperative." We toured the country giving management development courses to the managers of Culture Houses. We have also authored a course book on this topic.

One of the associate professors in education who was the driving force behind the research group was married to a professor of economics. She told me that her husband was thinking about breaking with the tradition of theoretical and statistical research in economics and wished to make a field study. He wanted to know how decisions are actually made in enterprises, not only how they ought to be made according to economic models of rationality. He did not know how to begin, she said, and wouldn't I like to help him to set up such a study?

Five years of learning how to conduct interviews and make observations paid off. Janusz Beksiak set up a big team of collaborators, and I started to coach field researchers. I did it strictly as an extra job, but when he said that even the theoretical part of research could use a chapter on how motivating are various incentive systems for managers, I was eager to help. We became good friends and I confided in him that evaluating the results of management courses proved to be a more frustrating type of research than I had thought. "Why don't you write a dissertation in economics instead, starting from your chapter?" A theoretical dissertation? I could not imagine what that would imply. Trained in writing papers that started with a problem, went through a literature review, continued with the formulation of a hypothesis, a description of the method, a report on the results, an analysis, and then a synthesis, I had no idea how to begin to write a book. It was Janusz who told me how to find a structure in the material itself, rather than to impose it according to a given format. He acted as my editor and my therapist when, with rather predictable regularity, I succumbed to bouts of depression over my inability to ever, ever write any doctoral dissertation. I imitate his example in my role as an adviser, and although I am sure that there are many other, perhaps better ways of helping people to write a thesis, what worked for me turned out to work for other people as well.

I was employed at Warsaw University but did research at Warsaw School of Economics, where I also received the title of Doctor of Economic Sciences in 1976. As our research concerned decision making, I read literature in the field and came up with two textbooks in this area. It was then when

I discovered the works of James G. March and his collaborators, and when the garbage-can model made its lasting impression on me, and on my first husband, the economist Maciej Ramus. Both of us incorporated the idea into our thinking and writing: I have produced a couple of textbooks on decision making in Polish, where I was slowly and surely approaching the understanding that matured only after I moved to Sweden: that decisions just happen, in life and in organizations.

Why Sweden? WSE had, since at least 1974, a cooperation with Gothenburg School of Economics and Commercial Law. Thanks to that cooperation I met a group of researchers who were to become my friends and colleagues: Nils Brunsson, Bo Hedberg, Sten Jönsson, and Rolf Lundin. During one of their visits, Walter Goldberg, the then chair of organization theory in Gothenburg, brought me a present. It was a book by Barney Glaser and Anselm Strauss, and its title was *A Discovery of Grounded Theory*. I was hooked. Many years later I read some anthropologist saying that Glaser and Strauss (1967) simply summarized the common sense of working in the field. The comment was meant as derogatory, but I feel that it is an extremely fortuitous description of the book. It legitimized the insights I was gathering through my research, which seemed to be at odds with various prescriptions of "how to." Of course, sense that is common varies from place to place and from time to time, but at least at that time, an official recognition and appreciation of what was a shameful practice was extremely liberating.

I did a study of management in Polish commercial enterprises using the grounded theory approach. I wrote a book that was to become a basis of the next step in my career, the so-called habilitation, which had to be recognized by a central qualifying committee to then qualify me for promotion as an associate professor. In Poland at that time people entered university careers as teaching assistants, doing research and writing their dissertation without a formal doctoral program. A PhD was a requirement for a position of an assistant professor, and another dissertation, for that of an associate. Talented teachers who failed to gain a doctor's degree could become tenured in the position of lecturer.

A colleague of mine, who received his PhD when I did, applied for recognition and was refused on the basis of his "young age." At the same time I published an article in the popular weekly *Politics*, which criticized the proceedings of the committee. "Solidarity" was afoot, and we were speaking our minds louder and louder. My friends suggested that it was as well to wait a little before submitting my product to the committee, and they recommended a visit abroad. (In spite of the common conviction, Polish researchers often traveled abroad. It was just that one never knew whether an application for a passport would be granted, and one never knew when and if the university administration will make the incoming grants accessible.) I applied for a travel grant from the American Council of Learned Societies. During the interview the representative of the ACLS asked me where I wanted to go. I said "University of California" because, to my knowledge, this was where Glaser and Strauss were. "Which of them?" I did not know there were several. "You and the Brits are all the same," chided the representative gently. "You want to go to California because of the sunshine. Did you think about the necessity of having a car?" So we compromised on Sloan School of Management, because David Kolb was there (by that time he had already left, but how was I to know?). I went home and checked my atlas. Boston was at the same latitude as Varna, the summer resort in Bulgaria, I was pleased to discover. I was to recall this piece of information acutely during Easter, when there was such a violent snowstorm that I couldn't turn the corner from Sloan.

Thus came 1981, one of the most eventful years in my life. I fell in love, I went to the States, and martial law was imposed on Poland. In the grand scheme of things, the order of importance should be reversed, of course, but both the chronological and the subjective orders of importance were as reported.

My contact person at MIT was Lotte Bailyn. She took good care of me and also gave me a book to read. It was Rosalie Wax's (1971) *Doing Field Research: Warning and Advice*. I finished reading it at 3 AM and was perplexed. Until then, professional reading was for me strongly differentiated from fiction reading. I never read professional books late at night or early in the morning, for fear of falling asleep after several pages. I often had to reread the same page again and again, as my thoughts ran freely to other topics, while my eyes perused the print mechanically. Wax's book confirmed my interest in anthropology and its method (to be developed later with help from, among others, Constance Perin), but it also made me question, perhaps for the first time, the sharp difference between the genres of science and literature.

Arriving at Sloan, I learned that most of my fellow guest-researchers, although arriving under the pretext of doing field research, had resigned themselves to taking some courses and spending their time in the library. I insisted, and Edgar Schein took pity on me. He made it possible for me to interview top managers in two retail corporations, closely resembling, in their tasks, those I had studied in Poland.

I was asked whether I felt that being a foreigner from a socialist country and, in addition, a woman, evoked any particular attitude in my interlocutors. Perhaps it did, but I was never able to distinguish between the two. This ambiguity remains with me to this day, although I changed the status of "being from a socialist country" to "being an immigrant." On the whole, I think that my gender is of more importance to the people I contact, whereas for me it is my foreign status that colors all my interpretations. At any rate, in professional settings the two seem to operate in the same direction. While interviewing the U.S. CEOs, I was not perceived as threatening, which caused relative openness and some degree of paternalism. I was instructed in detail on most matters (which was exactly what I wanted), and some remarks were usually made about the sanative effect of introducing U.S. management in Poland's troubled economy.

But doing fieldwork did not prevent me from attending seminars that were offered. I shared the life of the doctoral students at Sloan (Karen Epstein, Cynthia Ingols, Gideon Kunda, and Steve Barley were my chums), as they were closer to me in age and life experience than the professors. Also, I had a tendency to classify people according to the European order, where associate and full professors were one category, and all the rest another. We were especially interested in a seminar series organized by John Van Maanen. It was in relation to that series that I read *Social Psychology of Organizing* by Karl Weick. It so happened that I had translated Katz and Kahn's *Social Psychology of Organizations* into Polish, and its open system theory was my main theoretical frame of reference for many years. Reading Karl Weick was like reading science fiction and realizing that all this was already reality. I wrote an enthusiastic review for a Polish journal, but the book was translated into Polish only a couple of years ago.

It was also from Massachusetts that I paid my first visit to Canada and Nina L. Colwill, who was to become my friend for life.

U.S. television showed street executions in Poland (quite untruthfully, as I learned afterward). Going back meant to me a separation, forever, as I thought melodramatically, from the man I loved. I wanted to be close to him, in Europe, and spent some time in Berlin where, although much welcome at Science Center, I discovered that field research was not an option. I therefore accepted an invitation from Bo Hedberg, who was at that time professor at the Swedish Center for Working Life (the center changed its name several times afterward). I arrived in Sweden in February 1983.

One of the persons who was leaving the center at the time I arrived there was Rolf Wolff, who was to become my friend and collaborator. He told me about vicissitudes in the life of a foreign researcher in Sweden (Rolf is German) while packing his boxes. But my stay at the center meant first and foremost a powerful encounter with feminism.

As often in my life, my first encounter with feminism happened through a book. I do not remember its title anymore, but it was one of the first books that dealt with gendering of the language. I read it with fascination, while noticing that as English has a different grammar than Slavic languages, gendering operates differently in different languages. It was for the first but not for the last time that I observed that both gender discrimination and the strategies of coping with it differ across places and times. While I was still in Poland, after one of my lectures a group of female students came up to ask whether I would be willing to give a lecture on feminism. I was surprised: "Why me?" "Because you are the only feminist we know." "And why did you think I was a feminist?" They quoted at me many excerpts from my lectures, which to them was proof of my stand.

Before I managed to collect my thoughts on the matter, life swept me on; I went to the States, and it was not before I got to Sweden that I was confronted with this question again. Swedish feminists such as Annika Baude (who taught me not only feminism but also Swedish) and Wuokko Knocke became my friends, and through them I also met Joan Acker, who has been keeping me on the feminist track ever since. It was more than ideological support and guidance that I received from them, though.

While my first years in Sweden were very profitable in the professional sense, they were very painful in a personal sense. Immigration proved to be a very trying process, especially for a person who is so language-bounded as I am. I used to joke that while men helped me to make a career, women helped me to survive it. Nobody likes this joke. My men friends feel accused of lack of sensitivity; my women friends read in this a chauvinist undertone—only men can foster a career. I do not think either interpretation is right. It is not men's lack of sensitivity, but the surviving convention that does not encourage close friendship between the opposite sexes, the kind of friendship that goes deeply into everyday life. As to men as the only aids to a career, it is a topic often mentioned in descriptions of women who were helped in their careers by their fathers, husbands, or male mentors. This need not be explained by men's mysterious strength or women's mysterious weakness. No one makes a career on his or her own (this is a theme to which I will return often enough). And if a career happens to take place in a male-dominated world, it is no wonder that men are seen as aiding—or impeding—both men and women who are beginning their professional lives. If anything is changing radically, this is, as more women are able to help younger people.

After a year spent at the center, I moved to my second Swedish assignment at the Institute of International Business at the Stockholm School of Economics. There, Jan-Erik Vahlne assisted me in the same way Ed Schein had before—through a path of trials and refusals he helped me to contact the first Swedish company who agreed to be studied by me. At the same time, I was talking to Nils Brunsson, the head of another department at the school. He was willing to let me join his research group on two conditions: that I learn Swedish, and that I study public administration organizations. The first condition seemed sensible: I was clearly on my way to immigrate (in my case at least, it was never a decision but a process that ran more or less by itself) and learning the language of the new country made a lot of sense. But public-sector organizations? I was a product of the "industrial romance"; the public sector was boring and uninspiring. Luckily for me, I was given fifteen years to revise this opinion.

Thus I joined the "F-section" (the F does not stand for feminism, but for "administration" in Swedish), and the researchers there: Anders Forssell, Bengt Jacobsson, Rolf Lind, Björn Rombach, and Kerstin Sahlin-Andersson were to become my friends and collaborators in the years to come. It is ten years now since I left them to accept my first chair in management at Lund University, but I still consider them my intellectual family, if I may be forgiven such sentimentalism.

Upon my arrival in Lund in 1990, a woman who had never met me before, Margareta Bertilsson, now chair in sociology at Copenhagen University, gave me a room to stay in and her friendship. She was joined by Johanna Esseveld, who also acted on the recommendation of a mutual friend—Joan Acker—which seemed to be enough.

Many important things happened to me in Lund. One was my first encounter with doctoral students of my own. Now all doctors, my Lund students (and also my present Gothenburg students) are to me the best proof that what I am doing makes sense, in times of doubt, of which there are many. They seem to believe that I helped them along their way.

Lund, even before I moved there, was also the scene of my first participation in the Standing Conference on Organizational Symbolism, where I met the most amazing people, such as P.-O. Berg, Mary Jo Hatch, Kristian Kreiner, Joanne Martin, Michael Rosen, Howard Schwartz, Susan Schneider, and the late Barry Turner, whose death I still refuse to believe.

SCOS has also activated for me my latent Italian connection. It so happened that my friend since elementary school, Ania Biedzinska, married an Italian and moved to Rome in 1970. I went to visit her soon after, all eager to communicate in English, and discovered that either I would have to learn Italian, or I would never have the opportunity to speak to her new friends and family. So I did, but until 1984, at the SCOS conference, I never had the opportunity to speak the language in a professional context. SCOS made me meet Pasquale Gagliardi, Silvia Gherardi, Tatiana Pipan, and Antonio Strati, and soon I had all the possibilities and reasons to expand my Italian competence.

I also met Marta Calás and Linda Smircich through SCOS, and they came to visit me in Lund. They brought me a present—a book about Emily Dickinson—which I gratefully acknowledged, but being incurably curious about books I also wanted to know what gift they had brought for Mats Alvesson, who at that time lived in Copenhagen. It was Richard Rorty's *Contingency,*

Irony and Solidarity, and Marta and Linda allowed me to leaf through it, provided I did not smear the pages. (This was a wise condition, as my biography should be complemented with a shameful story from my childhood when I read a book, smuggled for me by a tenant who worked at a bookstore, while eating a hazelnut chocolate. This shocking accident cured me from chocolate but not from books. Think that it could have easily been the other way around.)

When I came to the end of page 73 in Rorty's book, I began to cry. This is what I read:

I shall define an "ironist" as someone who fulfills three conditions: (1) She has radical and continuing doubts about the final vocabulary she currently uses, because she has been impressed by other vocabularies, vocabularies taken as final by people or books that she has encountered; (2) she realizes that arguments phrased in her present vocabulary can neither underwrite nor dissolve these doubts; (3) insofar as she philosophizes about her situation, she does not think that her vocabulary is closer to reality than others, that it is in touch with a power not herself.

It is not that I am taken much to crying; quite the contrary. It is just that I realized that during the previous twenty-five years of reading scientific texts, I had always been making a rapid translation in my head, no matter what language I was reading. The texts said, "He who wants to be a scientist must realize that his life is going to be influenced by his choice," and I, so quickly that I ceased to notice it, was adding, "this goes even for women." It was the first time when somebody spoke about me, when somebody spoke directly to me, not to somebody who might be in some way similar to myself. It was the same feeling that one experiences in tender years, reading a poem that seems to have been written with the blood of one's heart (I was brought up in a Romantic tradition).

Rorty says that we read books with a purpose at hand, but that we appreciate most the readings that changed that purpose. He calls the first type of reading a methodical reading; the other, inspired. I do not think one needs to add anything to that, apart from the fact that, since then, I have read all Rorty's books. Among many other things that I found in them, there was the key to how to legitimize my secret passion: literature. Encouraged by Rorty's obvious approval, I started reading Jerome Bruner and other narratologists, and thus discovered the allure of the narrative approach.

But there exist inspired encounters not only with books but also with people. Through my second former husband, Bernward Joerges, I got in touch with sociology of science and technology, and the writings of such people as Karin Knorr Cetina, Simon Schaffer, Trevor Pinch, Michel Callon, and Bruno Latour. I find their work perfectly in tune with pragmatism, and if there is one thing that puzzles me, it is the reception of it. To me, far from being strange and deviant, they are describing the world just as it is, that is, just as I see it.

I left Lund after five years, but I remember it with fondness. Apart from Joke and Margareta, I enjoyed the company of Ron Eyerman, Jonathan Friedman, Orvar Löfgren, and Sven-Olof Collin. But I was attracted by an enticement that only Gothenburg can offer: the Swedish Film Festival.

People think I am being flippant when I mention this reason for moving to Gothenburg, but although not the only one, it was certainly the main one. I do like the city, though: it is big enough for variety, and small enough for comfort. It is pretty without being overwhelming (see Rome!). Inga Hellberg, professor of sociology, was a person who took me to her home and to her heart. My colleagues Sten Jönsson, Rolf Solli, and Rolf Wolff are very good to me, and it is fun to work in the Gothenburg Research Institute. I keep my international connections alive and burning, and it is another globetrotter, Guje Sevón (Finland/Denmark/Sweden/SAS), who is my closest collaborator at present.

When I look at my life now (and turning fifty provokes a lot of such looking), I see a clear analogy between my professional life and my personal life. In both, I move from one field to another, from one country to another, remaining a foreigner. But here the analogy ends, because the consequences are very different. Moving from one discipline to another creates forever-new sources of fascination. Moving from one country to another, and even from one city to another, means destroying the precious social web that one managed to spin in any given place. Unlike spiders, I seem to be unable to spin with the same intensity in each new place. Or perhaps aging spiders have the same problem. Traveling multiplies friendships; emigration decimates them.

I am as my mother wished me to be—single, traveling, a professor instead of a journalist, which I think she would readily have accepted. It amazes me how faithful I am to her wishes (Eric Berne would have much to say about life scripts), but also how I translated them into versions that are literally identical but profoundly different from her wishes.

It will be thirty years on October 1, 2000, since I started working at the university. No one will give me either a medal or a gold watch, and why should they: I was never faithful to any single organization. But I believe that I am faithful to the institution of the university, which may need a thorough renewal (what old institution does not) but which seems to me still a very good idea, especially if one allows women in. Perhaps "universitas"—a community of people working and living enthusiastically together in order to explore reality—never existed anywhere but in people's fantasy, or perhaps it is difficult to actualize in the mass education universities of today, but it does not matter. It is beautiful as an idea, and it should be cherished for that.

A young scholar who may be reading this autobiographical sketch might at this point become impatient and ask: Hasn't she ever done anything herself? I could answer him or her by referring the reader to Kenneth Gergen and to Gergen's idea of self as a net of relationships. I could also paraphrase Bruno Latour and say that I am but a network that is posing as an actor. Whichever way one looks at it, it takes a great many people—many more than I managed to fit onto these pages—to make one career. Thus although I am enchanted with the notion of a community of explorers, I have no patience for the image of a lonely genius, a heroic scholar who confronts the universe in an ivory tower (unless that ivory tower contains a telescope).

Exactly! I almost forgot. An actor-network theory puts much emphasis on the fact that a "socius" does not have to be a human being. Cats, dogs, horses, and, in this case, books and computers play an important part in a network. What surprises me sometimes is the fact that I do not remember my first encounter with a computer. I know that I typed my master's and doctor's theses on a mechanical typewriter, but after that, all is vague. Computers seem to have always been here. No wonder, perhaps, that I am looking forward to the era of the electronic book.

MARY JO HATCH

Commentary on "My Mother's Daughter"

I ADMIRED BARBARA from the start. The start I remember clearly. I had ducked out of my daily obligations at San Diego State University, to engage in a favorite activity—strolling through the stacks at the library. For those reared in the age of computer access to library materials let me say that, in my view, this pleasure has been too eagerly traded for the convenience of office delivery. Just think of the people you will never meet through chance encounters with their books. In any case, this was still an era of library stacks and impromptu (virtual) meetings with new authors. Moving down the aisle in one well-traveled section of the library I noticed a new book gleaming on the shelf. Its title beckoned me: *Ideological Control in Non-Ideological Organizations*. I had not a clue what that might mean but determined right then and there to find out. Snatching my prize from the shelf, I carted it back to my office.

It was usual in those days for me to keep library books on an office shelf for months at a time. There was already an inventory of twenty to thirty glowering at me from their lonely perch that day. I ignored their pleas for attention and packed this book in my bag. Over the weekend I read it with enthusiasm and some puzzlement; it was not like any other book I had read in that it combined organization theory with ethnography. It appealed to my imagination, though I remember wondering what sort of places Barbara was observing that sounded to my ears so completely mysterious. Still the terrain of her theorizing was familiar, even if her ethnographic haunts were not. I particularly remember being intrigued that sometimes I could not understand what she was telling me at all, while other times she seemed to be speaking my own thoughts. I was enchanted.

Some months later, as it happened, Barbara and I attended a small workshop of about thirty-five academics (a subgroup of SCOS, the Standing

Conference on Organizational Symbolism) held in Denmark, about an hour's drive from Copenhagen. All the participants met on the roof of the Copenhagen Business School's Institute for Organization where we had a toast to welcome one another. Then we took a bus ride to our meeting place in the countryside. When we arrived, we were instructed to take our room keys and stow our luggage before dinner. As I walked down the hall I saw a woman opening the door across from my room and we introduced ourselves. To my surprise and delight it was none other than Barbara (we had managed to miss one another on the rooftop) and to my utter shock she said how delighted she was to meet me and then referred to the one and only paper that I had ever published at that point in my life! Needless to say, I was flattered and somewhat overwhelmed that anyone had read something I had a hand in writing. I gasped out some awkward tribute to her book. She looked as shocked as I was feeling, saying how surprised she was that anyone had read her book since it had only recently been published. I silently formed a fan club.

In the days that followed I had several chances to work in breakout groups with Barbara and to admire her quick wit and enormous intellect. We talked and worked and ate several meals together with our colleagues, and my admiration only grew with each exchange. The workshop was the first of three that would be held over the next two years and I felt that Barbara and I might become friends. The next workshop confirmed this, at least for me, and when in 1990 I moved to take a job in Denmark, Barbara helped to guide me through the process of immigration. She shared her own wealth of experience in changing countries and gave advice and support to help me make sense of the changes I was facing as I adapted to my new life as a foreigner. Throughout this time she also continued to influence me with her writings, of which there was a constant new supply. I was in awe of the fact that she wrote books and stunned that she did so in several languages. I began to compare myself to her and fell far short on every dimension. What seemed worse, I soon discovered that every idea that came to me, came to her first. I used to joke that whenever I wanted to begin a new project I should write to Barbara and find out what she had just published on the topic. Only it wasn't a joke, it was true!

Reading Barbara's reflections about her life and her work has given me some new insight into my friend and mentor. We have shared time together over the years at conferences, visits to our respective institutions, and even at an art museum, but as writers know, reading allows a form of intimacy that can be had in no other way. Reading as a writer prompts me to compare my own thoughts to what it is like to think like someone else. The writer in me always tries to imagine how the writer I am reading thought or felt as they expressed their ideas with these particular words. Reading in this way, I become more than I was, stretched beyond my former limits by my images of the imagination of another. And Barbara's writing has always stretched my imagination in highly productive ways.

What I have learned from the narrative Barbara has written for this book, which I knew already at some level, has to do with the profound love of books and the lived life of narrative that do much to make Barbara who she is. Just as Barbara's writings have influenced and at times precluded my own, her reading has stood as an inspiration. She consumes books, great piles of them. And they consume her in turn. She reads not only academic literature but also fiction—voraciously. And as far as I can tell, when Barbara is not reading she is writing. I imagine her, day after day, banging out books on her keypad, one right after the other. I know she struggles, she has told me she does, along with stories I will leave for her to tell about the trials and tribulations of getting published when ideas come to you sooner than they do to so many others.

But above all, I would like to say what a joy it has been to meet an organization theorist with Barbara's range and pluck. I hope that her reflections will carry you to her work and that one book or article will follow the other as has been my experience. I hope that you will listen carefully and hear the sound of her voice in the narrative that explains how ideas are connected to and built on each other and how theory is not a sequestered place in the head, but tales told in interaction with many others. I can tell you that the voice you hear in Barbara's essay is the voice I know as Barbara. I also believe that what Barbara says about the people who form the web of her existence is mirrored in the way she does her research. Her personal narrative, printed here, is but one of many you will find when you meet her, as I first did, in the pages of one of her many delightfully important books and articles.

Traveling Solo

A Reflection on Barbara Czarniawska's Journey

I WASN'T SURE what to expect when I agreed to write a chapter "response" for this book, although I had some preconceptions. I knew the book was about academic renewal, and that I had been asked to respond to Barbara's Czarniawska's chapter because of my enthusiasm for her work. I also understood that Peter Frost had seen some parallels between Barbara's journey and mine, albeit mine is still somewhat short. I was intrigued. I began the chapter full of anticipation: the notion of examining the path taken by a much-admired academic to see the struggles she faced and, moreover, to discover how she hauled herself out of bad times and barren periods to move on, renewed and refreshed, was compelling. And this felt all the more exciting because I was sure that, being the discipline-spanning and perspective-challenging academic that she is, Barbara must have had more than her fair share of such struggles. I was also curious to detect the parallels to which Peter had alluded—I love Barbara's work but had never thought to identify with her.

I thoroughly enjoyed the chapter. I was delighted that it was the interesting, warmly written piece that one would hope—but could not be sure—a "narrative" writer would produce. From the first sentences, I saw it would be a personal account: immediately, I felt I understood something of Barbara's origins and her earliest influences. In particular, I appreciated the portrait she gave of her mother and the links she drew between her mother's life and values and the choices that Barbara went on to make for herself.

I also saw that it was not simply going to be a happy reconstruction of a life in which success was a foregone conclusion. But nor did it turn out to be simply a heroic tale of the determined scholar, battling against the forces: I especially loved the story of the oral exam for which Barbara found herself so ill-prepared, in which she was asked to "compare philosophical assumptions of two schools in psychology." I think I was particularly taken with this account because it is just the kind of question one would today readily associate with Barbara Czarniawska, and I enjoyed the insight into the time when it horrified her as much as it would have me.

Much as I took pleasure in reading Barbara's story, however, I gradually found myself asking "But where is the renewal?" Indeed, "Where are the fallow periods from which Barbara has emerged?"; then "Where are her struggles in the bleakest times?" And also, "Where are the parallels with my journey?" I reread Barbara's chapter several times, reflecting on these questions, and wondering how I would craft a response to Barbara's story of academic renewal.

In conversation with a friend, I realized the mistake I was making. Just as I have at times in my research, I saw that my error lay in setting out with a clear idea of what the answers would look like. To renew, I had assumed, means to have previously run dry. Reinvigoration and revitalization must come after impossible periods of low energy and decline. But perhaps this was not Barbara's story. I read the chapter again, this time seeking to explore rather than substantiate.

I have come to see Barbara's renewal as occurring, not through bursts of activity, but as an ongoing process made possible through the way she constructs her life—as a somewhat arbitrary sequence of events that inevitably contain both good and bad—and by her ability to develop and maintain so many rich, generative relationships.

Barbara's narrative has numerous subplots, each revealing a step along the professional path she has walked—or at times seemed to skip. I was struck by the often apparently arbitrary nature of these steps. For example, as an undergraduate, drawn to the experimentalist psychologists who brought with them the excitement of things American, Barbara made the decision to pursue her doctoral studies in social psychology. But because of the internal politics in her department, she ended up in industrial/organizational psychology, and from there shifting sideways to do a novel field study of decision making with a professor of economics. I am often curious to hear how an academic found his or her field, especially someone associated with a very distinctive approach, as is Barbara Czarniawska. I would never have imagined the consummate narrative researcher to have been once entranced by laboratory experiments!

Later she describes how—to pass time until she reached a "respectable" age to apply for promotion, and having her application for the University of California turned down—she ended up at MIT, where she had the enviable experience of working with Ed Schein. What she had wanted and intended, however, was to work with David Kolb, who had left by the time she arrived. Many people weave a strong thread of rationality and intentionality through their self-narratives. Barbara, in contrast, seems to revel in the capricious nature of her journey. As she observes, "Decisions just happen, in life and in organizations."

I reflected on what this way of constructing decision making, and decisions made, might mean for our understanding of renewal. Perhaps renewal, like other parts of life, does not have to be—perhaps cannot be—a very deliberate activity. Rather than making extensive arrangements for an upcoming sabbatical, or even planning a creativity-refueling vacation, we should be aware that renewal may occur as we set about doing something quite different. Renewal may be found in the most unlikely places.

Barbara's voice also caused me to challenge my earlier assumption that renewal must come after much struggle, as we finally succeed in pulling ourselves from a dark and difficult place. Barbara's tone is strikingly matter of fact: she recounts painful times without dwelling on them, and, in just a few pages, tells of her mother's miserable life and death, her own broken marriages, and the imposition of martial law in her homeland as simply necessary pieces of her story.

I wonder if this very way of speaking reveals something about Barbara's renewal, and about renewal more generally. Rather than construct her life as a chronology of highlights and hard times, Barbara describes a constellation of occurrences that simultaneously and inevitably must contain both pleasure and pain. She shows that renewal need not be about dragging ourselves out of the deep reaches of misery or despair, but rather about looking about the situation in which we find ourselves and spotting something interesting, or funny, or moving. For example, as she looks out from her "bouts of depression" when writing her doctoral dissertation, Barbara begins to learn the skills of advising that she now uses with her own students. In a similar fashion, as she tells of the demands of emigrating to Sweden, she simultaneously jokes and reveals what it taught her about herself and her relationships with women. Life is intolerable only if you construct it that way, and Barbara does not.

Especially significant is the part played by others in Barbara's journey and in her renewal. Most people have important relationships through which they have grown personally and professionally, but Barbara seems to have so many! Is this because she has traveled so much, or in spite of it? Both, perhaps. On the one hand, I am struck by the apparent ease with which she has moved about the world, seemingly unhindered by language or culture. On the other, she writes of the pain of immigration, observing that "moving from one country to another . . . means destroying the precious social web that one managed to spin in any given place"—something that resonated for me, a recent émigré to Canada. Yet Barbara's narrative is a portrait in connection: we meet the key people, colleagues who usually become close friends, who lead her to new intellectual adventures. These relationships seem very central to Barbara's processes of renewal. I see Barbara as enormously sustained by her ability to keep connecting to others who stimulate and support her. Toward the end of her narrative, Barbara suggests "A young scholar who may be reading this autobiographical sketch might at this point become impatient and ask: Hasn't she ever done anything herself?" For this young scholar that was not the question that came to mind. I have emigrated only once in my adult life and found it extremely painful, living Barbara's observation that while "traveling multiplies friendships; emigration decimates them." My question to Barbara, as I reflect on what I can take from her story to use in my own journey, is how she has managed to find and develop the wonderful communities she describes, and how she seems to have done so repeatedly in each place she has lived.

In my initial search for Barbara's "processes of renewal" I expected to come upon some terrible dark period, filled with emptiness and lacking in hope. From this desperate place, I anticipated a powerful experience through which Barbara had risen up, renewed and refreshed. I did not find any of this. I must have had my reasons for investing in this image of renewal; perhaps they are similar to Peter's for asking me to respond to Barbara's chapter. I am European, and a few years ago wrenched myself away from friends and family in England to come to live in North America. Doing so has been more of a struggle than I ever anticipated, dealing with my feelings of loss, at the same time as attempting to learn the rules of North American academia and to build a personal and professional community for myself five thousand miles away from what still seems like "home." When I think about it in the context of what I have just been writing, I realize that, in contrast to Barbara's arbitrary sequence of life events comprising simultaneous light and shadow, I have been constructing the last few years as quite a dark time, and hoping that if I just keep "doing the right things" and can have a bit of luck, I will "achieve" renewal, turn the corner, and see my new life laid out before me. But if I apply the lessons I have taken from Barbara's story to my own situation, I can see that as well as working hard at both my research and my relationships, I should perhaps spend some time thinking about how I am constructing my life. I know, of course, that it wasn't simply glorious then and difficult now, but rather joyous and demanding at different times in both places. It also seems unlikely that how I feel is a matter of whether I am currently making the appropriate moves: getting it "right" is not what explains the times I have felt the greatest growth. Renewal is, I am learning, what you make it, not just what you do.

Discipline and Practice

The scholars represented in this book, and the field as a whole, strayed from the path of science as described by Kuhn (1962). In leaving behind their disciplinary origins in psychology, sociology, or economics, they abandoned the comforting umbrella of a well-developed paradigm. They have traveled fresh paths, sometimes bushwhacked new trails.

We continue to look over our shoulders to the base social science disciplines for theory and methods, the tools to sustain us on our journey. Even so, while individual scholars were better equipped in micro or macro, psych. or soc. or econ., most believed in the possibility of a wholistic study of organization that embraced multiple perspectives in a single conversation. Looking back over forty years of organization studies, Lyman Porter (1996) identifies the development of a truly multidisciplinary field as our most significant accomplishment. But this multidisciplinarity is not trouble-free or easy to maintain. As March observes, "As the field has grown and elaborated new perspectives, it has continually been threatened with becoming not so much a new integrated semidiscipline as a set of independent, self-congratulatory cultures of comprehension" (1996, 280). March (1996) applauds two forces that limit the tendency toward fragmentation. One was present in 1965, when he edited the *Handbook of Organization*. The second reveals the development of an organizational studies pedigree that did not exist in 1965: "The balkanization of organization studies has, however, been limited by two traditions that developed early and have been maintained. The first is a tradition of intellectual openness, of relatively promiscuous borrowing across disciplines and across subfields. . . . The second tradition is one of intellectual path dependence, of maintaining continuity in ideas" (March 1996, 280). Also in 1996, the editors of the next *Handbook of Organizations* (*Handbook of Organizational Studies*) described the same growth of perspectives in number and variety. They write, "[We chose the book title *Organizational Studies*] to embrace the many and varied approaches to the study of organizations" (Clegg, Hardy, and Nord 1996, xxiii). "We rejected 'organization theory' because we do not believe there is a theory, in the singular, of organizations . . . we rejected 'organization science' because science is in the singular, it is surrounded by cultishness and talismanic recitation as to who has it, what it is, and what it isn't" (xxiii). "The Handbook consists of a series of coordinates of the terrain of organization studies which revolves around: *organizations* as empirical objects; *organizations* as theoretical discourse; and *organizing* as social process" (xxiv). They add that the intention of the book is to "stimulate and engage conversations at the intersection of multiple narratives, multiple sites, multiple practices" (xxiv).

The field of organization studies of the 1965 March *Handbook* did not have the range of intellectual and cultural diversity and abundance of the current era, which is not to say that there were no differences. It also did not have the same range of controversy as currently exists about the nature and value of the contributions within the field. The 1965 and 1996 *Handbooks* reflect very different visions for what constitutes meaningful conversations about the phenomena, the measurement, and the nature of proof when the focus is on organizations. March worries about fragmentation. Clegg, Hardy, and Nord (1996) worry about exclusion.

The business school departments of organization management have trained a new generation of scholars. But is there a new discipline of organizations? There are some signs of discipline, a professional association, and a system of peer-reviewed journals. But closer examination does not reveal a singular body of knowledge.

Perhaps we need more time to build a traditional discipline. However, two factors in the environment of the business school lead us to believe that there will never be a management/organization discipline. First, we agree with Zald (1996) when he argues that we must respond to the broader intellectual currents of the twentieth century. Postmodern thinking has eroded the solid foundation of the Enlightenment project, the belief that rationality could conquer all. We use the term broadly to encompass diverse theoretical movements including phenomenology, constructionism, existentialism, poststructuralism, and so on. Burrell (1996) and Reed (1996) describe the movement from functionalism to paradigms to the postmodern European social theories of Foucault and Derrida. Sometimes, these observations lead to alarm. We think there is nothing to fear. The "death of reason" will not destroy science, but it will change it, just as the scientific revolution did not eliminate religion.

The second environmental consideration that we face is the insistent feedback from the business community that our knowledge is simply irrelevant (Porter and McKibben 1988; Rynes, Bartunek, and Daft 2001; Starkey and Madan 2001). The academic study of organizations arguably owes its existence to the failure of the traditional disciplines to understand the significance of, or even be curious about, the phenomena of large, complex organizations. For example, the very rich knowledge of economics about the behavior of the firm as a profit maximizer in perfectly competitive markets is largely irrelevant to top management decision making in the multinational corporation. Many critics contend that business school research is headed in the same direction.

These realities have generated a variety of responses. Some senior members of the field respond to fragmentation by looking to the history of the natural sciences and economics. Pfeffer (1993) argues persuasively for the benefits of a singular paradigm to compete successfully for resources against the dominance of the economics tradition. But the intellectual and practical landscape has changed. There is no candidate for a unifying paradigm.

In the eighties and nineties many relied on the paradigm incommensurability position (Burrell and Morgan 1979). By arguing for independent knowledges with unique methods and criteria for evaluation, new modes of inquiry were able to establish a foothold. But paradigm incommensurability cannot be justified (Hassard and Pym 1990; Weaver and Gioia 1994). Now paradigm differences must be taken seriously, not ignored or granted "separate but equal" status (Reed 1996). Today, we are left with the uncertainties that characterized the end of the 1990s regarding definitions, meaning, method, the nature of theory, and the role of the theorist (Clegg and Hardy 1996).

Several commentators have argued for moving beyond these paradigm debates. Moldoveanu and Baum (2002) provide a provocative and interesting analysis. They argue that we often speak past each other, rather than to each other, because we answer the criticisms we imagine the other party to be making. For example, they argue that realists attack social constructionists as relativists (when they need not be) and constructionists attack realists as positivists (when they are not). Poole and Van de Ven (1989) frame the solution as dealing with the "paradoxes" presented by multiple theories. Martin and Frost advocate "appreciative critiques" that "seek to advance a field rather than a particular point of view" (1996, 616) by challenging assumptions and inspiring new ideas. Morgan (1983) and Clegg and Hardy (1996) call for developing research conversations. Clegg and Hardy write about perspectives rooted in different theoretical camps:

They are that, just perspectives, we see different things with them, different facets of that which is represented. They are voices in a conversation but they are not the conversation. Energy and vitality derive from the difference rather than the similarity, the contrasts and the contradictions rather than the agreement. We can use that energy to learn more about what we do, who we are, what we can achieve and where we have failed. (1996, 703)

Baum and Rowley (2002) propose a similar view on perspectives, but they emphasize the complementary, rather than the competitive, nature of the perspectives. Balogun, Huff, and Johnson (2003) suggest some methodological responses.

Another approach has emphasized rapprochement with the practice communities of management, drawing on the new production of knowledge thesis (Huff 2000; Gibbons et al. 1994). They contrast Mode 1 and Mode 2 knowledge production. Mode 1 is knowledge production in the normal, discipline-based mode. Mode 2 is knowledge production in application to a core problem or project. Team members draw from several Mode 1 disciplines to create a transdisciplinary knowledge that may not feed back into the contributing disciplines. "It includes a wider, more temporary and heterogeneous set of practitioners, collaborating in a problem defined in a specific and localized context" (Gibbons et al. 1994, 3). Exemplars of Mode 2 knowledge production include the human genome project and the development of the ramjet engine.

We have already noted that organization studies has always been multidisciplinary. It has never been Mode 1, so there may be a temptation to describe organization studies as Mode 2 where the phenomenon of organization is the core problem. However, in contrast to Mode 2, we continue to rely on the organizational structure of a Mode 1 discipline, that is, quality control and communication of knowledge via peer-reviewed journals. In Mode 2, knowledge is captured by those involved in its production, but it is difficult to communicate to a broader community because of its transdisciplinary and project-specific nature. Many commentators are calling for a movement toward Mode 2, for example, organizing research around practitioner-defined problems. However, one of the consequences of moving more fully to Mode 2 is the difficulty of translating our findings into the kind of knowledge we are used to writing up for the journals.

Whatever our response to these pressures, we think it is important to keep in mind that the field needs powerful theories (Gagliardi 1999). Gagliardi argues that "a theory empowers organizational actors when it spurs their imagination, points out new opportunities and ends, unveils new paths and new means to ends, increases their freedom of action and their will to act" (1999, 143). Empowering theories are persuasive.

Persuasive theories acknowledge their audience and the local context by engaging with the tangle of intellectual, emotional, and moral experience. He argues that we should accept the status of our theories as cultural artifacts that have the potential to mean more than the sum of their logical co-herence and empirical validity (Gagliardi 1999). We agree.

Like many commentators (Weick 1989B; McCall and Bobko 1990; Clegg and Hardy 1996), we are unsure of the contemporary efficacy of traditional approaches to better understanding organization. However, remember that organization studies have never been particularly traditional. As the stories in this volume reveal, it has been an innovative, developing, growing community of scholars. Now is a time for renewal. It is not quite a journey into the dark, but we know that there are new, exciting, and unimagined vistas ahead.

ANDREW H. VAN DE VEN 6

"Don't Do Longitudinal Research" Nonsense

IT IS IRONIC that while there is a growing need and call for longitudinal research to understand dynamic organizational processes, few management scholars engage in it. In fact, many colleagues tell me that they advise their doctoral students and junior faculty colleagues not to undertake longitudinal research. They argue that longitudinal research jeopardizes career advancement and promotion prospects for young scholars because it entails a significant investment of time and defers publication of study findings. Instead, they advise undertaking cross-sectional organizational studies in order to achieve demands for immediate publication and career ascendancy. I believe this advice is misdirected. In fact, it is sheer nonsense!

Let me take this opportunity to argue the case for doing longitudinal field research especially if you are just starting your career as a doctoral student or junior faculty member. It provides a fast track for the advancement of knowledge and prospects for career promotion. Let me caution you that my recommendation goes against the advice of most of my colleagues. I apologize for this long answer, but I feel I have much explaining to do to challenge the institutionalized wisdom of our academy.

Specifically, my claim is that scholars who undertake longitudinal research will be more prolific, make higher-quality contributions to knowledge, and will therefore advance faster and farther in their professional careers than scholars who conduct cross-sectional studies. I base this claim on three premises. When compared to cross-sectional studies, longitudinal research:

- Promotes writing a stream of articles on a research theme over time.
- Is more productive; it permits devoting relatively more time on the substantive research question and less time on administrative research tasks.
- Facilitates deeper learning and understanding of a research topic.

1. Longitudinal Research Promotes a Stream of Articles on a Theme

Longitudinal research in organizations entails repeated observations of selected organizational units over time on a question or topic. Repeated waves of data collection using interview and questionnaire surveys and organizational records are typically used to make these observations. The tasks involved in designing a longitudinal study, preparing funding proposals, and negotiating access are not much different from that of conducting a cross-sectional study in organizations. After the first wave of data collection the findings can be analyzed and reported as a conventional cross-sectional study. However, the benefits of longitudinal research increase exponentially after the first cross-sectional study. The second data collection wave provides opportunities to report findings on a before-and-after study by analyzing changes between the first two data collection waves. With the third data collection wave, one can examine and report findings on trends in the three-period data. Thus, after three rounds of data collection, the longitudinal researcher can write a series of papers that triangulate on the research question or topic with cross-sectional, before-and-after, and longitudinal trend analyses.

By this time most longitudinal researchers will have studied the research question in sufficient depth to develop a much richer appreciation of the research question or topic than she or he had after the first (cross-sectional) set of observations. At this stage the researcher is able to make a significant theoretical contribution by crafting an original theory or reconstructing an existing theory. Because this new theory represents a major departure from the past, it merits further empirical development and elaboration. Doing so may require substantial revisions in the design and conduct of the longitudinal research. It also represents the launching of a deeper and more fundamental cycle of learning in the ongoing longitudinal research program.

2. Longitudinal Research Is More Productive

After a single wave of data collection, most cross-sectional researchers conclude their studies by analyzing and reporting the findings, and then moving on to their next topic of investigation with another cross-sectional study. Each study entails significant "administrative" tasks of designing the research, preparing funding proposals, and negotiating access to organizations to conduct the study. Longitudinal research typically entails the administrative tasks of conducting periodic reviews and seeking approvals to continue the study. However, the administrative tasks of maintaining a five-year longitudinal study, for example, are relatively less time consuming than the administrative tasks of conducting five one-year cross-sectional studies. Hence, longitudinal studies permit researchers to devote relatively more time in productive study of the substantive research question or topic and less time on administrative tasks in comparison to cross-sectional studies.

Another indication of research productivity is the kind of knowledge that is gained from the study. My experience is that it takes more time to understand and ground a research question or topic in its natural field setting than a cross-sectional study either permits or is designed to uncover. Study of any question or topics requires a set of categories or concepts. These concepts provide selective focus for observing the topic being investigated; one cannot study everything. When a deductive approach is taken, the researcher assumes an understanding of the concepts by developing clear operational questions and indicators in survey instruments. When completed by organizational participants, the researcher analyzes the data to determine if his or her measures and hypotheses are valid. However, learning this does not tell the researcher how organizational participants might frame the research concepts or questions. The researcher only learns about his or her concepts and theories, not those of the organization being investigated. As a consequence, the researcher can only draw claims about his or her conceptual model, and not that of the organization being studied. More extended periods of field observations are typically needed to sensitize and ground constructs in their natural field settings.

3. Longitudinal Research Facilitates Deeper Learning and Understanding

Herbert Simon (1991) argued that it takes ten years of dedicated work and attention to become world class in a domain. While we might quibble if it takes ten, seven, or five years, the point is that cross-sectional organizational studies typically take less than a year to conduct and represent a single snapshot on a subject being investigated. As a result, cross-sectional studies do not provide researchers sufficient time and trials to become world class in their research topic. Longitudinal research promotes deeper learning because it provides repeated trials for approximating and understanding a research question or topic.

Seldom does a one-time study produce a world-class product. I think that far too many management scholars dilute their competencies by conducting an eclectic and unrelated series of cross-sectional studies in their careers. Becoming world class involves a path-dependent process of pursuing a coherent stream of research questions over an extended period of time.

A basic, but often overlooked, fact of organizational research is that re-

searchers are exposed to only the information that organizational participants are willing to share. Interviews in cross-sectional studies or initial interviews in longitudinal studies with organizational participants tend to be
formal and shallow. Greater candor and penetration into the subject matter
only occurs several years into a study when organizational participants have
come to know and trust the researcher. Perhaps the "one-minute manager"
is an unfortunate social construction of the one-minute researcher.

One indication of comfort with a researcher is how respondents treat
you. A few months ago I conducted the fourth yearly interview with one
manager. When greeting him he stated, "Normally I wear a coat and tie
when outside visitors come. This morning I noticed that you were coming.
So I decided not to wear a coat and tie." Candid information comes not
only with familiarity and trust but also with more knowledgeable and pen-
etrating probes in responses to questions. A common self-assessment of field
researchers is "If I only knew then what the study findings would be, I
would have asked more probing questions." Repeated interviews and meetings with organizational participants in longitudinal research provide important opportunities to penetrate more deeply into the subject matter being
investigated.

Qualifications

I have argued that scholars who undertake longitudinal research will be
more prolific, more productive, and come to understand their subject more
deeply than scholars who undertake cross-sectional research. As a result, longitudinal researchers will make higher-quality contributions to knowledge
and will advance farther and faster in their careers than scholars who conduct cross-sectional studies.

I confess that my argument may be one-sided because I have been engaged in longitudinal field research for most of my career. Longitudinal
fieldwork is a normal part of my everyday work. In addition to professorial
teaching, writing, service, and administration, a normal working week includes about a day of fieldwork in conducting site visits, interviews, observing meetings and events, and talking to people related to the organizational
changes that are unfolding in real time. Trained initially in traditional approaches to studying variance theories, as Larry Mohr (1982) calls it, I have
tended to launch my field studies with a specific research question and some
general concepts and propositions that were derived from the literature. But
as field observations began I found it necessary in each case to alter some
initial conceptions so they might better capture the process dynamics being
observed. While frustrating at times, some of my greatest insights have come

from field research, and they strongly influenced a growing appreciation of dynamic organizational change processes. These experiences lead me to suggest that letting go of initial conceptions and remaining open to new ideas and directions from field observations are important dispositions of longitudinal field researchers. I recommend undertaking longitudinal field research, for it provides a rich laboratory for personal learning and development.

Transitions Revisited

DESPITE MY SUPPORT for this book's agenda, I found it hard to begin my chapter. The transitions I could think of from my own career fell under rather mundane headings. While their pleasure and pain were real to me, my stories seemed too generic, too similar to others. Even worse, I realized I had faced each transition more than once, using similar strategies to move on, which is hardly the stuff of high drama.

I have had this feeling before, and my humorous conclusion is that we all are the creation of a grade-school class on a far more advanced planet. They are just beginning to write fiction. It is not surprising that their scripts are repetitive and obvious—they are beginners who should get better with practice on us, the creatures of their imagination. This image encourages me to mentally give a grade of "needs improvement" to far-away authors when I find myself participating in particularly inept transitions.

But these fanciful thoughts also bring me back to the more serious belief that each of us contributes to context and has choices about what we do, even if we cannot control outcomes as we might wish. What follows, therefore, is an examination of three particularly important turning points in my career: gaining entry into a field I wanted to study; maintaining energy for the work to be done; and connecting it to the work of others. Because I have been involved in each transition more than once, I have presumed to give some advice to others who find themselves in similar situations.

Transition into the Field

Ideally, firm connection with a field of study is part of doctoral education, but I was not so lucky. Even after I began my first academic job at UCLA I was not sure what areas of inquiry interested me most, and I was very unclear about the career implications of the choices I could perceive only dimly. Strategy was still known as "business policy" when I began work, and few were trained in the newly required course of that name. My multidisciplinary background offered either not enough or too many anchors to begin work in this ambiguous environment. I could not tell.

Although I wanted to do well, I also was aggravated by academic elitism. I had studied philosophy and sociology before getting a PhD in business and accepted philosophy of science arguments that a field of inquiry necessarily establishes rules of the game and standards of performance. The academic groups I could identify, however, seemed more like "old boys' clubs" than the lofty intellectual groups described in books. There were interesting conversations going on, but a great deal of comfortable superiority as well.

There had not been a woman on the tenure-track faculty in the business school for many years, and only one female adjunct was in evidence. Not surprisingly, my new colleagues and their systems were not completely ready for me, or Carol Kovach who also joined that year. For example, Carol and I were confused quite often. I was surprised, amused, but also angered by being perceived as interchangeable with a woman born in England, who had a different hair color, height, and style, and also different academic interests.

Being young and female also seemed part of my own confusion. I would not have gotten where I was if I had been inclined to follow rules. The very things that had led to my success up to this point now seemed to be roadblocks. For example, I had "escaped" my father and hometown by honing a reflexive "no" to almost everything he asked me to do, followed by a scramble to find as creative an alternative as I could devise. The same attitude helped me move quickly through college and graduate school. In my first job, however, the strong advice I received was to conform. I was urged to abandon qualitative work in favor of more acceptable, and faster payoff, quantitative methods. It was suggested that I stop looking at not-for-profit organizations and turn to business. There was a definite feeling that I should move from a sociological perspective to an economic one. It was not clear to me whether I wanted to be a part of a profession that asked me to do these things. It was not clear how much I could make the transitions suggested.

Strategy, as it came to be defined in many schools by the end of the 1980s, is certainly more clearly defined today, but identifying the field that one is joining, no matter how clear the contours to incumbents, is always difficult. Figure and ground have to be identified, and accepted, by every new entrant. Research and teaching are unlikely to go well until firm transition into a specific field of study has been accomplished.

I began to make that transition largely because I was genuinely excited about many things I read and heard as a new assistant professor. While I was learning new things, I also began to think I had something to contribute from my somewhat atypical experience and training, even though I was not sure which part of the elephant to grab hold of.

These are issues of identity and identification. At the beginning of my career I did not have those categories and was deeply confused by being simultaneously worried about whether I could or wanted to succeed, excited by the subject matter I was discovering, and unclear about what I was going to study. Doubts about whether one can belong interact with doubts about whether one has the requisite skills and insights to belong and doubts about whether one wants to belong. We all know enough social science to recognize that uncertainty about the resolution of the first question can lead to negative answers to the second and third questions.

Gradually, however, I overcame some of my doubts in all three areas by realizing that I wanted to say "yes" more often than "no." In response to generally well-meaning advocates of more established epistemologies and methods, I argued the need to develop my own point of view and pointed out that "proving myself" with other mind-sets would make it more difficult to develop my own contributions. I did begin to think about private organizations but still used the qualitative, longitudinal methods I had learned. Over time I realized that I was interested in social, political, and cognitive conditions that give individuals the confidence to act in new ways. I have explored different aspects of this broad agenda ever since.

It was not easy. I would offer four pieces of advice to those similarly troubled by the transitions required to enter a field of study

I. STAY CLOSE TO THE WORK, BUT ALSO STAND BACK

The world is an interesting place. I rediscovered the reasons I went to graduate school by paying attention to what was happening around me. Read the newspapers. Talk to colleagues. But most important: start talking to and working with people in organizations.

Howard Becker, a well-known sociologist at Northwestern, also taught me that a back door to insight might be found by analyzing another subject. If you are interested in strategy implementation but your work is not going well, he said, take time out to think about interactions among children on a playground or in some other very different social system. Do not worry about finding parallels to your subject. The detour should be refreshing, and exercise analytic abilities that may have lain dormant. Often, however, the remote subject will suggest some new avenues of analysis in your own work and reconnect you to your primary interests. The further implication, for me, has been to have more than one project underway. If progress is slow on one, the other may be more energizing.

2. CHOOSE A CONVERSATION

Two insights, which took several years to discover, were critical to my finding an academic home. First, many people around me were assuming their perspective was the only viable one. It was necessary to realize that in fact there is no one arbitrator of standards, no one source defining field boundaries. Instead there are many rich, semiconnected arenas of academic inquiry. Some are parallel; many are orthogonal.

Once I began to map some of this out, I realized that I could make choices. More to the point, I had to make choices. The first commitment to the strategy field had to be followed by finding a more specific subarea, in my case, strategic change. As that more specific area of inquiry came into focus, the numbers involved become more manageable. It was easier to identify people who were doing the kind of work I wanted to do, from perspectives that I found compatible. Contemporary authors became real people as I started to attend conferences, especially small ones. Some of these people continued to strike me as elitist, but many others were welcoming.

Second, I began to get work published only as I realized that the conversations I was hearing at UCLA, the ones I heard at conferences, and the ones that echoed in my head, could be connected to the work I was reading. I began to think of academic work itself as a large number of conversations, of varying interest to me. This idea has become a central organizing metaphor for my academic work. It does not matter if the author of a particular piece of research has died, or moved on to other areas of inquiry. As a specific article or book is cited, it becomes alive; the written work is in conversation with other evidence, other points of view. The basic research and teaching tasks of the academic are to engage and contribute to this live conversation.

3. IDENTIFY FRIENDS AND MENTORS

I would not have lasted long enough to become involved in academic conversation if various people at UCLA had not befriended me. My list of debts is too long to recount in detail here, but they were critical to my survival. For example, Jim Jackson, a member of the faculty who unfortunately retired a few years after I arrived, was interested in teaching a core course with me. We not only traded ideas, but he invited us to the mountains where his wife Virginia made osso bucco and other unfamiliar, delicious dishes. Joan Lasko, the one long-term female adjunct on the faculty, was a valued friend and confidant. Dick Rumelt joined the faculty and was assigned an office next to mine. In talking and socializing with him I began to see the contours of the strategy field more clearly. Bob Tannenbaum, Dick Goodman, Dick Mason, and many others helped me in various ways to put what I was thinking about into context.

External contacts were also critical. Charles Summer made enthusiastic comments at my first professional presentation at the Western Academy of Management meetings. Praise from this well-known person was critical, especially since the paper was about organizational politics, and I knew just enough to know that politics was not a mainstream subject in business policy/strategy. Lou Pondy was similarly positive about a paper I gave at the Academy of Management meetings the next year, and I began to realize there were conversations of interest in organization theory.

I mention specific names and events in gratitude, and to remind myself and others how important personal connections are to people entering our profession. A great deal has been said about mentors. The mentorship that was helpful to me was part of increasingly rich, informal, ongoing connections. Given my antiauthoritarian tendencies, I doubt I would have gotten much benefit from formal mentorship. However helpful assigned programs are, the larger issue is intellectual exchange. A positive nod from the audience, a note in response to a publication, a request for a syllabus—these are the things that facilitate the transition of new members into our fields of inquiry.

4. FIND HEROES BUT MAINTAIN AN INNER COMPASS

A few people observed from a greater distance have also been very helpful to me—especially Jim March and Karl Weick. I can't remember being enthralled by heroes in childhood (perhaps that is one advantage of being a girl?), but both of these men write in a complex, multilayered way about subjects that interest me. They treat these subjects in original ways. Their themes reappear in later work with instructive new insights. It was very useful to find these heroes as an assistant professor; I still find their work inspiring.

However, my advice to myself and to others is to look inward more than outward. Precisely because they are so unique, direct emulation of well-known people in an academic conversation is unlikely to lead to success. My senior seminar as a philosophy student focused on a book by Ludwig Wittgenstein, the *Tractaus Logico-Philosophicus*. Toward the end of the book, he writes that he intends his propositions to be a ladder that the reader will move beyond. I have taken this advice to heart; it makes sense to move beyond mentors and heroes, circling back for additional input, but not staying too long.

5. PAY ATTENTION TO PERSONAL LIFE

I do not want to make these early years seem too easy. A few years after I arrived, senior faculty at UCLA began to discuss a "revolving door" policy for assistant professors in response to the rising proportion of tenured faculty.

Noting the behavior of a few top schools, they mulled over the idea that tenure should be rarely conferred, allowing them to continuously hire new and interesting young faculty. It was extraordinarily distancing; I fell back on earlier interests in art and literature to put together a collage of photos and poems that began with a duck swimming alone in a vast expanse of water. Rhetoric about "there are many wonderful jobs out there" was disingenuous to those of us without tenure.

Luckily, I lived with Jim, someone who was following the same path, working by the same calendar, with whom I had a life beyond work. I do not think I would have stayed in my first academic job without this pole of gravity. Our children became even more helpful balancers. I can renegotiate promises I make to Jim, because he faces the same kind of pressures I do. In fact, I do it too often. Betsy and David are not as patient. They help me pay attention to NOW. My advice to others is to maintain some other engaging life as a counterpoint to academic fixations and frustrations.

I am speaking primarily in the past tense—perhaps it should be present tense, for I still occasionally feel the tension of negotiating belonging. Moving to a new job obviously requires negotiating entry again. Less obvious, perhaps, are the requirements of beginning work in a new area of inquiry. That requires finding and making connections with a new group of people, identifying major players, discovering how the conversation is turning. Just reading journals is not sufficient; they catalog the history of past enthusiasms more than point the way toward current and future ones. Participating in meetings, reviewing papers, establishing networks, and other entry activities are critical.

A more interesting echo comes from questions about the way out—questions about when and why to leave a conversation. Many things encourage remaining within an academic home. Students seek advice and possible coauthorship. Colleagues suggest symposium, conferences, and other joint projects. Course contributions are expected and facilitate further exploration. These and other things reinforce a field choice and make it more interesting, but they also contribute to filtering schemas that receive less and less reexamination. The framework creatively invented to answer the needs of a first project begins to reappear in others. If I start to anticipate myself, I get bored, and so do others.

Thus I have discovered perplexing reversals to the questions about entrée posed by my first attempts to forge an academic identity. Once I do belong, do have some skills and insights, should I choose not to contribute? This question came to the forefront when we began thinking about leaving

UCLA. We wanted to go for two primary reasons. First, our daughter was two years old, and Los Angeles was very different from our hometown. Second, Jim had gotten tenure, but it seemed much less likely for me. Luckily, we both were offered jobs at the University of Illinois, a good fit for us both. The move meant that I could reexamine my commitments, and it also facilitated beginning a significant new research project based on theoretic foundations I had not explored before.

I skim over six months or more of tension and uncertainty here. All the questions of where to be, how to be, did we want to be, were raised again. Now they were stay-or-leave decisions, for two. I was lucky that Jim was willing to leave his recent tenure. I was lucky that we received offers from a well-regarded institution and that we both quickly and uneventfully received tenure there. It helped that we were both active in our fields, that we had networks and established research agendas. It seemed easier that our subjects fell within different colleges. I wish I had better advice to give others trying to navigate from two careers, but I do not. It is a transition facing many academics that needs more attention.

Discovering Sources of Continuing Energy

An unanticipated benefit of my move to Illinois was a surge of energy that turned out to be a noteworthy transition in the most positive sense. I had been chosen for research and teaching I could now demonstrate. No one at Illinois had witnessed my early faltering steps; that meant I could put them more firmly behind me. I loved having colleagues with interests and enthusiasms that were new and engaging.

About the time of my arrival, the department decided to establish a separate strategy area. I had input into the formation of a group that included Howard Thomas, Charles Schwenk, Irene Duhaime, Marjorie Lyles, Ming Tang, and Joe Mahoney. We had a loose decision-making focus in common, but diverse interests and backgrounds. Developing a doctoral program took a good deal of our time, but the contributions of doctoral students amplified the group. We were convinced that we were one of the (if not the) best strategy groups in the world. There is no better platform for getting work done.

A second source of energy was a major research project, with Lou Pondy as coinvestigator. It was an intensive field study funded by the National Institute for Education, which followed the strategic decisions of three well-regarded school superintendents. (Note that with a change of place, and more seniority, I was able to think more freely about the public sector again.) The project generated a number of articles, which we authored individually, jointly, and with others at Illinois. I am still interested in the theoretic and methodological puzzles we were working on and think some of the work from this project is among the best I have done.

But, Lou and I did not accomplish as much as we anticipated. The weight of the project was itself a factor. We underestimated the time demands of our design, which not only took us to each site every two weeks but also required extensive data gathering from secondary sources. We overestimated computer support, as well as our own ability to track detail. We were excellent colleagues in the field, good at playing off each other's insights conducting interviews, and we were inventive when analyzing the data afterward. We were much less spectacular as coauthors. Gradually we became de-energized.

The original idea for the project was the outgrowth of a much smaller project I had completed at UCLA. I am sure that Lou's reputation was an important part of gaining the larger second grant, and he significantly expanded my horizons as we developed the second proposal. I was unhappy, however, when he expected that I would do most of the administration and writing that a large grant requires. I was also surprised and aggravated when outsiders sometimes assumed that the project was Lou's idea, the writing driven by his insights, the methodological decisions under his control.

To be fair, Lou was increasingly distracted by divorce, a new marriage, adopting three young "at-risk" boys, and becoming head of our department. Jim and I also had another child. The research came to a formal conclusion, and I turned my attention to other work. The book we planned never materialized. Over time, I become more aware of helpful things Lou did that I had not even realized were useful or necessary. Lou and I continued to enjoy occasional intense academic conversations. He was a helpful advisor and certainly would have done more for me, if I had let him. We might have resuscitated ideas we had not completely explored from our joint project, but Lou was diagnosed with a late-stage cancer. It was a significant loss to the field, and to me, when he died.

By that time a new project was in full swing. The cognitive revolution was having an impact on many areas of management inquiry, including strategy and organization theory. I had worked with several cognitive mapping methodologies in the study shared with Lou, and doctoral students in the strategy group had developed others. Full of missionary zeal and community spirit, I wanted the cognitive perspective to be more widely appreciated. I also wanted our work to be recognized, and journals were not yet welcoming. Editing a book was an obvious solution.

Putting a book together is not easy, especially in a new area. It took much longer than I expected and was much harder than I thought it would be, but it was published at an important time and still continues to be cited. The volume, and the conversations it led me to, vastly expanded my horizons. But by the time I completed it I was exhausted and not sure what I wanted to do next.

I love the energy of academic thinking and am surprised when I do not feel enthusiasm for work that I felt not long before. The triggers do not have to be large. I have come to accept that there is a natural ebb and flow in my work. Sometimes I wake up feeling that I can see for miles; at other times it is as if I am coming down with the flu, but the malaise is in my work. As I look back, I wish I had understood more about the necessity of energy and paid more attention to maintaining it, from the beginning of my career.

I mentioned doubt in the context of the search for identity as I began my career. Doubt also interferes with the ongoing course of the most established scholar. Lou Pondy amazed me one day when he said his reluctance to write a first draft was psychological. I went to Illinois primarily because Lou was there. I admired him as someone who was instrumental in broadening organization theory and methods. But he was not as sure of himself as I had assumed. He moved between enormous confidence and debilitating disbelief in his abilities and contributions. The tension had some benefits, but on balance it slowed him down.

He was working in the wake of past success. Trained as a physicist, he understood regression to the mean and worried that his next paper would not be as good as those that had been so well received in the past. This particular fear of failure has not been one of my stumbling blocks, but I have found it hard to move away from the mind-set of a completed project. Even a positive event—getting tenure, being promoted to full, finishing a job like the Academy of Management leadership sequence—requires transition.

It is not easy to think of something new, and interesting, to say. Many smart people are and have been at work. Even when I've found the energizing germ for what may be an original contribution in this daunting environment, I sometimes stumble when I see too many possible connections to other work. Focus is difficult.

But focus is required, and pressures to produce can be problematic. Too much pressure reduces the pleasure that feeds long careers; it also cuts the discovery process short. The current environment pushes us toward taking smaller, safer bites of the projects we imagine. I know that many academics, at all levels, are de-energized by this context.

I do not have brilliant suggestions for maintaining critical enthusiasm, but I can identify several things that have been helpful to me.

1. IDENTIFY QUESTIONS THAT DO NOT YET HAVE ANSWERS

The easiest research project to initiate is the one with results that seem secure. But this kind of project can be hard to complete and is unlikely to lead to other compelling work. When researchers try to "prove" what they already believe to be true, it is hard to establish a credible position as a researcher; observers are more likely to wonder about possible bias in many decisions, from sample selection through analysis of data. If the project does not develop as anticipated, the researcher with an early commitment also is less likely to recover, because they are so invested in the project design.

More important, following an expected path tends to be boring. Low enthusiasm means less energy for the research task. Editors, reviewers, and other readers are more likely to respond in kind. As an editor, I have rejected several manuscripts that had a "scripted" feel. As a researcher, I choose to wait to begin a research project until it focuses on a question that I genuinely do not know how to answer.

2. MAINTAIN A PORTFOLIO OF PROJECTS

Most advisors in today's world council that business scholars should work on journal articles. Period. But I have benefited from writing things (like this chapter) that increase my reflexive understanding even though they do not "count" for much in salary calculations or business school rankings. As another example, few would advise the investment I made in the cognitive mapping book I edited, yet the book showcased my work and the work of other people, including recent Illinois graduates I wanted to facilitate. It helped establish a new area of inquiry, now well represented in the academy. The methodologies it compared are still influential. Thus, the work was and continues to be energizing.

My advice to others and myself is to maintain a portfolio of projects. Try to be strategic and not allocate too much time to projects that have less instrumental payoff, but lead a well-rounded academic life. Today's pressures are risky in themselves—they lead to one-dimensional careers that are hard to maintain. Think about work that will be sustaining, as well as work that will be immediately rewarding.

3. CONTINUE TO BE AN APPRENTICE

Haskel Benishay, who taught statistics at Northwestern, gave me the single most important piece of career advice I every received. I was agonizing over several possible offers for my first job. "Go where you will learn the most," he told me. "Don't think about geography. Don't be blinded by the prestige of the institution. Don't worry about the proportion of women on the faculty. Just think of yourself as an apprentice." It is very good advice. I regularly pass it on to students and continue to rely on it myself. I took my most recent job in the United Kingdom precisely because it met Benishay's test. Following opportunity can be overwhelming, however, which leads me to the last transition I want to briefly consider.

Leveraging Impact in the Face of Competing Demands

In the early days of my career, it was as if I faced a set of tunnels, each with unknown payoffs in its depths. It was difficult to make a decision about which dark path to follow. Over time choosing a tunnel—a metaphor for everything from committing to an overall area of inquiry to beginning work on a specific article before one can know how well it will be received—does get easier. Opportunities increase as contacts, reputation, and information increase, and the possible payoffs of different choices become clearer. That is the good news. Mentors and fellow travelers tend to be less helpful as the landscape becomes more complex, but we do not need them as we once did, which is also good news. However, the stakes, and expectations, go up, though this is rarely overtly discussed. This is bad news, if the opportunities for further transition are not recognized.

I was slow to realize the increased opportunities and responsibilities that accompany tenure. Being female and still relatively young may have been part of the problem. More influential, in retrospect, are the facts that I was raised in a large family in the western United States and was part of a growing but still young field of inquiry. This background emphasized hard work, but strongly de-emphasized self-promotion. My values still lean away from aggrandizement, yet it has been instructive to recently be responsible for promoting the quality, quantity, and impact of management research in the United Kingdom. I now worry that as part of a young field management researchers have to collectively be more assertive. We are relatively new to academic institutions, and relatively unknown to the world of policy. We can, and should, do more with what we know.

Academic fields need leadership. Providing leadership requires an important transition from finding and energetically maintaining direction, to helping set direction. I believe that it is important for more senior members of any academic community to begin to ask bigger questions. Established faculty should not only continue to seek answers to their own research questions, but also begin to help others identify their own point of view. These are not incompatible objectives. Calling a specialty conference, editing a special issue, and other projects are examples of fieldwide contributions that can advance an individual's specific research agenda but link it to the work of others to broaden and intensify academic conversation.

However, at later career stages there is less time to make more significant contributions as the number of demands goes up. Many promising contributions to scholarship are not made, or made once but not continued, because of opportunities not recognized, or not seized. Even in research-oriented institutions, tenured faculty often shift their attention toward teaching, administration, consulting, or other tasks. Many scholars lose a research focus.

In addition to the availability of professional alternatives, personal lives offer other paths to follow. Lovers, families, friends, hobbies, and other strong commitments can (and, in my opinion, should) be as compelling as the multiple roles academic life offers. Their siren calls are frequently reinforced by internal and external voices that suggest, "You are the only person who can meet this need!" In short, life becomes increasingly complicated, despite the naivete of the young scriptwriters I imagine writing our lives.

Why are these alternatives to research so distracting? Each job offers its own rewards, of course. Less obvious is the fact that the positive and negative feedback of most other forms of employment is so immediate that the loop back to research is often not completed. Other jobs also tend to provide more emotional content than intellectual work offers. In addition, they can be easier to control; satisfaction from developing a new syllabus, arranging teaching schedules, leading girl scouts, skiing, wine tasting, and other pursuits tend to be more reliable that chasing noteworthy empirical results.

Other paths may provide a needed break that revitalizes a scholarly agenda. My interest in organization politics, for example, has deepened and strengthened from administrative and service assignments. The day I decided I had to leave my administrative assignment at the University of Colorado, however, was the day I went home with a feeling of accomplishment—then realized in describing my triumph to Jim that I had succeeded in getting one of my colleagues NOT to write an inflammatory memo. It just was not enough.

I now realize I never made contact with administrative conversations that might have made the work more interesting. I have just made an administrative choice in the United Kingdom where impact, on research, seemed more likely. It is this focus on impact that I want to recommend. For many of us, it is another point of transition.

Academic work does not necessarily support cumulative effort. Early in my career I was on a committee to fill a chaired position at UCLA. One candidate, who we initially thought might fit very well, did not get the job. Each reference we called had approximately the same response. "I know who he is," they would say. "He hasn't made that much of a contribution to my area, but I am sure he has done a lot more in others." It was a sobering experience.

The message from this search experience is about impact. Most academics I know worry about the choices they make when confronted by distracting alternatives. Too few of us, in my opinion, step back to think about overall direction even when committed to academic endeavour. We think too much about specific requests and not enough about the cumulative result of what we do. The tunneled choices we perceive in increasing number are intrinsically misleading.

I have several last observations about how I am trying to make better choices; "make" in the sense of create, as well as more passively choose.

I. THINK BIG, BUT FOCUS

The disadvantage of being a reasonably imaginative person is that I can think of, and even start, far more things than I can actually accomplish. The obvious antidote is to begin only what has a reasonable chance of seeing conclusion. That is not good enough. Over time I have prepared and delivered many presentations, written and finished many articles, chapters, and even books. Too many. They have contributed to more conversations than I could maintain over time. Thus the considerable effort involved had too little impact. I got into a conversation for a time, but did not stick around to understand its depths, or make deeper contributions myself. In some cases the conversation did not seem important enough to maintain; in other cases I was distracted by something new. My advice to myself and others is to make longer-term commitments and then think seriously about the work that really needs to be done within that area.

It is a collective as well as an individual task. Management research is at a crossroads. We have never had a central place in the conversations of policy and practice, but globalization and increasing access to the tools of knowledge production have made us even more peripheral. What management academics think about has little chance of an audience outside academia. I believe we have to push ourselves, and those around us, to identify the really important questions, then find the stamina and insight to answer them. Though I have been writing about recurring transitions, I hope that we are able to significantly increase our impact, and not revert back to the comfortable, but less impactful life of the past.

2. PLAN

Planning has not fared well in the strategy literature. In practice, it tends to be too formulaic, which makes it easy for participants to separate planning exercises from day-to-day activities. When conditions change rapidly, the most positive case for planning, in many people's minds, is that the process of considering new responses can be worthwhile, even if the plans that are made quickly become obsolete. I am a fan of the process school but have also found that old-fashioned goal setting and other tools of planning help me, if I resist, first, getting into too much detail, and second, putting my plans on the shelf.

It has been particularly useful for me to decide what I do not want to do, so that I have a ready refusal at hand. The "cis" root of "decision" means "to cut." It is also found in the words "incisor" and "scissor." Often my hardest task, in accomplishing the things I want to do, is deciding what I will not do.

But I have also become much more active in shaping opportunities. I ask if an attractive possibility could be made better. More important, if I see someone doing something that looks attractive, I am less likely now to try and copy it, and more likely to brainstorm other paths to even more attractive outcomes.

3. HELP MAINTAIN COMMUNITY, BUT KEEP BOOKS

The ability to say no is a necessary skill that must be continually sharpened, but as I observed at the beginning of this essay, life requires "yes" more than "no." Thus I want to contribute to the communities that are important to me, but my "rule" has been: one contribution at a time. Within my university, for example, I try to limit committee service to one committee at the department, college, and university levels. It may seem too selfish, but I am involved in many other communities, including editorial boards and professional associations.

Requestors inevitably only see the part of the pie that concerns them. I have come to see that I must keep the books on the overall service load. If everyone involved in each of the communities that are important to me were to make one contribution, the most important work would get done. Of course it is not as easy as that, and I do sometimes get much more involved, but I try not to drift or be pressured into that position.

4. SACRIFICE QUANTITY AND TIMING BEFORE QUALITY

When Jim and I thought about having children, the time costs were very clear. We continue to be delighted that we made this balancing choice; we know that our family led not only to our most rewarding jobs but also to the jobs that are least transferable to others. Both of us had to accept, however, that once we had children we could not move as fast as our fast-track colleagues. We focused instead on trying to maintain the quality of our professional work, even if it was delivered more slowly.

Tenure pressures in many universities make the decisions we made as assistant professors more difficult today. I stand against current standards I believe are generally too oppressive and hope that more reasonable demands will emerge. The current climate exhausts people and drains needed energy from the field among survivors as well as those who leave. It also discourages well-rounded life choices that create better researchers. The study of human organizations requires being human. Personal choices are not a distraction; I believe they are essential to the work we must do.

5. ENDURE

Carol Gilligan (1982) observes that young boys argue endlessly about the rules of the games they play, complaining loudly if they do not get their way, but when young girls do not get their way in play, they tend to more quietly move to another game. A similar pattern can be found in some of the stories I have recounted here. When I was unsure as an assistant professor, I thought about leaving academics. When I was unhappy about the balance of power with Lou, I moved to other projects. If this were a book, I could add other details.

Walking away stands in the way of making an impact, because academics is a social activity. Cohen and March (1986) make the observation that those who influence the path of decision making in academic institutions are those who persist. The same is true of scholarly contribution.

Conclusion

The three questions I have taken as transition points are basic questions of academic life:

- In which academic fields will I work?
- How will I maintain the energy to explore challenging questions?
- How can my work, linked to the work of others, make a difference?

These are questions with many answers. Few individuals I know are totally satisfied with the ones they find or develop. My purpose has been to suggest why these questions have been challenging for me to address, and to outline strategies I use at crossroads that often feel familiar. Luck has an important role to play. I was lucky that Charlie Summer happened to attend my first professional presentation. I was lucky to be at Illinois with a group of people who were particularly interesting and productive. I am lucky to now be at London Business School. I am especially lucky to have a sustaining life at home that continues to draw my attention. I have also been frustrated, of course, when luck did not go my way. I did not understand, revise, and re-submit conventions as a young scholar and did not pursue what might have been important early publications. I wasted time on projects I could not complete due to circumstances largely beyond my control. I am sorry not to have gotten several jobs I wanted, because they might have moved me in interesting new directions.

Over time, however, I have learned not to focus on anticipating or analyzing such turns in fortune in favor of making something of current circumstances. This is "make lemonade out of lemons" advice—easy to say, often hard to do. Over time I have learned more about how to extend and build on negative, neutral, or even obviously positive events. Most of all I have come to see that good career strategy is about thinking and acting—catching a wave and then shifting one's weight as the surf moves on.

With surfing as the model, each of us has to keep track of where we want to go, even though we are not in control of all significant factors. For example, I have deliberately maintained some interests that are not "smart" because they are interesting and informative. I try to balance them against more mainstream endeavors. I try to help others, because that is the kind of world I want to live in. I try to follow intuition but beware of self-indulgence and avoid doing the easy thing again and again. At a time when publications are too often counted rather than read, I push myself to do quality work, all of the time, even if the project seems to be on the periphery of other peoples' radar screens. Above all—I turn myself toward energy and try to pass energy on. I choose academic life because I thought it would be interesting. It continues to interest me. It is a pleasure to work with people who also love their work. Over time I have found multiple homes that I thought might elude me when I first was trying to enter the field. I wish you as reader the same good fortune.

KATHLEEN M. SUTCLIFFE

Transitions Revisited

An Unexpected Evocation

---

surprise   (i) to strike with a sudden feeling of unexpected wonder   (ii) to come
upon or discover suddenly and unexpectedly   (iii) to attack without warning . . .
Webster's Ninth New Collegiate Dictionary, 1987

Transitions Revisited utterly surprised me. I'm still puzzling over my first reaction. Perhaps I expected the ordinary, was primed for the ordinary by the
author herself who in the first paragraph describes her transitions as "rather
mundane." I guess I expected another self-help guidebook filled with admonitions and prescriptions for navigating various passages through one's
academic life. I expected the rational, reasonable, and logical. And that is exactly what I *saw* the first time through the essay. But after I went back to
reread and reflect and took a second and third look I began to see something
entirely different. I was surprised when I realized that my first impressions
were unfounded. When our expectations are not confirmed (and we realize
it) we naturally feel a little *attacked without warning*. But the crux of my *unexpected wonder* comes mostly from the profound wisdom that Anne Sigismund Huff shares with us in her essay. Perhaps you, Anne Huff herself, and
other readers might be surprised by how I have interpreted her insightful
work. If so, so be it. I'm grateful to have the chance to reveal the insights that
were revealed to me.

Perversely Huff's counsel is antithetical to what I imagine the editors of
this volume hope to accomplish (that is, to provide a developmental
roadmap for graduate students and new scholars). Her message is clear and
concrete: each of us alone has to figure out our own path and on our own
terms. "The realities of professional academic life are that no other individual or group is responsible or can be that helpful. Although general guidelines are available, accepted wisdom in one place is often not followed in

others. Especially when the subject is *how* to achieve, rather than *what* to achieve, we are on our own." As Huff counsels, each one of us needs to maintain our own inner compass.

Huff's words resonate with my own experience and with the many frustrations I have encountered in creating my scholarly life. I am a skeptic when it comes to prescriptions—either giving them or receiving them. I doubt that I know what is right for someone else or that someone else knows what is right for me. But if there are no general guidelines, then what is there to be learned from Anne Sigismund Huff's essay?

Plenty!

transition   (i) a passage or movement from one state, condition, or place to another; change   (ii) a movement, development, or evolution from one stage, form, or style to another usually of a later time or period   (iii) a passing from one subject to another especially without abruptness . . .
Webster's Ninth New Collegiate Dictionary, 1987

Huff's essay is organized around transitions, "turning points" in her career. She uses the term to mean discrete movements from one state to another. But if you focus simply on the discrete milestone events (her first job, first move, first promotion and tenure, first book) and the aspects of change, development, and passage as she describes them (entering the field, continuing to explore challenging questions, leveraging impact), without digging deeper, you might miss the contrasting and metaphorically contradictory more important themes related to coherence, perseverance, tenacity, and permanence. In the process of describing the parts (that is, her transitions), she reveals what it takes to fashion the whole: how to create and nourish a fluid, coherent life (academic and personal), how to persevere and endure through multiple competing demands, slights, and various disappointments, and how to sustain critical enthusiasm and energy for work and life in the long term. In sum Huff's advice touches on both the individual and social conditions that foster human potential and personal well-being.

It is more the norm than the exception that humans are inclined toward proactivity, engagement, vitality, mastery, and applying their talents responsibly; but it is also the case that humans have a vulnerability to passivity (Ryan and Deci 2000, 68). As Ryan and Deci (2000) highlight, self-motivation is not simply the result of particular dispositional or biological endowments. Rather, it is influenced significantly by the social-contextual conditions in which people are surrounded. People's inherent growth tendencies, their positive human tendencies toward activity and curiosity are fostered under social contextual conditions that support the development of their competence, autonomy, and relatedness (Ryan and Deci 2000). Contexts in which people's competence, autonomy, and connectedness are thwarted seem to exploit their vulnerability and diminish these positive natural tendencies. It is under these conditions that human beings may well reject growth and become apathetic and alienated.

At its core, Huff's essay focuses on what we can do to create conditions that foster our own human potential and what we can do to create social contexts in which others' can grow, develop, and function at their peak. Huff's specific suggestions seem to mirror the three conditions cited above as being crucial for promoting the positive potential of human nature. She tells us to develop competence, claim our autonomy, and do our relational work by staying connected. Perhaps this was Huff's intention, but I suspect that it was not. No matter by design or by chance, we are lucky that Huff has taken us down this path because I cannot imagine wiser advice than advice concerning how we can elicit and sustain our curiosity, vitality, and self-motivation throughout our academic lives.

To those of you struggling with entering the field, for example, Huff suggests keeping close to the work and paying close attention to what is exciting and engaging. To those of you struggling with faltering enthusiasm she suggests identifying questions that don't have answers and continuing to be an apprentice. At the heart of these suggestions is the notion of continuously developing our *competencies*. The more we are excited and engaged with an activity and the more efficacious we feel with respect to doing it, the more likely we are to do it, simply for the inherent satisfaction of doing it. Learning fuels doing, and doing fuels learning. Huff highlights the importance of *autonomy* when she writes to colleagues concerned with entering the field to find heroes, people that you admire and inspire you. Attend to the themes in your heroes' work. But she goes on to counsel, don't try to emulate your heroes. Move beyond them and find your own voices. The focus on *relatedness* shows up in her recurring suggestions to attend to relationships, both in one's personal life and in one's professional life. Pay attention to family, find friends, find mentors, and facilitate others.

Huff suggests that her essay is concerned with three basic questions of academic life—(1) In which academic field will I work? (2) How will I maintain the energy to explore challenging questions? (3) How can I connect my work to the work of others so that it makes a difference? To those of you concerned with these questions she proposes potentially useful survival strategies that come straight from her experience. Yet she readily admits that these questions have many answers and many solutions. There is no one right way. In the end we are left to tailor our own solutions to fit our unique problems and contexts.

But we aren't left stranded. The deep enduring themes woven throughout the essay are relevant to all of us. Creating, persevering, and sustaining an academic life requires that we feed our needs for competence, autonomy, and relationships and pay particular attention to how we can create social-contextual conditions that fulfill these needs rather than undermine them. Although Huff may not realize it herself, she has wisely counseled us to develop our resilience.

resilience   (i) the capability of a strained body to recover its size and shape after deformation caused especially by compressive stress   (ii) the capability of a strained body to withstand a shock without permanent deformation or rupture   (iii) an act of springing back . . .

Webster's Ninth New Collegiate Dictionary, 1987

Huff's essay is distinctive by what is not there: a single prescription and step-by-step guide for managing our career transitions. And it is distinctive by what is there: enduring and universal ideas on how we can continue to breathe life into our lives. "Academic life is complicated . . . by multiple role demands and opportunities," she writes. It is filled with pressures and standards that some people think are becoming too oppressive and unreasonable. Some people snap when confronted with these hardships, others snap back.

Resilience results when people positively adapt to adversity (Luthar, Cicchetti, and Becker 2000). Huff in her ultimate wisdom understands that. She encourages us to seek our own path and deal with its exigencies in our own ways. But she also knows that positive adaptation emerges from ordinary factors. And she encourages us to develop these factors such as our competence, efficacy, and meaningful relationships. Huff doesn't just give us some ideas for managing crossroads, she reveals what it takes to endure the journey.

PAUL M. HIRSCH

Commentary on Anne Huff's Transitions

Dear Anne,

I read your reflections on transitions with great interest. You are very modest. The "transition" to your role in our field as acknowledged leader and elected president of the Academy of Management is left to the reader's imagination. Like David Whetten, who, in his address as president of the AOM reflected that he never imagined he would rise so high, your essay reminds us that while we focus our attention on the process of managing from day to day, what the outside world notes and rewards are the outcomes of these efforts. So, let me begin with a salute to the high level of your accomplishments, as the outcome of the more day-to-day transitions you have shared with us.

To construe these concerns and transitions as "mundane" is a key point for our students and colleagues to grasp. You sound a tad disappointed there is not more high drama to report. But I think that is an important point. Just as you note, very rightly, how we all "contribute to context and have choices, even if we cannot control outcomes as we wish," I think much of the difference in the crossroads and turning points that follow later on stems from exactly what we all do in our largely mundane surroundings at earlier times. It is when the bright lights are *not* on, working outside the limelight, that we take the decisions and start up the projects that later on lead to the reactions we all wish for. As you rightly note, again, it is important to plot and plan while also realizing we do not control the outcomes, which may even turn out to be positive for reasons we did not anticipate. The energy side of your insight is that we are certain to get nowhere if we do not put in the time and effort, *on faith* that these efforts will lead somewhere we will be pleased with.

Between the time we write something, and it gets submitted, reviewed, published, and then read, there can pass at least two years. What else besides faith and blind commitment would lead young scholars to be willing to wait so long before learning if the work they have invested so much in is going anywhere? The good news is that journals need papers, and somewhere along the way, if we do the work it will get published. That is an important point for students to learn. It reduces terror about "all for naught" if (as should be expected) the first submission gets less than a unanimous and positive response.

Part of the complications you capture so well about the entry transition is that we simultaneously face demands to be modest and respectful, on the one hand, and to be self-confident, original, and creative, on the other. Graduate school is designed to make students believe they must start over intellectually. If we professors like their work and they do right, then prelims will be passed and senior faculty may take them on as assistants. Then, with no transition, the same students are expected to produce a publishable dissertation on their own and go off to be original and creative scholars and teachers.

But just as you noted—if you follow all the advice given to you in the dependent role (student, female, young professor), the outcome will not be what others see as strong, creative, and independent. Just as we learn about our parents, sooner or later, they really do not have all the answers. I tell my students to "take an arrogance pill." You rightly counsel yours to not forget what they are interested in. A secret of good work in our field is that often those writing about a topic have been there; they did not leave it behind forever when entering graduate school, for what we know from our past can be utilized for later research contributions.

One advantage to being able to find life mundane is that seriously negative jolts are not there to distract us. Having triplets, losing siblings, or working near what were the Twin Towers in New York City distracts one immensely from getting his or her "normal work" done. In my view (and in my own case), it is when such disruptions do not occur that we are best able to focus and get done the kind of work our colleagues tend to value the most highly.

But losing the energy to keep it up is inevitable at times. (The question for me here is not so much will it happen, but rather when and for how long.) The ebb and flow you note as part of your transition is admirably described and formulated. But—just as you regret the "mundane" aspects of your transitions, you also seem upset at the lapses of energy you report experiencing. But I say to both: CONGRATULATIONS! For the question is not if we encounter these (all do unless they are crazy, says I), but rather how one deals with them. And it is here that you have done such a terrific job of keeping going, not losing faith (for long), and going on to (among other things) be elected president of the Academy of Management.

An important moral here is that to project out one's bad times as lasting forever is a foolish enterprise, a self-defeating self-fulfilling prophecy to undertake. Much better to take the view "this will pass," like the flu in your metaphor, from which one goes on and gets back to getting his or her work done.

My last observation is that once we have committed to the blind faith that goes with being an academic, I think it important to remember it is "just a job." Of course the manuscript we began so excited about gets boring over the two years of work that is required before its publication. The art of what we do must then become its craft. In many ways, what advantages our field is not that the mundane is present, but that the moments of fun and excitement we fear have left do reappear, to be savored and enjoyed, even if they are not there all the time. If life is a postdoc, then we are indeed privileged, for (as my father once noted) we get paid for it!

I benefited from seeing the potential chaos of academic careers while still a graduate student. It helped a lot to have few illusions along the way. But when I told a friend I was cynical about academia, he joked that if that were really so I would not work so hard and so secretly enjoy it. He was right. Your third turning point of having conversations with others who are interesting and generally supportive is also critical. Our profession is a social one, even if we write alone in our offices. The access to e-mail, professional meetings and networks, and the books and journals we read are all invitations to communicate with colleagues and contact those we seek to be in touch with. I agree with your advice to use them. In some ways, the alternative would say the field is as lonely as we make it. Better to be a pest (even) and contact others.

Your transitions and "take-away" points of advice are important and should help all who read them. They are a refreshing testimony to the idea that our field still remains open, that hard work and innovative contributions get noticed and rewarded. Your essay shows well how "backstage" we don't expect this, that we work hard on faith. Your optimistic message is that the ideas one has and conversations with others do not go unnoticed, and that if we succeed in keeping our energy level up when these rewards are not apparent, good things may follow that even leaders like yourself may not have seen coming.

This is the good news I take from your candid comments and reflections.

With best regards and affectionately,

Paul

Images of Scholarship

We are struck and intrigued by the variety of images that people use to describe scholarship. Starting at the beginning, Jane describes her research garden and Jean responds with images of detours, clocks, decay, and a harbor, while Kevin works the gardening metaphor. Joanne swims against the tide. Christine externalizes her images with paper and scissors and magazine. Steve describes his academic life as a series of puddles. Denny ironically describes a renaissance self and reflects on an ambiguous photograph with a postmodern sensibility. Barbara uses book titles to stand for movements in her intellectual life, while Sally travels solo. Anne draws on physics: balance, energy flows, tension, and resistance. In response, Paul plays with the genre of letter writing and Kathleen makes ample use of the dictionary.

These images churn and collide with each other and our own images of research and scholarship. We are reminded of writing on improvisation (Kamoche and Pina e Cunha 2001; Hatch 1999; *Organization Science* 1998) and the promise of novel theorizing from the edge via transgressing boundaries and genres hinted at by Clegg, Linstead, and Sewell (2000). We are sure you will have your own reactions. Our guess is that mixing metaphors could be a winning renewal strategy.

These images invoked in writing about research are relevant to doing research, too. As the academic-writing genre evolves, our writing practices are becoming more explicit (Rhodes 2001). We are realizing what an important role images, metaphors, and narrative play in our research. For example, Golden-Biddle and Locke (1997) use storytelling to organize their book on writing qualitative research: Barbara Czarniawska (1998) describes the ways we use referencing as storytelling. Even quantitative research often relies on a story line to present results and attach meaning to them (Ragin and Becker 1992).

In our previous book, *Doing Exemplary Research*, we described research as a journey. We followed the journeys of seven research projects. For this volume, we expanded the notion of journey to encompass the research life. Taking a cue from Kathleen, we explored the etymology of the word "journey." We discovered it originally meant a day's travel by land. Journey shares its root with other daily turns: sundial, diary, diet (Morris 1980, 1511). The use of the word has expanded to a "spell" or "continued course of going or travelling, having its beginning and end in place or time, and thus viewed as a distinct whole" (*OED* 1971, 1515). As early as the thirteenth century the word had expanded from a day's travel to the whole of a lifetime.

We like the fact that the definition of journey relates to cycles. It meshes with the series of progressive transitions that Anne describes. However, sometimes, when we get stuck, the positive, progressive connotations of journey get replaced by sense of déjà vu. We have been here before and we are traveling in circles. Maybe that is the time to visit the other images our authors have offered.

Journeys are tentative. When on a journey, we're separated from routines of the every day and more open to chance and serendipity, to Kathleen's surprise. We get opportunities to see new things and explore new places. Perhaps, like Steve, we can explore a puddle or two.

Some of these journeys may be read as quests, the hero's adventure (Campbell 1949). The hero's adventure has a standard structure: "A hero ventures forth from the world of common day into a region of supernatural wonder: fabulous forces are there encountered and a decisive victory is won: the hero comes back from this mysterious adventure with the power to bestow boons on his fellow man" (Campbell 1949, 30). All our contributors are significant, successful scholars. Some have been identified as intellectual heroes of the field. They have all worked long and hard to make their contributions. They have paid the price, survived the ordeals of journal review and tenure and promotion committees. They have brought us the boons of new methods, better constructs, and deeper understanding of organizational life. They deserve our admiration.

However, we warn against exclusively reading these stories as the spoils of many an intellectual battle. We need to avoid the retrospective reconstruction of success as planned, rational, and under control. The lessons offered here derive as much from the incidental, the coincidental, the pragmatic, and the adaptive as they do from the sustained unwinding of a rationally planned career. With Bateson, we advise scepticism of heroic adventures:

I believe that our aesthetic sense, whether in works of art or in lives, has overfocused on the stubborn struggle toward a single goal rather than on the fluid, the protean, the improvisatory. We see achievement as purposeful and monolithic, like the sculpting of a massive tree trunk that has first to be brought from the forest and then shaped by long labor to assert the artist's vision, rather than something created from odds and ends, like a patchwork quilt, and lovingly used to warm different nights and bodies. (1989, 4)

Bateson writes these lines in the introduction to her book on the lives of five successful, nontraditional, academic women. She argues that the hero's adventure is an inappropriate model, especially today with the faster pace of life and especially for women who frequently have not followed a linear path or made independent decisions about career.

There is a tension to explore between the masculine image of a hero's journey and the feminine image of a quilting bee. It is not an issue of which image is right, in either the empirical or normative sense. Acknowledging the importance of uncertainty and adaptiveness is not an attack on those occasions when there is a correlation of vision, persistence, and achievement. For most of us, the scholar's journey is not larger than life, nor is it smaller or less significant than life. It is a real life. As Anne suggests, our hero's trials and contributions may inspire our own efforts, but we must be wary in adopting the same tactics. Changing times and stable expectations is a recipe for disaster and bad advice. "Do as I did" will guarantee failure as the times they are a changing. We need to ask, What do these accounts offer for my journey? Can I match them to the pattern of my quilting? Is this the fertilizer for my garden?

Bateson does invite us to consider the gendered experience of research journeys. We invited four men and four women as the main contributors for this volume. Their sex was a minor factor in our selection process. We did want to represent some diversity, but we did not a priori decide on a 50/50 split or consider the contributors' gender identity in our equation. Similarly, we invited seven women and seven men to serve in the role of commentators. This fact we did not know until we prepared this essay. We did not ask our contributors or commentators to consider gender issues.

Some of our authors have explicitly drawn the reader's attention to their gendered experiences. Not surprisingly it is women who did so. Not surprising, because we continue to understand the field as dominated by men, who often unconsciously universalize their experience, which forces women to notice their gendered experience, while allowing, and making it difficult for, men to see the gendered aspects of their experience.

Our sample is small. Gersick, Bartunek, and Dutton (2000) had a bigger sample. They interviewed thirty-seven faculty members in a variety of departments from six U.S. business schools. They report that men and women academics tell of different relational work experiences in business schools. On the whole, the difference is not positive. Men were three times more likely to tell stories of receiving career help. In contrast, women's helping stories "often described help as a rare extended hand in a hostile world" (Gersick, Bartunek, and Dutton 2000, 1036). Women were four times more likely to tell stories of receiving career harm in their workplace.

One other finding from this study is truly important for readers. This finding does not differentiate men and women faculty members: "Our findings are saturated with the interviewees' depictions of relationships as ends in themselves, from the preeminence of collegiality as a reason for relationships' importance, to the across the board significance of stories about joint work and colleagueship" (Gersick, Bartunek, and Dutton 2000, 1039). This finding relates to another connotation of journey that works for us. We like the notion of the journey as an experience in itself, perhaps more important than the destination. When it comes to our research journey, we know that we will never reach the destination. We know that we will never fully understand organization. Yet we have already learned a lot along the way, usually working across a desk, or across the Internet from our colleagues.

KARL E. WEICK 8

How Projects Lose Meaning
The Dynamics of Renewal

THE PURPOSE of this chapter is to provide a way to think about the dynamics of renewal that will encourage empirical investigation and reanimate projects that have stalled, turned sour, or become meaningless. Although that aspiration may sound abstract, the dynamics discussed here come out of my own experience as an academic who battles continuously with such things as a sluggish imagination, self-doubt, dead-end projects, rejection letters, low teaching ratings, indecision, blank stares, dismissive critics, a limited vocabulary, and all the other things that make scholarly work, anxious work.[1]

What annoys me about the idea of "renewal" is that it always sounds like such a big deal. It sounds like something that should be approached in awe and spelled with capital letters and done once or twice in a lifetime when the stakes are really high. If we think of renewal that way, then we hold it at arm's length, we fear trying to do it, we deny the need to do it in the first place, we do it almost as if we were invoking magic, we often do either too much of it or too little of it since we don't know when to stop, we repeat everything that seemed to happen the last time we renewed since we don't know exactly why we were successful, and we measure our success at renewal against unrealistically high standards.

It never dawns on us, for example, that under some circumstances we could simply declare ourselves renewed and move on. Or that renewal resides in the small details that lead to small wins. Or that the topic of renewal may be just another conversational gambit like the weather . . . and no more controllable. Or that renewal creates experience rather than responds to ex-

---

1. I am grateful to Jane Dutton, Peter Frost, Ralph Stablein, and Karen Weick for their help in revising earlier versions of this chapter.

perience. Or that renewing is all we ever do. Or that the problem is not so much fresh starts and renewing, as it is fresh endings and "reolding." We are big on beginnings, but lousy on endings, which may mean that we can't restart something until we finish off something else, heedfully and thoroughly. "The End" may trigger the definitive infusion of energy.

Even though renewal is elusive, it lurks somewhere in these three examples.

"Marion has a son Michael, who is hyperactive. After trying various failed medications, she decided to use her deep love for him as her primary treatment. Whenever he began to lose control of his impulses, Marion would scoop him up and sit him in her lap, place his head against her chest, and rock, and rock, until, she said, he could remember who he was" (Muller 1999, 151).

In December 1939, Duke Ellington enlarged the saxophone section of his orchestra from four men to five when he added Ben Webster. "When Webster joined, there was written-out music initially for only four saxophones, none for him, and he had to find a fifth note that would work, while avoiding the jealously guarded parts of the other saxophonists, who kept accosting him, 'Hey, you've got my note!'" (Hasse 1993, 240). The resulting music, once Webster found the fifth note, contained some of the most glorious, rich, original chords that were ever recorded by any version of the Ellington orchestra. Both Ellington and Webster experienced fresh starts.

Warren Bennis, when he was president of the University of Cincinnati, gave an evening lecture at the Harvard School of Education. Everything came together in a superb performance. During the upbeat Q-and-A session after the speech, Bennis was startled when the dean, Paul Ylvisaker, asked quietly, "Warren, do you really love being president of Cincinnati?" Bennis did not have a snappy answer. He didn't have any answer. After an interminable silence, in a room that quieted dramatically, Bennis finally said, "I don't know." Shortly thereafter, he came to the realization that he loved being a college president but hated doing a college presidency, so he resigned.

Diverse as these examples may seem, they share some interesting features. They vary in scale, but not in their structure. In each instance, something is made new again (renew) and living is refreshed. In each case, work and living are fused. When one of these two begins to fall apart, the other one does too. Each episode involves being thrown into the middle of something unexpected. There is a sense that fragments and parts have replaced flows and wholes. Attention is flooded with questions: What's the story? Why are we doing this? Where am I? In these examples, small acts of holding, fitting, and questioning begin to restore the sense that has been lost. People seem to move away from the strictly logical and sequential, toward the intuitive (Marion's touch), the balanced (Webster's harmonically interesting notes), and the vital (Bennis's linkage of being and doing). The movement toward resolution seems to consist of going back to earlier moments as well as going deeper, both of which seem to engage more fundamental "truths" involving relationships, harmonies, and values. The solutions feel "wise" rather than smart. But, for all their intensity, these disturbances are also bounded and relatively short-lived, partly because people continue to act. These continuing actions generate new meanings. And the participants move on to calmer parenting, more complex jazz arrangements, and more focused mentoring.

In each example, a choice that was originally meaningful and emotionally charged, gradually makes less sense and gradually builds pressure for a fresh start. Throughout this chapter I will refer to these choices as "projects." I adopt this noun to preserve the point that the diffuse entity that is being renewed consists of some contemplated venture, conceived reflectively and appreciatively, that has some risk and uncertainty connected with it. As time passes, people may become less aware of their projects, but only until they begin to break down. At the point of breakdown, deliberate attention to direction appears once again. Since people tend to be conscious of projects, both when they start and when they break down, and since these moments are key markers in the progression of renewal, it seems preferable to conceptualize the phenomenon as if it were mainly conscious, deliberate, and effortful. When I talk about projects I will not neglect the importance of tacit knowledge. But I am more concerned with locating renewal in some story that serves as a frame of reference within which activities make more or less sense. That vessel is the project. The word "project" has obvious meaning for those who live amidst research projects, but it also has meaning for those who live amidst everyday projects of concernful coping (Dreyfuss 1995, 61). My goal is to develop ideas that appeal to readers with diverse interests.

In the three examples at the beginning of this chapter, the original choices and projects might have been to wade in and cope with hyperactivity, to create original music by playing unique variations on traditional melodies, and to put into practice the very theories of leadership that one had espoused. Over time these choices feel less sensible as unanticipated consequences appear. Medications for hyperactivity fail; playing the arranged notes in the Cab Calloway orchestra (Webster's employer just before Ellington) leaves little room for creative expression; and doing the presidency of a college turns out to involve more than leading. These developments weaken the context of the initial choice and render it less meaningful. In extreme cases, each person is saying to him- or herself, "I have no idea where I am, who I am, or what I am doing."

Stated informally, the story of renewal starts when projects begin to lose earlier sources of energy and meaning. The attendant feelings of ennui, melancholy, and concern may signify a need for reattachment to some of those earlier sources of energy. By reattachment I mean going back, reinstating, and reconstructing the beginnings of the project in a more heedful manner. As people reexamine that earlier period, and see it more richly, this deeper noticing may produce deeper appreciation and deeper acceptance of the present difficulties. If that happens, then one's present living is made new again. And renewing takes place. But sometimes, deepened noticing has a different effect and the earlier decision is actually remade or updated. We see hints of this in these three examples. The earlier choice to cope with a hyperactive child through medication becomes remade as a newer choice to enfold, love, and rhythmically move that child toward calm remembering. The earlier choice to make original music by being a reactive sideman is remade as a newer choice to find a meaningful place for oneself as a proactive sideman in the challenging environment of jealous musicians and traditional chords. And the earlier choice to walk the talk of leadership is remade as the newer choice to mentor leaders in all sorts of settings rather than to model leadership in just one setting.

Stated more compactly and more formally, the story line of renewal seems to be this. As earlier projects begin to unravel and turn sour, there is the perception that activities are becoming less sensible. That perception is the result of fragmentation produced by a loss of context, ineffective sensemaking, or inattention to the world. Each of these three sources for fragments will be explored shortly. The feeling of disorder is reflected both in questions (for example, what's the story, why are we doing this, what's wrong) and in assertions (for example, I have no idea where I am, who I am, or what I am doing). To reduce this disorder, people need to act in ways that reconstruct context, strengthen sensemaking, and restore attention. In the following sections I argue that renewal seems to be a story with a finite number of plausible plots and some workable tactics that shape these plots. I will discuss briefly three different developments in any project, including scholarly ones, that seem to increase the felt need for renewal. These three story lines include the loss of integration and patterns, the weakening of capacities for sensemaking, and the disconnection of preoccupations from attention.

These basic ways in which projects weaken and lose sense can be reversed by tactics such as listening, writing, goal setting, and dialoguing.

Plot Lines in Narratives of Renewal

The question—when does renewal start?—is almost as puzzling as the question, when does it end? Both questions are best answered retrospectively, which means that the actual immersion in an episode of renewal is not clear-cut. It can be difficult to distinguish episodes of renewal from ordinary setbacks, problems, hassles, and speed bumps in daily life. However, we can feel the difference even if it is tough to articulate. Episodes of renewal tend to be anchored by a context that pulls together an initial set of choices, meanings, and activities into a frame of reference that resembles a project. When projects begin, they typically make sense because they are free of "unanticipated consequences." As the project unfolds and as these unanticipated consequences begin to pile up, questions about the wisdom of the choice, the meaning of the consequences, and the worth of the activities also begin to build. As questions build, so too do feelings that the project might benefit from a restart, a redirection, or a rethinking. As all of these forces continue to build, the phenomenon of renewal becomes easier to distinguish from everyday hassles and problems.

There are at least three ways in which meaningful projects begin to lose some of their meaning. First, the initial big picture in which everything found a place may begin to fracture into parts, such that it becomes harder to see why the project is being continued. Second, the full set of tools mobilized for sensemaking in the initial stages of the project may become differentially available over time, such that it becomes harder to make sense of what is happening. Third, the tight coupling between preoccupations and attention that tied the project into the current environment and gave it meaning initially may loosen such that relevant updating seldom occurs. Each one of these unfolding plots sets in motion a series of events that seem to correspond with what people have in mind when they talk about "renewal." There obviously are many other plots.

Projects that Lose Integration

When people initiate projects, they often do so for more reasons than they are aware of. For example, I began to puzzle over wild-land firefighting crews in 1992 for many more reasons than were obvious to me at the time. Initially, I wanted to understand their work because it seemed to embody sensemaking, a small group, thinking under stress and in danger. But as I dug deeper I also began to realize—as Norman Maclean had in the book *Young Men and Fire*—that their fatalities tapped my own troubled feelings about death. Furthermore, the firefighters were the pretext to grapple with my own ill-defined feelings about macho subcultures, physical work, vicarious adventuring, the qualities of heroes, decisiveness, arrogance, doing rather than saying, respect, fictions sustained by detachment, and the eerily resonating line in Pablo Neruda's poem that reads, "When a decent house catches fire, / instead of the fireman I summon, / an arsonist bursts on the scene, / and that's me" (Weick 1995, 19). Neruda's poem, titled "We Are

Many," affirms the many selves we have. Many of those selves are active in project selection, although we may not realize it at the time. Thus, even though there were explicit reasons why I chose to focus on wild-land firefighters when I began the project of writing the Katz-Newcomb lecture, that choice meant more to me than I could say at the time.

But those silent bases for choice were still active, meaning that my choice of the firefighter project was overdetermined. It was driven by a set of interrelated tacit and explicit hooks that, in combination, provided a meaningful frame of reference to think about firefighters directly and the human condition indirectly. Given these densely integrated relationships, a loss of either explicit or tacit meanings would likely be felt as a loss of sense and energy for the project, and as an occasion for renewal. But there is a tricky issue here. If the project makes sense because it is a meaningful whole, then efforts at renewal that focus solely on parts may be self-defeating. If people try to explicate wholes and put them into lists, or disassemble them for repair, these efforts may be destructive. Reflection changes intuitive knowing into something that is logical and stepwise and reasoned and different from the project with which people started. "An unbridled lucidity can destroy our understanding of complex matters (Polanyi 1967, 18). . . . Deliberate conscious reflection does change the nature of knowledge: it becomes no longer tacitly held, but intellectually reasoned" (Pye 1991, 112). Thus, to reflect, even if it is reflection-in-action, is to change the nature of knowing and to put the understanding of wholes out of reach.

To move away from this potential for collapse, and toward resolution, we need to deepen our respect for tacit knowing and our skills at managing it. When wholes begin to lose their coherence (that is, when projects seem to make less sense than they used to), the strong temptation is to undertake analysis and identify the parts that are causing the trouble. That approach may be of some help. But the help is only partial because much of the coherence in the initial project was based on tacit knowing. Tacit knowing does not take the form of separable, meaningful parts that are assembled into a whole. Instead, tacit knowing is "that which dwells in our awareness of particulars while bearing on an entity which the particulars jointly constitute" (Polanyi 1967, 61, in Pye 1991, 108). The knowledge in tacit knowing is relational. Particulars bear on an entity and that entity is jointly constituted by particulars. Thus, the project is founded as much on simultaneity and intuition as it is on linear sequence and intellect. The project is tied together as a whole by people who know more about that project than they can tell.

If a project begins to make less and less sense, this could mean that something is wrong with relations, tacit knowing, and intuition. Analysis won't touch any of those three. What will have more of an effect are tactics that can restore relations, strengthen and enrich intuitions, reinstate a big picture, substitute aesthetic appraisal for rational appraisal, and tightly couple the general with the specific. Many of these changes can be understood as efforts to enrich a story of what the person is up to by connecting the subthemes and strengthening the plot line. Narrative enrichment sets multiple themes in motion, themes that develop and define one another. It is the jointly constituted motion that re-creates a meaningful project and a good story.

To return to the example of wild-land firefighting, that project seemed to be running out of gas when there was little I could think of that would move beyond my initial reframing of *Young Men and Fire* (Weick 1993). But a trip to a smokejumper base in Missoula, Montana, conversations with firefighters, free association, free writing, and mental stimulation drove me deeper into themes such as "drop your tool" (Weick 1996) and "never hand over a fire in the heat of the day" (Weick 1998). What seems to have happened is that deeper pursuit of these narrower slices reanimated *both* the explicit and tacit attractions to wild-land firefighting. It was as if the complete pattern in my initial fascination had been restored and the human condition was once more visible in people trying to outrun an exploding fire. Mann Gulch once more became the representative anecdote for people everywhere who are frightened and confused. In Mann Gulch, as in life elsewhere, "individuals who are strangers to one another are spread out, unable to communicate, unfamiliar with the terrain, in disagreement about who their leaders are, and they're told to do something they've never done before, or they will die. They don't do it. They die" (Weick 1999, 55).

Tactics that successfully accomplish such reintegration differ across people since all of us live in different realities. So I can't finger the one best way to reverse a loss of integration. In the section on tactics, I will mention several things, some of which help me rebuild wholes, and some of which may help others to do the same. Right now I am more concerned with suggesting a generic story line for renewal that highlights the patterned quality of projects. In this story line, if the pattern begins to deteriorate then people become more concerned with making the project new again. But if they try to do this by means of reflection and analysis, the problem could get worse. Reflection and analysis are blunt instruments when it comes to pattern recognition and pattern restoration. To make a loss of integration new again requires heightened trust in tacit knowing, tying experience more richly to projects, and more deliberate use of images and words that treat complex wholes with respect.

Projects that Lose Sense

As we have just seen, any project has content. And that content is a mixture of the tacit/explicit and the intuitive/reasoned, which forms a meaningful pattern. Fluctuations in the pattern trigger attempts to restart the project.

But other story lines of renewal are possible.

Any project becomes a project, and continues to be a project, in part because it "makes sense." And it makes sense because one or more of at least seven resources inform it. A project makes sense to a person because there is some combination of social validation, confirmation of important identities for that person, raw material that permits retrospective judgments of elapsed events, cues that enable diagnostic trial and error, updating that keeps pace with ongoing developments, plausible explanations for what is happening, and actions that enact events into recognizable forms. These resources can be summarized by the acronym "SIR COPE." If we assume that the more resources committed to sensemaking, the richer the sense that will be made, and if we assume that a loss of resources is accompanied by a loss of sense, then the felt need to restart something may stem from a loss of sensemaking resources rather than from a loss of a strong narrative line. It is not the story that falls apart. Instead, it is the capability for "storying" that falls apart.

In the early stages of a project, we can safely assume that there are sufficient resources to engage and hold attention. Otherwise, there would be no focus of attention and no project. Thus, beginning makes sense, even if part of that sense consists of wishful thinking or doing something simply because it is fashionable or exists as a target of opportunity. Whatever the case, the initial sense is the product of one or more sensemaking resources. It is the fate of those resources over time that determines whether moments of renewal are needed and what those moments may consist of.

There are obvious ways in which resources can weaken. There can be a loss of social resources as when interactions decrease in frequency and consensual validation weakens (for example, people begin to wonder if their work is accepted by others as being in the mainstream). Identity may become more insecure (for example, people question whether they have lost their distinctive "voice," or whether they ever had a voice to begin with). Retrospect may be neutralized because the new project has accumulated relatively little history that suggests an emerging direction (for example, one begins to read a new literature, but themes do not seem to recur and the question soon becomes, what's the story and why am I doing this?). As a sidelight, retrospect plays an interesting role in renewal. If people learn what they think by seeing what they say, then there isn't much to see for significant stretches in some projects because not much is said. If not much is being said or seen or thought, then not much is created that could be made sensible. Earlier, we saw that "unbridled lucidity" is harmful because it undermines the restoration of wholes. But here, in a different story line built around the loss of sensemaking processes, "unbridled lucidity" might be much more of an asset since it refreshes retrospect by supplying more raw material for it to process.

Cues that once were trustworthy may become equivocal in the context of a newer project (for example, the occurrence of human errors was once a trustworthy cue that accidents were likely to happen, but now those errors are treated as consequences rather than causes). The ability to keep pace with unfolding events may disappear when a person thinks of one thing too long or of too many things too fast (for example, by the time one has written a solid contribution for the magazine *Fast Company*, the fad-makers are breathless about something else and the writing has become dated). The resource of plausibility tends not to disappear as quickly as do other features of sensemaking (for example, one can always be plausibly working to understand the human condition even if no one else sees it quite this way). So long as the project retains some plausibility, fresh starts can be postponed even though they may seem increasingly attractive. Finally, sense tends to decrease when there is a loss in the level of activity associated with the project (for example, people keep thinking up clever ideas and concepts but fail to test them). If people act their way into meaning, then a high level of activity should delay the need for renewal, and a lower level hasten it.

A personal example may make this clearer. In 1969 I wrote a book called *The Social Psychology of Organizing*, revised it in 1979, and it seemed natural to do a third edition in 1989. But as the 1980s unfolded, they did so in a way that steadily pulled sensemaking resources away from this project. We moved from Cornell, where the second edition was written, to Texas, and from Texas to Michigan, meaning that *social* resources changed. We moved closer to and then away from a communication group at Texas that had provided an *identity* that sustained the organizing book. The evolutionary epistemology that was central to the second edition was annexed by institutional theory and population ecology during this period, which made microevolutionary processes less *plausible*. My research was being *enacted* in the newer setting of high-reliability organizations, which meant that the *cues* I had available for *retrospect* were different from those laboratory-based cues (for example, prisoner's dilemma, common target game, triad table) that had guided the organizing book. I was seeing more surprises, sensemaking, and improvisation, and fewer loosely coupled systems, double interacts, and assembly rules. Doing a third edition because the calendar said it was time made less sense because several sensemaking resources had disappeared or changed radically. What made more sense was to do a short article (Weick 1989a) that said in essence, I haven't learned enough to warrant a third edition, but I have reconnected with an even older project, namely, trying to understand jazz improvisation. In 1989 I was beginning to see improvisation, bricolage, and embellishment where it wouldn't be expected, in elaborate hierarchical systems such as flight operations on a carrier, air traffic control, and nuclear power generation. And sixteen years after 1979, I did do a book on sensemaking (Weick, 1995) that retains a flavor of the second edition.

To move back to the more general argument, when a project begins to feel senseless and flat, that may have nothing to do with content and everything to do with process. Resources for sensemaking may have weakened or disappeared. But moves toward renewal need not be large or dramatic. They consist of small changes that refresh SIR COPE, small changes such as writing to authors of influential articles in an effort to initiate a discussion and strengthen social validation; searching autobiographies to spot newer identities that can be tried on for size; keeping more detailed records to enrich retrospective revisiting of earlier events and to suggest new cues that foreshadow significant changes; enriching the variety of verbs in one's vocabulary in order to heighten sensitivity to rates of change in ongoing events; reconceptualizing plausibility as approximations to accuracy in an effort to think more carefully about the evidence (or the lack thereof) that the project continues to be worth doing; and allowing the computer to go dark so that one can push away from the monitor and experience the project tactually.

What is important in a story of renewal based on sensemaking processes is that people remain alert to gradual deterioration of any of these seven components. To spot and remedy an early loss of a single component may not be a big deal or consume much time. It truly is a "moment" of renewal. Its significance lies in the fact that it is a small change that can have large consequences. For example, once a project is underway, coworkers may become less available for interaction, as the excitement of beginnings gives way to the tedium of middles. This is a weakening of social resources that seems trivial in the short run. But if this component is left unrepaired, the project can rapidly collapse into nonsense. Recall that in the Mann Gulch wild-land fire disaster, sensemaking started to deteriorate when interactions became less frequent and occurred among smaller numbers of people with less and less information being exchanged. Social resources, which were shaky to begin with (for example, the firefighting crew had not worked together before), were allowed to weaken even more until sensemaking became lodged in small subsets of the fifteen crew members, some of whom were working at odds with one another. In the early stages of the Mann Gulch incident, the six components of the sensemaking process other than social resources were functioning adequately. The problem came when the failure to repair social resources eventually disabled the other six components. The resulting senselessness of an exploding fire left people with no remaining resources that could direct survival.

The Mann Gulch incident is an extreme example of what may happen on a much smaller scale when sensemaking processes become compromised, sense is lost, and the urgency to restart increases. It is important to reiterate that the point being made here is that renewal involves something beside an issue of content. In the case of sensemaking, the problem is not so much that the content of the story no longer coheres, but that the capability for building a sensible story has diminished. The senseless story is not a compromised whole, but rather a byproduct of flawed sensemaking processes. The story will continue to be a puzzle until resources improve.

Projects that Lose Attention

Many story lines of renewal involve efforts to rebalance some duality such as theory-practice, spectator-participant, superiority-inferiority, work-play, or obedience-rebellion, where one pole has come to dominate the other one. For example, Fritz Roethlisberger, in his work as a counselor at the Harvard Business School, came into contact with a large number of student clients who were sufficiently preoccupied with issues of success-failure that they couldn't focus on their studies. The interesting feature that was common among these cases is that students essentially said to themselves, if this project is not an absolute success, then it is a failure. Since this is a tough criterion to meet, most of their projects felt like failure. Roethlisberger called this form of thinking "false dichotomies" because people were treating success-failure as a contradiction rather than a contrary. When people conclude that everything that is not a success is failure, they act as if they face a duality where, if one pole is false then the other one is true. There is nothing in between. What they fail to see is that projects can be both a success and a failure, or neither a success nor a failure. These additional possibilities are contraries rather than contradictions. Mistaking a contrary for a contradiction can happen with any duality (for example, everything that is not safe is dangerous). The tragedy in all this is that "in the thinking of such people the notion of adventure is lacking. There is little or no place for exploration and experiment. They work so hard in preventing themselves from making mistakes that they never learn anything at all" (Roethlisberger 1968, 90).

Roethlisberger argued that this tendency to elaborate contraries into contradictions seemed to occur when a person's attention to self became disconnected from attention to the world. Preoccupations with the self focused on significant personal questions and values about which people have strong feelings (Roethlisberger 1977, 43). When people became obsessed with their preoccupations they ignored the current situation and their ongoing work. With less input from the current external environment, preoccupations tended to be overelaborated. Small bits of data were elaborated into overblown significance. Thus, for example, what looked like a partial success (for example, an invitation to "revise and resubmit" a manuscript) might be elaborated in terms of the many ways it "actually" signified failure. When Roethlisberger looked more closely at the form of thinking that accompanied false dichotomies he found that preoccupations took the form of "an overelaboration in logic of an oversimplification in fact." Instead of treating the world of fact as complex and keeping his thinking about it simple, the student tended to treat the world of fact as simple and to complicate his thinking about it. As a result he was "complicating" his life not in relation to the complexity of relations that existed in "matters of fact" but in relation to an oversimplified logicization (relation of ideas) of them. The products of this kind of thinking I called "false dichotomies" (Roethlisberger 1977, 39–40). The remedy is this: "Instead of treating the world of facts (the territory) as simple and making the map complex, one should treat the territory as complex and keep the map simple. A simple map applied to a complex territory could do wonders" (Roethlisberger 1977, 139). Thus, a story line of renewal begins with a project whose execution has an initial mix of success-failure, safety-danger, and theory-practice. Over time these dualities may become unbalanced and frozen into false dichotomies from which contraries are excluded. To renew is to restore contraries.

The ups and downs of one of my own ongoing projects seem to track Roethlisberger unusually well. The very first project I undertook as a graduate student, in conjunction with Harold B. Pepinsky, was a project on the determinants of productivity. "Productivity" is an academically acceptable label for the often much more personal issue of success-failure. Interestingly, my very first publication was a theoretical piece on impression management among seemingly productive researchers. It's obvious that I wanted to study what most preoccupied me at the time, namely, the question of whether I could hack it in graduate school and what the "secret" was of being productive. The tricky part is that I often did just what Roethlisberger's clients did, namely, personalize this issue, ignore the world, and overelaborate small outcroppings of qualified successes into distinct failures. For example, my acceptable though undistinguished performance in my master's thesis oral exam got overelaborated into a miserable failure that left me wondering if I should leave graduate school. As the failures piled up, so too did the need for renewal. In this case, renewal meant moving from overelaborated logic to simpler logic, and from simpler perceptual inputs to more complex inputs. It meant paying more attention to the world and less attention to the self in order to weaken the false dichotomy that I kept reinforcing. Over the years, my ongoing efforts to treat success-failure as a contrary, rather than a contradiction, have had varying success. I have tried to articulate contraries surrounding success-failure with such ideas as the surprising virtues of doubt, the aesthetics of imperfection, the role of ignorance in wisdom, ambivalence as the optimal compromise, task enhancement as a controllable source of success, action rationality, and retrospective justification. The idea of small wins is a perfect example of the point I am making. A small win "is a concrete, complete, implemented outcome of moderate importance. . . . Small wins are like miniature experiments that test implicit theories about resistance and opportunity and uncover both resources and barriers that were invisible before the situation was stirred up" (Weick 1984, 43–44). A small win is both a success and a failure. It is a success because something was improved. It is a failure because the something that was improved was small and not especially important considered by itself. A small win can also be seen as neither a success nor a failure, since it is a miniature experiment that produces information rather than an evaluation. In either case, a small win is an event in the world that draws attention away from preoccupations with success-failure and toward ongoing events in the external world. The beauty of small wins is that they draw attention and action into the world, while at the same time they demonstrate that something that is not an absolute success is also not a failure either. Small wins refute false dichotomies. In doing so, they reconnect preoccupations with perceptions, they open those preoccupations to modification, and they make projects new again.

Roethlisberger is not the only person to suggest that complication and renewal are tied together. The work of William Schutz also implies that some complications encourage renewal while others discourage it. Schutz has argued that the act of understanding progresses through three stages: superficial simplicity, confused complexity, and profound simplicity. In my own work I have argued that those in need of renewal should follow the advice, "complicate yourself" (Weick 1979, 261). This counsel derives from the idea of requisite variety and from my interpretation that it takes complex thinking and perception to register and adapt in a complex world. Thus, if a project begins to stall and become senseless, this may be the result of a failure to update and register the complexity of the environment. To renew the project, people need to enact a more complicated conceptual scheme so that they see more of the complications that interfere with progress. But my counsel, considered in the context of Schutz, may stop too soon. I treat complication as the end point of understanding, under the assumption that once your thinking is as complex as the environment, that's all you need. That is wrong because there are no end points. Instead, there is life beyond confused complexity. We may call it profound simplicity, or we may call it wisdom, or we may call it small wins enacted with full attention to the here and now.

To restart projects that are stalled by false dichotomies and logical overelaboration, people need to replace contradictions with contraries, cultivate a deeper appreciation of simultaneity (for example, this project is both a success and a failure), and go for the small win. This suggests that to move in the direction of renewal is to move toward profound simplicities. And to move in this direction means that people have to connect their preoccupations more closely to what they notice and do right here and now. If the connection between attention and preoccupations weakens, then self-absorption increases and learning decreases. Projects lose their energy and their relevance. To strengthen the connection between preoccupations and attention takes perceptual enrichment and conceptual simplification. Or, as Roethlisberger puts it, it takes simple maps to navigate complex territories. But what simplicity means in this context is subtle. Simple maps have fewer contradictions but more contraries. They have fewer superficial simplifications but more that are profound. They are general-simple explanations, but those explanations also contain inaccuracies. They contain knowledge as well as ignorance. They are wise, rather than smart or dumb.

Tactics

Renewal may be a big deal, but it is often accomplished by small changes that influence integration, sense, and attention. My basic assumption is that renewal is more successful when people do less, but do it more often, than when they do more, but do it less often. There is seldom a one-to-one relationship between a specific story line and a specific remedy. More common is the case where some seemingly autonomous tactic supplies a crucial whole or sensemaking resource or connection that has been missing. For example, a loss of integration through inadvertent tinkering with tacit knowing may be reversed by something read, or something heard, or something said, or something desired. To reintegrate is to become more mindful of wholes, intuitions, relations, and contexts, but the precise remedy that can produce this kind of mindfulness varies across people and situations.

Thus, the tactics to be discussed in this section represent potential means to restart any of the story lines mentioned above, as well as others not discussed. What I have tried to do so far is to suggest a finite number of ways in which projects may begin to unravel and a general set of remedies that focus on the locus of the unraveling. Thus, a loss of integration is made new again by something that affects relational sensitivity; a loss of sense is made new again by something that strengthens sensemaking; and a loss of attention is made new again by something that curbs overelaboration. The present section is a brief discussion of what those "somethings" involve. My concern now is with the pragmatics of renewal.

Renewal Through Reading

Whenever my projects stall, I read (for example, Berlin, 2001). And I read about reading (for example, Gass, 1999). And I read people who are skeptical about the value of reading (for example, Schopenhauer, 1851/1970). Reading seems to help renew projects, regardless of how those projects have lost their vividness. For example, at various times my reading has provided an allegory that reintegrates fragments (for example, Maclean, 1992), a biography that reinstates possible identities that restore sensemaking (for example, Haase, 1993), or an analysis that reconnects preoccupations with attention (for example, Hillman, 1999). Reading can renew because it is a form of active listening. Attentive readers hear such things as tacit knowledge that knits events together, trusted intuitions that encourage one to duplicate the trust, conversational partners who enable one to see more clearly the thinking that is implicit in what is said, or tales of complexity that disconfirm the superficial simplicity of an either-or dichotomy.

But the reading that facilitates renewal is not just any old slacker reading. This is evident in E. B. White's (1954/1975) wonderful essay on "The Last Reader," written nearly fifty years ago. White worries over the future of reading "in these audio–visual days" where AV devices "ask no discipline of mind and . . . are already giving the room the languor of an opium parlor." True reading "is the work of the alert mind, is demanding, and under ideal conditions produces a sort of ecstasy." These are outcomes capable of restoring projects. These outcomes are hard to come by. "Indeed, there is very little true reading, and not nearly as much writing as one would suppose from the towering piles of pulpwood in the dooryards of paper mills. Readers and writers are scarce, as are publishers and reporters. The reports we get nowadays are those of men who have not gone to the scene of the accident, which is always farther inside one's own head than it is convenient to penetrate without galoshes" (551).

To go "to the scene of the accident" in search of context and renewal, and to locate the scene of that accident deep inside one's own head, is to discover the power of imagining to renew, and the power of reading to animate that imagining. A true reader is an armchair ethnographer, able to catch the significance of the accident scene and to use that significance to reanimate a floundering project. The significance may reenact wholes, strengthen sensemaking, or redirect self-absorption back into the world.

To pick up a book at the moment when a project is dying may seem like the ultimate act of escape and denial. It could be that. But it could be something more. When a project shudders, the temptation is to wade in and fiddle with some parts and tweak other ones. This temptation to meddle is antithetical to being still and listening and recapturing wholes. Reading fore-stalls direct meddling, quiets the chatter of logic, and redirects meddling into imagined worlds. Reading tends to stir up intuitive understanding, tacit knowing, and wisdom. It is hands-on renewal done vicariously through someone else's hands.

Renewal Through Writing

Whenever my projects stall, I also write. I write free-associationally to see what relates to what and what those relationships might mean. I write volu-minously in the hope that I might generate some variation that will prove to be a more attractive whole, a more sensible starting point, or a more com-pelling outcropping for a languishing project. I write allegorically to capture small moments that may embody more vivid summaries of ongoing proj-ects. I write continually to find better words and clearer ways to join them that improve the wisdom, sense, and relevance of projects. I write indiscrim-inately in order to stumble onto themes that would not normally show up given the limits of my frames of reference. I write respectfully to get hints of the tacit knowledge that might form part of the infrastructure of events. And I write passionately to discover the "voice" that I may bring to an issue, and what the resonance in that issue may be for me.

I want to say a bit more about "voice" because it seems to figure in so many occasions of renewal. "Speaking your voice has to do with revealing what is true for you regardless of other influences that might be brought to bear" (Isaacs 1999, 159). William Isaacs describes the following incident to il-lustrate voice. It involved his colleague, Michael Jones, who is an improvisa-tional pianist. "Once, while playing, an older man came up to him and they began to speak. The man asked about his work and what the music was that he had just played. 'That was an arrangement of "Moon River,"' Michael said. 'No, before that,' said the old man. 'That was some of my own music,' Michael replied. The man then said, 'You're wasting your time with "Moon River."' He then continued, asking Michael, 'Who will play your music if you don't do it yourself?'" (Isaacs 1999, 169).

Projects often begin with "one's own music," or at least a hesitant claim that one has something distinctive to contribute. But as the project unfolds, its integration or sense or connection with one's own music may begin to weaken. And with this weakening, people sometimes begin to question the distinctiveness, quality, and size of their own contribution. This is when peo-ple can become preoccupied with issues of voice and withdraw attention from the very ongoing events that could pull them out of this overelabora-tion (for example, unless my idea is very good, it is very bad). Writing can take a preoccupation with voice and reconnect it to the world, if the following description is taken seriously: "The original style is not the style which never borrows of anyone, but that which no other person is capable of reproducing" (de Chateaubriand quoted in Platt 1989, item # 2075). People get messed up on issues of voice because they feel that imitation is antithetical to the development of voice. Since it's tough to avoid imitation when you read your way into renewal and write your way into preexisting topics, people get stuck in preoccupations with voice. The twist is to pull together what you read in such a way that no one else can imitate your expressing. This is what Duke Ellington did when he lifted phrases from some of the solos played by his musicians and combined them in a manner no other composer could imitate.

What is intriguing about unreproducible imitating is that it creates original continuities. The imitation provides the continuity; the unreproducibility provides the originality. To craft original continuities, at least in academic work, is to be engaged in projects that are widely and durably valued. Writing sustains and restores academic projects, because the words that develop the project are words that recur in the mainstream. This is the continuity. But if those words are handled associationally, voluminously, allegorically, continually, indiscriminately, respectfully, and passionately, then the recurring words will have been rearranged into new and original phrases that point to new wholes, new sense, and new objects of attention. Those rearrangements are the essence of renewal.

Renewal Through Goal Setting

The tactic here is straightforward, but it involves a reversal that may not be obvious. Normally, we think of present activities as a means to attain some future goal. For example, impatient MBAs plow through a business school curriculum as a means to gain future entry into fast-track positions. Currently, they find themselves tempted to short circuit MBA work in order to get on the even faster tracks (up and down) of dot.com firms. In either case, they still think in terms of means-ends linkages and tolerate a miserable present because there is the promise of a much more glorious future. The whole notion of a project is permeated with the means-ends language of intentions, activities, and outcomes. Most of the examples in this chapter presume current sacrifices for future rewards and pleasure deferred until a later moment. The implied picture was much like one painted by Dorothy Parker when she said, "I hate writing, I love having written."

One tactic to create renewal is to reverse the way you think about means and ends. This insight is Roethlisberger's and again comes from his contacts with MBA students. Recall that many of them were preoccupied with how to be successful in the future and this made it difficult for them to relate to the present. As Roethlisberger described it, people who have excessive pre-occupations with success "do not seem to have the capacity for easy, inti-mate, and friendly association with other people. . . . [T]hey become enam-ored about words rather than the things to which words refer. As a result they have a greater facility in relating themselves to words and abstractions than to concrete events, things, and people" (1968, 89). Roethlisberger argues that people who are preoccupied with success ask the wrong question. They ask, "What is the secret of success?" when they should be asking, "What pre-vents me from learning here and now?" To be overly preoccupied with the future is to be inattentive toward the present where learning and growth take place. To walk around asking, "Am I a success or a failure?" is a silly question in the sense that the closest you can come to an answer is to say that everyone is both a success and a failure.

One way to renew an obsessive preoccupation with success is to alter the idea that the present is a means and the future is an end. The problem with this way of thinking is that, when the future comes, then it too becomes just another present that is yet another means to yet another future. To act as if the present is nothing until we achieve success is to take all meaning and sig-nificance out of the present. "When the future comes, it will be a present, and as we have taught ourselves to treat the present as insignificant, won't we have to posit more and new goals, bigger and better goals to strive for—ad infinitum?" (Roethlisberger 1968, 92.) To avoid this fate one can treat the future as a means and the present as an end. Future goals are selected for their capability to create a meaningful and significant present, one in which growth, learning, zest, and a sense of adventure are commonplace.

What are those goals that allow for zestful living in the present? Roesth-lisberger admits that this is partly an unanswerable question. But he also in-sists that it is a better question than the question, "What is the secret of suc-cess?" It is better because it

at least implies that the satisfactions we get from the present are relative to the ex-pectations we have and the demands we make of the present situation. It also implies that goals are not static things—like most other matters they are subject to change. It suggests that occasionally they need renovation and that they can be renovated in the direction of making the present more significant if we so choose. . . . Lastly I think this is a better question in that it is one to which at least each person can ob-tain a partial answer for himself in his own experience. (1968, 94)

Notice that in each of the three story lines for renewal, when a project is going well, it is not just because it is goal-driven. Projects also go well be-cause they cohere and utilize tacit knowing, because they make sense here and now, and because preoccupations are meaningfully tied to current on-going events. In none of these cases is the project purely instrumental to something else. Instead, it makes sense, right here and now, and continues to make sense.

A robust project contains goals that infuse the present with meaning. For example, my goal is to create a picture of renewal that will fit into Frost and Stablein's concept. But my goal is also to grasp an elusive phenomenon that annoys me and fascinates me and seems to defy articulation and is also one of the last lines of defense between despair and hope. The unrenewed life, in William James's image, may not be a life worth living. So renewal is not trivial stuff. But it retains its meaning for me, moment by moment, not because I am trying to please two editors, but because I am trying to craft meaningful phrases that evoke its nuances. In that sense, my goal is to create enthusiasm for renewal as a resource and as a topic for inquiry. And each sentence I write becomes a sensible attempt to pump up enthusiasm for renewal. In a way, I keep renewing my own quest to grasp renewal by worrying word by word. It is conceivable that when I finish, I will have crafted a chapter, each sentence of which has been a meaningful struggle for me, but the net result of which is not what Frost and Stablein want. My meaningful early morning hours of phrase making become their senseless late-night editorial nightmare. What they will have in hand is a heartfelt depiction of renewal, whose heart is unusually cerebral. The depiction is heartfelt because I took Roethlisberger seriously.

In my project to better understand renewal, some of my future goals actually served as the means to reach the present goal of meaningful moment-to-moment writing. Some of those future goals included discovering what I think about renewal, discovering possible order inherent in renewal, and experimenting with words, concepts, and comparisons that wrestle this tentative understanding into ideas that resonate with the experience of readers. Phrase by phrase, this project retains wholeness, sense, and a tight linkage between preoccupations and attention. I am not writing this solely to get Peter and Ralph's praise or to get another publication for a resume. What I am writing may fail to get either one, though I would certainly be disappointed if that happened. But even if things work out, all that means is that their praise and one more line on a resume become a short-lived present, haunted by the future-oriented question, whose praise am I next aiming for?

Goals that make for an interesting here and now forestall the unraveling of projects. Those who talk about pleasure in the process or about journeys being more significant than destinations (for example, Cavafy's poem called "Ithaca" in the second edition of the organizing book) understand that goals are crucial for their effect on the present rather than the future. They understand that there is more to instrumentality than meets the eye. The present is not the means to a meaningful future. Instead, the future is the means to a meaningful present. That reversal is a tactic that slows unraveling and hastens reraveling.

Renewal Through Dialogue

In each of the preceding three tactics, there are implicit conversations with authors (reading), colleagues (writing), and self and editors (goal setting). These implicit conversations are openings for dialogue, but they tend to be narrowly drawn. The conversations that lie at the center of my chapter are quite different from those that lie at the center of Jane Dutton's chapter. I single out her chapter because I read it before drafting this one, because Jane and I have had an ongoing conversation about the nature of renewal for years, and because the contrasts between her chapter and this one give readers some idea of the range of options available for renewing.

The feedback I sent to Jane after I read her chapter shows something of the differences that are involved. A portion of this feedback, edited out of an e-mail message sent on January 19, 2000, reads:

Garden framing works uncommonly well, largely because you take it seriously throughout and nuance it. I love the heading "rarely in the garden alone." Most meaningful section for me was weeding and saying no. . . . Weeding is tough for those of us who love variation, richness, surprise, novelty. But too much novelty can overwhelm and be self-defeating. . . . I think there are interesting touch points between us. You work on longer projects (e.g. 6 years) than I do. You think of renewing a life. I think of moments of renewal, which occur more often. Your garden is full of people. My garden is full of books. Your relations are face to face. Mine are vicarious. You weed in order to sustain large projects. I shrink projects in order to accept more of them. We both are co-created in dialogue, but your dialogues are continuous and mine are intermittent (a little dialogue goes a long way for me). You renew by grounding yourself in a customized barn, I renew by moving from one barn to another . . . and grow weary of the costs in such renewal overkill. . . . You know what you think when you see what they, your collaborators, say. I know what I think when I see what I say. . . . And we both get renewed by seeing what we say to each other.

A further contrast in our two styles of renewal, discussed in the same e-mail message, dates back to March 31, 1990, when we both were on the program at the fifth annual Texas Conference on Organizations. The conference theme was renewal. Jane had just purchased a new pair of glasses and the lenses were tinted with a faint rose color which, literally, meant that she saw the world through rose-colored glasses. The glasses I wore were reading glasses, whose lenses were ground so that I could see the small print in my notes, but nothing else. We literally held different lenses up against the world of Texas. And it is this difference that is the context for a continuation of the e-mail message to Jane about her chapter.

At the Texas conference, you saw the world through rose-colored glasses; I saw the world through close-up reading glasses, which meant that the audience that looked rose-colored to you, looked blurred to me. That has an uncanny carry over to the present. You have your renewing garden which you attend to alongside other people who are viewed by you appreciatively, supportively, as a rose-colored set of contributing companions. I have my renewing bookshelf, whose authors are blurred and who are brought to life by my projections and interpretations of what they might be saying that had never dawned on me before. Whatever tools we may drop [refers to firefighter fatalities that occur when people run from a fire but are slowed because they refuse to drop their tools], we probably should keep the rose-tinted glasses that enchant things and the reading glasses that blur things. Or perhaps, another wave of renewal will occur when you and I switch glasses. I see the rose-colored world and grow in appreciativeness. You see a blurred world and grow in structuring.

There are lots of contrasts here that could be pursued. I leave those to the reader. The point I want to make is that human relating is ground zero in renewal. In the Mann Gulch disaster, it was the partnership between Bob Sallee and Walter Rumsey that kept them from experiencing the full impact of the cosmology episode that killed the other thirteen crew members. I have tried to show that projects become more puzzling when there is a decrease in their integration, sense, and attentiveness. These are not abstract possibilities. They are concrete ways in which my own projects have fallen apart. Projects unravel for lots of reasons including ignorance, self-absorption, hubris, complacence, blind conformity, and distraction. It takes a partner, with a different set of lenses, to spot these lapses, to correct blind spots, and to make things new again.

I can think of no more basic source of renewal than dialogue. My wife, Karen, has been a steady source of alternative lenses and renewing throughout all my writing. If Frost and Stablein really want to know the secrets of renewal, then my compact advice is, "everyone needs a Karen." As in any long-lasting partnership (we were married in 1957), little rituals encrust the relationship and customize it, channel it, and stabilize it. In our case, there is a curious ritual in our dialogue, which I have tried over and over to stop, but which recurs nevertheless. Out of thin air, without any provocation, without any warning, and without any context, I find myself saying to Karen, "Do you have any words?" Say what? I'm never sure what words I am searching for or want to hear or what kind of magic those words might perform. And neither is she. I suppose it's not surprising that someone as invested in words as I am would blurt a plea for sense by asking for any old words. Yet, if I think that any old map will do if you're lost, then it's not much of a stretch to think that any old words will do if you're scared. How can I know what I think until I see what Karen says? Strange as all of this may sound, it seems to lie on top of a profound simplicity. The name of the game, triggered by my unfathomable query, "Any words?" is intimacy, not content. Whatever Karen's response, there is an affirmation of contact, of connection, of struggles, of interruptions that will pass, of sense that will be restored, of cocreation, of not being alone. That is sufficient bedrock for any renewal, at least as it plays out in my life.

DAVID BARRY

Mountain Dancing

A Reflection on Karl Weick's Work

HOW IS IT THAT Karl Weick consistently rates as a favorite read in organization studies? Is it his relentless pursuit of organizational knowledge, his discovery of profound truths, his wide scholarly grasp of organizing processes? Those of you who know his work will probably shake your heads "No." While Karl actually does all these things, and does them well, they aren't what people remember. Rather, it is that feeling of surprise, of having our heads turned around by his quizzical yet grounded ideas that we recall. Weick's work typically has an upending yet muted playfulness about it, a rich, living quality that variously flies, walks (often backward), and occasionally stops dead in its tracks to look in the rearview mirror. Unlike his opening remarks here, my students never groan, come back with blank stares, or fail to turn in their Weick-related assignments. On the contrary, his works always stir up chatter, invoke other stories, and spark speculation. In fact, I would say it is this "on-the-contrary" quality that both lies at the heart of his work and makes it a timeless favorite. Karl Weick's art is the art of paradox, of gracefully taking us left and then impishly calling from behind, "Look out on your right!"

Take this chapter as an example. It opens with Weick facing a tortuous state of affairs: "sluggish imagination, self-doubt, dead-end projects, rejection letters, low teaching ratings, indecision, blank stares, dismissive critics, a limited vocabulary, and all the other things that make scholarly work, anxious work." That, combined with a title which promises considerable depth—renewal in the face of loss—leads us to anticipate a soul-searching journey. Yet moments later, we're told that renewal is no big deal and that attempts to make it so are irritating. Just declare yourself renewed and get on with it, he suggests in his best salt-of-the-earth, Stephen King voice—big boys don't cry or succumb to the willies, they get up and play ball. "Well, this is a surprise," I think to myself. And then go on to conclude, "Okay, so maybe renewal *is* like burping the baby or blowing my nose. I never thought of it that way, but yes, I can empathize. Why must renewal necessarily be a grail-like quest accompanied by Hallelujah choruses?"

Yet, just as I conclude that renewal is going to be a walk down Easy Street, I'm thrown into a maelstrom of complex speculations. My surprise is even greater when I stop to consider that these speculations are born of a sluggish imagination and limited vocabulary! It looks like I have grossly underestimated things. Yes, renewal is indeed a small and simple thing. But it's small and simple the way microorganisms are small and simple—until they're put under the microscope. As Karl suggests, maybe renewal lies in small details. Maybe it's simply cocktail talk, an icebreaker—"Looks like fine weather for renewal, don't you think?" Maybe it's one of those backward sensemaking processes that creates more problems than it solves. Or maybe renewal is a fresh ending (rather than a stale one?), or even more teasingly, a "reolding." My left turn onto Easy Street abruptly ends with this startling precipice on the right.

This same surprising, contrary quality appears again and again at the micro-, meso-, and macrolevel. At the level of the paragraph, a triumphal mother, a grateful Duke Ellington and a reflective Warren Bennis are first proffered as grand exemplars of renewal, only to be reframed as instances of thrownness, of fragmentation, and of decisions that seem "less sensible as unanticipated consequences appear." Renewal goes from the felt to the logicked, from the earthily storied to the succinctly hypothesized, and then to the narratively analyzed.

At the level of theory building, what starts off as seemingly progressive deduction zigzags back on itself; just as we think we're going to hit the next step, we find the terrain has changed. For instance, in discussing the category "Projects that lose integration" Weick introduces the idea that losing meaning in thick relationships may feel like losing energy, which in turn can spark a push for renewal. Then, rather than leaving this as an established point, he pulls away the rug, saying, "But there is a tricky issue here. If the project makes sense because it is a meaningful whole, then efforts at renewal that focus solely on parts may be self-defeating. If people try to explicate wholes and put them into lists, or disassemble them for repair, these efforts may be destructive." Look out on your right!

Even at the larger level of the chapter, what seems to begin as autobiography hops, spins, and morphs into something altogether different. Self-admission turns into an academic treatise on renewal, one so engaging that we forget to ask where Weick went until we see him starting to reappear in little vignettes about his research.

In many ways then, we are repeatedly left whistling the chapter's refrain:

"What's the story? Why are we doing this? Where am I?" There seem to be echoes of his old-maps story here, where soldiers find their way out of the mountains, only to discover they've been using the wrong map. Here, he seems to be saying, "Don't rely on my map—your best bet is to just start walking." So, faced with many possible directions, we begin tacking back and forth along the mountainside, abandoning hope that the helpmate SIR COPE is going to amount to anything more than a wry smile carved in the rock. Gradually, after much backtracking through retrospective slopes, we find our own way out. And when we finally meet up with others at the Lodge, we have a good time telling each other about the various flowers or gems-in-the-rough we found along the way, and about how good it felt to walk without a guide after all.

Achieving all this is as much the writer's work as it is the theorist's. Yet it is not the work of any old writer, a mere "setting multiple themes in motion, themes that develop and define one another." Rather, it is more the work of a Dostoevsky, where multiple themes develop and define one another in surprising ways, where dailiness is turned into something extraordinary, where heavy-handed holding is replaced by a light dance step. It is truly dialogical work, the work of many logics seeking to turn one another into something new and fresh. This is at once its pleasure and the challenge it offers us—how can we hold our work lightly enough so as to hear other tunes, yet not so lightly that it goes fluttering off the cliff? How can we juggle our time so as to read widely in our field, and still read elsewhere, bringing these far-away worlds into our professional homes? How can we step away from ourselves enough to embrace others' perspectives, yet not lose our own voice in the process? While each of us must work these things out in our own ways, I'm nevertheless grateful for having seen Professor Weick's artful, balanced dances through the mountains—he lets me know it can be done.

An Invite to You the Reader

When I was first learning to paint, despairing over muddy canvases, a roommate suggested that I try copying some of the artists I liked. I came up with some mediocre renditions of Rembrandt, Monet, and Hopper. While the results were sad to say the least, the learning that resulted from this was surprisingly great—I got a much stronger sense of my own preferences, fears, and even a feeling for how these artists might have felt as they grappled with questions of light and dark. As I went on to experiment with my own style, I found that if I was stuck, it sometimes helped to ask, "Okay, how would old Claude have tackled this? . . . What might Rembrandt advise here?"

Similarly, I would invite you the reader to ask what your own work might be like if you followed a Weickian dance step—for instance, bringing in the contrary, engaging in multiple theming, getting deliberately lost in other writings, or being deliberately found by a Karen (or a Karl). You might do the same with the other researchers in this book, walking for a little while in their shoes, not with the intent of selling reproductions, but to acquire a more usable shoe collection of your own—sturdier hiking boots, more comfortable Lodge loafers, and maybe even some lighter dancing shoes.

JAMES D. LUDEMA

The Process of Renewal
Breathing New Life into Old Projects

IN CHARACTERISTIC style, Karl Weick has written a chapter that will be a source of renewal for many readers. It certainly renewed me. His superior blend of theoretical connections, practical suggestions, and personal stories enabled me to see and act in new ways on projects of my own. Specifically, after reading Karl's chapter, I reprioritized some projects by revisiting how each makes sense in the context of the past, present, and future; I began to experiment with writing associationally, voluminously, allegorically, continually, indiscriminately, respectfully, and passionately; and I read some works I've been longing to read for some time (which was truly a gift) and incorporated them into this document. More than anything, Karl's chapter inspired me to pick my nose up off the grindstone and reflect on which of my projects and which aspects of those projects energize me and give me life. This was an important step toward renewal.

In this sequel I want to invite you, the reader, to take a similar step. I will highlight three of Karl's ideas that I believe hold particular promise for the process of personal and professional renewal—narrative enrichment, original continuities, and dialogue. Along the way, I will invite you to apply Karl's ideas to a project of your choosing by responding to a short series of questions. The questions are adapted from appreciative inquiry (Cooperrider and Srivastva 1987; Ludema, Cooperrider, and Barrett 2001) and from Anne Huff's (1999) work on writing for scholarly publication. The purpose of the questions is to assist you in renewing your projects through narrative enrichment, original continuities, and dialogue.

What's Your Story?

I found Weick's notion of "narrative enrichment" to be particularly compelling. Weick suggests that when people initiate projects, they often do so for many reasons, some of which are available only at the tacit level of awareness. A project "makes sense" because it is held together by a set of interrelated tacit and explicit story lines that, in combination, provide a meaningful whole. There can come a point, however, when the story loses its coherence and the project begins to surrender its meaning. It becomes less vivid and less connected to the big scheme of things, and consequently, it loses its attractiveness and its ability to engage the creative passions. In essence, it runs out of gas.

The remedy for this is not reflection or analysis, which Weick characterizes as "blunt instruments when it comes to pattern recognition and pattern restoration." Rather, the solution is narrative enrichment, or reenchantment of the stories that gave life to the project in the first place. Two kinds of reconnection occur when we enrich our narratives. First, subthemes, both tacit and explicit, that animated the original story are reconnected with one another to strengthen the story's plot line. Fragments that lay disconnected and therefore diminished in meaning come together once again into a coherent and compelling whole. Second, we reconnect with the sources of energy embedded in the story. As we revisit and reconstruct that which attracted us to the project in the first place, we begin to remember it more fully, see it more richly, and appreciate it more deeply. This restores a body of knowledge (social, emotional, intellectual, spiritual) that appeals to us and draws us back in.

At this point, I'd like to invite you to begin a process of narrative enrichment as a first step toward renewing a project that, for whatever reason, has lost some of its meaning. In keeping with Weick's idea of opening up to intuition, I'd encourage you to pick a project that appeals to you intuitively, one that inspires you and that, no matter how many other things get in the way, keeps calling to you from the margins of your imaginings. Whichever project you chose, make it something that in one way or another excites and delights you. Then, consider the following questions. You may certainly do this alone and ask the questions of yourself, but I would encourage you to involve a friend or a colleague, someone with whom you can openly share your aspirations and who will help you advance your ideas. You or your colleague may want to take notes so you are able to refer back to them.

Question #1—What attracted you?

Take a moment to reflect back to when you first decided to embark on your project, and ask what attracted you. What were your initial excitements and sources of joy?

Question #2—High point

During your project, I'm sure you had some ups and downs, some peaks and valleys, some high points and low points. I'd like you to reflect for a moment on a high point, a time when you felt fully alive, engaged, and fulfilled by your involvement. What was going on? What made that moment possible? What was it about you that made it possible? Who were the significant others (individual and institutional), and what was it about them that made it possible?

Question #3—Your gifts

As it relates to this and other projects like it, what are the things that you do best—your gifts, abilities, hopes, aspirations, commitments, values, approaches, best practices, and so on—things that you want to preserve and strengthen as you move into the future?

Who Will Play Your Music if You Don't Do it Yourself?

The second idea from Weick is his notion of "original continuities." He suggests that because we as scholars are always building on the ideas and contributions of others, there are very few truly unique projects. This need not be a cause for anxiety or disappointment. It can be a powerful source of renewal. The opportunity is to imitate others in such a way that no one else can reproduce. Unreproducible imitating creates original continuities. The imitation provides the continuity; the unreproducibility provides the originality. This, claims Weick, is what Duke Ellington did when he lifted phrases from some of the solos played by his musicians and combined them in a manner no other composer could imitate. Here, I want to focus on the idea of originality and leave a discussion of continuity for the final section.

In recent years, compelling research on positive emotions has begun to emerge in the fields of psychology and organizational behavior. Fredrickson's (1998) broaden-and-build model is one exemplar. According to the model, negative emotions (for example, fear, anger, sadness) narrow an individual's momentary thought-action repertoire toward specific actions promoting survival (for example, running, fighting, withdrawal). Positive emotions (for example, joy, interest, contentment), by contrast, broaden an individual's momentary thought-action repertoire. In the context of a project, for example, joy creates the urge to play, physically, socially, intellectually, and artistically. Play, in the short term, gives rise to increased levels of imagination, invention, and experimentation, which broaden a person's thought-action repertoire. Over the long haul, as a person continues to play, he or she will develop enduring physical, social, and cognitive resources that can be drawn on later, creating an "upward spiral" (see Aspinwall 1998) of joy, play, imagination, and experimentation.

Interestingly, Fredrickson (2000) found that the best way for a person to create and sustain positive emotions is to search for positive meaning. This can be done by appreciating the "meaning of life" on religious, spiritual, or philosophical levels; reframing adverse events in a positive light (positive appraisal); infusing ordinary events with positive value; building meaningful relationships with others; or imagining and pursuing a meaningful purpose (Folkman 1997; Folkman et al. 1997; Frankl 1959; Affleck and Tennen 1996; Davis, Nolen-Hoeksema, and Larson 1998). This final option, imaging and pursuing a meaningful purpose, can be a powerful source of energy for a project that seems to be losing steam. It allows you to reconnect with the deeper significance of your work and to infuse your current activities with new meaning by placing them in the context of your aspirations. In turn, this allows you to revitalize your project by reconnecting it with a sense of novelty, excitement, possibility, and forward movement. In Weick's words for us here, a robust project contains goals that "are selected for their capability to create a meaningful and significant present, one in which growth, learning, zest, and a sense of adventure are commonplace." He adds, "The present is not the means to a meaningful future. Instead, the future is the means to a meaningful present."

The following question is offered as a way for you to reconnect with your image of a meaningful future for your project and, more broadly, for your professional contribution. In a playful way, it invites you to look to the future and imagine the project in "full bloom"—its activities, its impact, and its significance to the field and to the world. Read the question, and then take a few minutes to imagine the project in it fullness in such a way that it fills you with joy, excitement, and a sense of adventure. You may want to block out distractions and sit in a relaxed position with your eyes closed to allow your imaginings room to roam and freedom to cohere.

Question #4—Image of the future

Imagine that tonight you fall into a deep relaxing sleep, and when you awake, you see that a miracle has occurred. Your project is in full bloom, and it has become everything you ever hoped it could be. You can truly say, without reservation, that this *is* the project of your dreams. What do you see? What does it look like? What's going on around you? What are you doing? Who else is involved and what are they doing? What are the products? What impact is the project having in your life . . . in your field . . . in the world at large? What is the original contribution of which you are most proud?

Do You Have Any Words?

The third idea from Weick is his notion of "dialogue." He says that human relating is ground zero in renewal. There are three ways in which this is true. First, relationships are a source of novelty. When we are stuck, stymied, or derailed, reading or having a conversation with a friend, colleague, or stranger can introduce fresh ideas and create new connections that help us restart, clear up the confusion, or get back on track. I love the way Weick puts it when he says that for him reading "quiets the chatter of logic, redirects meddling into imagined worlds . . . [and] stirs up intuitive understanding, tacit knowing, and wisdom."

Second, relationships provide a sense of wholeness. They are an essential source of assurance that our lives and work somehow have meaning in the larger scheme of things. I appreciated Weick's description of his relationship with Jane Dutton. It is clear that their conversations have been a source of enjoyment, growth, and creativity for each of them. As a result, they and their writings have been a source of learning and inspiration for many others. I was also touched by Weick's description of how his relationship with his wife, Karen, provides "an affirmation of contact, of connection, of struggles, of interruptions that will pass, of sense that will be restored, of co-creation, of not being alone." In this sense, his question, "Do you have any words?" seems perfectly reasonable to me. It is an implicit recognition that to be complete, we all need to be joined and supplemented by others.

Third, relationships are a source of social validation. This brings us back around to the idea of continuity in the phrase "original continuities." Weick suggests that projects often begin with "one's own music," but as the project unfolds, one's own music begins to fade. People question the distinctiveness, quality, and size of their own contribution, and they become increasingly preoccupied with issues of voice. Self-absorption increases, learning decreases, and projects eventually lose their energy. This happens because people allow their attention to self to become disconnected from attention to the world. With little input from the external environment, projects lose their connection to other people's work, and their resonance and relevance are diminished.

To restart projects that are stalled by self-absorption, people need to connect their work more closely to the external world. Weick makes a compelling case for how this can be done by reading, writing, goal setting, and dialogue. Reading allows us to engage as "active listeners" with other authors and to learn from, imitate, and extend their ideas. Writing enables us to put our ideas out into the mainstream to see how they are received and supplemented. Goal setting permits us to locate our projects in a place that is meaningful to us and to others. Dialogue with colleagues makes it possible for us to see with a different set of lenses, to spot our lapses, to correct our blind spots, and to engage in the co-construction of novelty and renewal.

Anne Huff concurs with Weick on the centrality of dialogue in scholarly projects. She claims succinctly that "scholarship is conversation" (1999, 3). The content and process of scholarship is learned from other scholars. They shape the way one understands the world, define the issues worth our attention, and provide an essential audience to appreciate, assess, and interact with one's work. But, she says, the idea that scholarship depends on interaction with other scholars is often forgotten in the research and writing process. To help overcome this omission, she offers a series of small exercises to jumpstart the conversation process. As a final step in your project-renewal process, I offer one of Anne's exercises and one of my own. I will shape the exercises in the form of questions. The purpose of the questions is to assist you in identifying a group of conversants who can help you revitalize your project.

Question #5—Primary conversants (written works)

Imagine yourself at the door of a crowded room of conversing scholars (past and present) in the process of choosing which group you want to join. Which three or four written works produced by these scholars would you like to be the primary conversants for your project?

Anne writes (1999) that in her experience, this is not an easy question because most scholars are interested in many topics and additions that distract from their primary message. This is precisely why it is important to force yourself to focus on a limited set of works to get started. She recommends:

- Weed out conversants that define a large field and look instead for those written specifically about your topic of interest.
- Choose conversants that you find most interesting, even though you do not necessarily agree with the points made, rather than conversants that support your point of view but do not add much to it.
- Include a new voice or two in your conversant list but lean toward well-known works that a broader audience will recognize and find interesting. (48–49)

The final question is an invitation to enact Weick's proposition that "human relating is ground zero in renewal." It invites you to identify a small group of collaborative partners with whom you can converse (talk, e-mail, imagine, dream, analyze, doubt, start, stop, advance, stretch, inquire, wonder, explore, read, and write) to begin the renewal of your project.

Question #6—Partners in dialogue (people)

Imagine that you move on to a smaller, quieter, more intimate room that contains all of your most-esteemed friends and colleagues (old, new, and possible). Which three or four people in this room would you like to be you primary dialogue partners for your project?

This question, like the previous one, is not an easy question to answer, primarily because different projects require different kinds of dialogue partners and because different people have different levels of interest in person-to-person dialogue. However, I encourage you to:

- Choose partners who share your interests. To the extent that your project will help to advance their projects, they will be more passionately invested in the conversation.

- Select at least one leading scholar in your field. To engage with "the best minds" is a great way to stretch your thinking, writing, and excitement about the project.

- Include at least one person who will support you unconditionally through the highs and lows, ups and downs of the project. There is no greater gift than a person who will be a steady source of affirmation, contact, connection, cocreation, and words when your own resources simply are not enough.

To conclude, renewal, when it is at its best, is ongoing and ordinary. It is something we do each day to infuse meaning and vitality into our work, our relationships, and our lives. I agree with Weick that "renewing is all we ever do," that it "resides in the small details that lead to small wins," and that it "creates experience rather than responds to experience." My hope is that Karl's chapter and this sequel have, in some small way, allowed you to renew your projects so that they energize you and give you life.

Toxins and Antidotes

Parting Thoughts on Researcher Resilience and Renewal

A colleague of ours once commented: "I think academic life is a privileged life, and I am either amused or outraged, depending on my mood, at my colleagues who have somehow persuaded themselves that it is a burdened, difficult kind of career. Few people can earn a living doing things that are so close to their major life interests. Instead they pour their energy into tasks defined by others. As academics, we have a high degree of choice. We ought to be profoundly grateful" (Quinn, O'Neill, and Debebe 1996, 427). By and large, we agree with this sentiment and think that you will find that this freedom to pursue intellectual pursuits in this way is reflected in the stories of the journeys in this book. However, as we also have seen in this volume there are aspects of researchers' lives that create burdens, that cause emotional pain and suffering and that become toxic, draining vitality and productive drive. Some of this drain comes from the impact of negative feedback on our work. Some comes from the very opposite, enthusiastic acceptance of what we create. And some flows from institutional demands that we, as researchers, face. As we noted in our conversation about the community of scholars, these experiences become toxic when they generate in us a loss of self esteem, or confidence or we feel hopeless, overwhelmed or undermined by them (Frost 2003). Then perhaps, we lose our way; we find we are not doing fresh work; we are caught in the grip of other people's agendas. Among many possible arenas for discussion as we move to close this book on scholarly renewal we have chosen three in which these hazards present themselves: Getting Published; Getting Noticed; and Getting Used. We believe these have resonance for each of us at some point in our researcher journeys. We will also discuss possible sources of prevention, intervention, and recovery within each of these arenas (Frost 2003).

Getting Published

"Self disclosure puts it on the line. . . . Writers, especially poets and novelists, spill the essence of their souls into immutable black and white" (Clinton 1995, 246). While we, as researchers may not quite be writing poetry or novels, we do reveal ourselves in our creations and none of us likes to be told that our work is flawed or that it has failed to measure up to some standard held important by our peers. This is so particularly if professional acceptance of our work is also a means to tenure or promotion, ensuring a guaranteed livelihood.

A process of reviews, revisions, and rejections is vital if we are to have a robust, vibrant field of enquiry. Submitting one's work for peer-review ensures that there always will be feedback that may not please us when we receive it. Given the amount of intellectual and emotional effort we put into our work and the time and grind it inevitably takes to prepare a submissible manuscript, it is perhaps not surprising that, at least initially, we tend to respond to criticisms more viscerally than to words of encouragement. "This is my baby! This is a reflection of me!" However rational we might be about the feedback experience, however many times we have been through this process, and however constructive the feedback from editors and reviewers might actually be, dealing with criticism is rarely something we do with equanimity. (The situation is made worse if the dignity of the researcher is shredded by personal attacks by editors and reviewers.)

In response to editorial feedback, we resort, perhaps to shoving the manuscript in a desk drawer after we have taken a first cursory read through the letter from an editor and the accompanying reviews, only returning to the package much later when we have the courage to absorb its messages. This may be good practice. Sometimes, however, reactions to this feedback creates an unfortunate stumbling block to a productive research journey. We may not open that drawer for months or even years, losing valuable momentum and find that the time has passed for our ideas and findings to be a useful contribution to our professional community. Receiving the reviews to her initial submissions, then–assistant professor Joan Gallos commented:

Three letters came. I quickly interpreted them as flat rejections—letters that I now realize, years later as a journal editor myself, were encouraging, complimentary, much more suggestions for refocusing and revising than recommendations to throw in the towel. But, inexperienced and too quickly discouraged, I stopped writing articles. I put the three letters, my three initial journal submissions, and notes for additional pieces in the bottom drawer of my desk. (Gallos 1996, 11)

Getting Noticed

There comes a time, sooner or later for most researchers in our field, that their work gets noticed. It triggers a positive reaction in someone, somewhere. The recognition may be international, or our work may attract national or local attention. The approval may come from peers, funding agencies, sometimes from practitioners or from the general public. Such attention can be very gratifying. After all, one objective of having one's work published is to have it read and even remembered (as Denny Gioia suggested) by others. This perhaps confirms that we are doing valued work, and may help us to discover where we need to go next.

Getting noticed can lead to additional, important benefits for our work. We find potential new collaborators and more confidently seek new resources for future projects. We may be invited to become reviewers of the work of our peers, or to participate in topic-specific conferences or to appear on select panels to discuss our own and others' work. Doctoral students may seek us out to be their mentors and supervisors. All this is good, for our work, for our profession, and for our egos. However, the increased visibility that accompanies good work has its downside. The pull of invitations can link us with new contacts but it can also wreak havoc on the time and space that the researcher needs to develop new ideas, to get studies launched, to bring a project to completion and to complete or revise a manuscript. The pile-up of manuscripts to review for editors with deadlines and authors with expectations can inform us on emergent research in our field but often reviewing can simply bog us down as we wade through submissions that may or may not pass muster or need a great deal of repair. Having students to supervise is a wonderful part of our profession. It helps us renew ourselves and the field. It can also take time from work we seek to develop and do as we attend to the important mentoring and training of others.

The point here is not to demean these sources of being noticed. The problem we see is that one can become overwhelmed with the demands of others to the detriment of our own needs, especially if we find it difficult to say "No!" We live in an over-enriched world. There rarely is anyone to help us establish and maintain boundaries to limit what we take on board professionally. Everything looks inviting and when we are approached to do some new project, we are good at dropping from our short-term memories the countless other commitments we have to meet. (They return with a vengeance later as the apparently far-away deadline suddenly looms on the near horizon.) We can become creatively constrained by these conditions. One colleague recently commented that he was being "eaten alive" by all the demands on him and had to escape to a period of seclusion to re-discover his own voice and to get on with important work that had been side-lined for months because of other deadlines.

Getting Used

Most of us researchers live and work in formal institutions that have as their mandate delivering teaching and doing research. Teaching is a vital and important part of our contribution to our students, to our institutions and to our field. (See Andre and Frost 1997.) Similarly, we are citizens of our schools and our civic contributions through committee work, and other collegial inputs help keep resilient our places of work. So what are the "getting used" issues? The drain on our research comes in part from over-exposure to teaching and/or to citizenship activities. This may be particularly true for women and for members of minority groups. They are often underrepresented in the demography of the institution but over-utilized on committees and on special institutional assignments since there is a press on university institutions from various stakeholders to show strong representation of women and of minorities so they look "right" to outside interest groups. So, for example, the lone female professor (or, the small cadre of women on the faculty) may find herself on many committees and asked to make many presentations on behalf of her faculty, so that the female voice is represented and heard. The same can occur for members of minority groups. There is then precious little time left over to devote to read, to think anew, to reflect on things, to create new work unhurriedly. Productive work gets jammed into "extra hours" of a day or a week, at great personal cost to the individual.

Joanne Martin speaks poignantly about such pressures:

Sometimes this welcome (from women, minorities, and some white men, from all over campus) overwhelmed me. There was no way I could create a research publication record sufficient to get tenure and be responsive to the number of students who wanted to contact me. . . . When I held office hours, the line of students wound around the hallway and out into the terrace.

A second source of institutional toxins is the competitive ethos engendered in the cultures of many well-known business schools and associate research institutions. In one sense this is as it should be. The drive for high standards can add to the already present inner work ethic of most scholars and creates an ongoing "buzz" of energy and application from those who are in the organization. There is precious little time to "rest on one's laurels," as everyone works long and hard to do good research. So collectively, productivity increases. This condition can become quite "intoxicating," as everyone joins in the frenzy and feels the press of continued high expectations from their culture and from the institution. A researcher's application to his work can become all-consuming. There is little time for enjoying other facets of living (the aesthetics that Denny Gioia talks about, the time with a child, as Joanne Martin observes, and the "getting of a life," as Anne Huff urges) and there is little opportunity to replenish one's creative juices or just having time to "be." The signature of this life is ceaseless pursuit of output and striving to stay with the relentless and often oppressive norm of publish or perish (in the sense of falling behind the pack).

This press becomes even more intense when the institution joins some rating game and inevitably introduces more, different, and more frequent evaluations of the work of its researchers. The problem is not with evaluation. This is a normal part of taking stock in any organization. The problem comes in the potential focus of the criteria (how does this help us in the ratings?) and in the creeping mindlessness of the process (Gioia and Corley 2002). Large amounts of time are devoted to having members of an institution evaluate one another, at the expense of attending to the work of research itself. Even scholars with established reputations, whom the field needs for their considered and wise contributions of ideas and insight, can find themselves wearing down on a treadmill of production and evaluation.

While everyone needs to get feedback and to be evaluated from time to time, there is an urgent need for thoughtful, humane, and flexible systems of assessment in many of our institutions. We think many existing systems foster isolation, workaholism, and burnout. The institution may prosper, at least in the short-run, but we fear that a process that burns up well-trained human beings and replaces them with eager new recruits is not healthy. Nor is it necessarily the best way to nurture creative and productive researchers over the long term. In many hard sciences the best work is done by researchers who are relatively young. This is not necessarily so in our disciplines. Many good ideas and breakthroughs come from more experienced members of the community who have been thinking and publishing over a protracted period of time, if they have not burned out along the way.

Toward Solutions that Restore and Renew

> When I am feeling overwhelmed and have lost my way, I start somewhere, anywhere and proceed from there.
>
> Aileen McMorran

GETTING CLEAR

We can lose our way at almost any point in our journeys as scholars. Feedback on our manuscripts that freezes us in our tracks, finding ourselves overwhelmed by the seductions of our emerging or established visibility, or feeling oppressed by the excess of demands our institutions place upon us. At these points we may find ourselves wondering how we got to this point and—importantly, from the point of view of feeling creative, vital, and empowered—who we are and where are we going to move forward constructively. Finding effective ways to emphatically say "NO!" is an essential element of maintaining or regaining clarity and space for ourselves.

Feedback on our work will always have an inside track to our emotions. Our defenses will always rise up as we first encounter the judgments of others on our work. Acknowledging this likelihood is a first step to dealing with our fears and anxieties. Assuming, until proven otherwise, that our peers mean to be constructive and helpful is another step toward being receptive to this information and gaining clarity to its meaning. Having strategies to deal with feedback in an emotionally effective way becomes important as do techniques to cognitively process the observations, concerns, and recommendations of reviewers and editors. Susan Ashford provides some useful advice on this count.

The Emotional Component: Protect Yourself

"I always read my reviews in a secluded place (not in my office). I know several others who do this as well." She points out that when she does not do this, perhaps opening and reading a feedback letter, mistakenly taking it for copies of reviews on others, she takes in the feedback on her own work "intravenously," that is without being mentally prepared for it. "This feedback is always toughest on my soul" (Ashford 1996b, 124). She continues: "So what preparation do I do in this secluded place, with my reviews sitting unopened on my knees? I tell myself that the feedback I am about to receive is about my work, not about me, that my work is only a small part of myself. . . . I prepare myself for pain and I open the letter. . . . Recognizing that the review process has some inherently negative aspects makes it easier to deal with." (Her strong admonition here is that one *not* take the feedback process personally.)

The Intellectual Component: Be Open; Be Persistent

Openness

Shortly after I receive my reviews, whether the decision is a revise and resubmit or a reject, I break up each review into specific points. I then create a setup for responding to each review . . . a template in which I state the reviewer's points in order, each followed by "Response:" and room for my future response. Thus I create a lengthy document, most of it blank, awaiting my responses. No matter how gloomy I feel after receiving the reviews, I get this done. Then after several days (sometimes weeks), I pick up the response templates and begin by answering those points that are easiest. Once I am engaged in the task and the task is broken into small pieces, I generally can keep going and soon build a head of steam to deal with the more difficult issues. (Ashford 1996b, 125)

Persistence

The most important advice I can give is to keep going, whether it is in redoing the study with better measures and more constructs or in revising and resubmitting it to the journal (or to another journal following a rejection), the important thing is to keep moving. (Ashford 1996b, 126)

Saying No!

Another aspect of clearing space is to find ways to tap our own instincts and intuitions about what we need to do next, to begin to listen to the ideas we might have for next steps or new inspirations for our work. This is pretty tough to do when we have made commitments that stretch endlessly ahead. The poet David Whyte observes that we cannot find or rediscover our own voice until we start to clear space for it by saying "No!" sufficiently often and forcibly, so that there is room for the "Yes" inside us to be heard. This "Yes" is our connection to our creativity and to finding new ways to develop and present new work.

The *via negativa* is the discipline of saying *no* when we have as yet no clarity about those things to which we can say *yes*. Not only is it bound to turn up by the law of averages, but it will also appear *because* we have said *no* to so much. . . . One way to come to *yes* is to say *no* to everything that does not nourish and entice our secret inner life out into the world. (Whyte 1996, 137–38).

This is hard to do but it can be accomplished with determination and persistence. Jane's weeding out non-productive projects and tasks is another way of doing this. Karl talks of shrinking projects to accomplish the same end. Joanne creates five-year plans to provide a strategic focus for her time and work. Steve knows that he is good at working in puddles and avoids getting trapped in long runs of work on the same topic. If a research agenda does not "speak to him," it will not endure and he lets it go.

Sometimes the decision is made for us, through outside events. One of Peter's big noes came from an encounter with cancer. All preset yeses vanished from the table for a while to make way for surgery and physical and emotional recovery. Somewhat ironically, this time of more easily managed es opened up a space in which having quiet time to reflect and explore possible meanings of the cancer episode. The "yes" space it produced for him was the impetus for a stream of research on the topic of toxic emotions and their implications for workplace outcomess (Frost 2003).

Getting Connected

No one makes a career alone.

Czarniawska, *Narrative Approach in Organization Studies*

Researchers vary in the degree to which they prefer to work alone or with others and for many of us the choice to work by oneself or in a dyad or in a team may vary according to the nature of the research project. Yet it is abundantly clear that our contributors here frequently look to others for advice, encouragement or support as part of the process of maintaining perspective and to keep alert and refreshed in their work. We talked earlier of the role of a community of scholars as an important factor in the lives of all researchers. Finding helpful connections within that community is one antidote to the isolation that we sometimes feel when things are going badly (or too well, so that we lose a sense of proportion or direction). Support networks of colleagues on site or virtually (connecting with colleagues at other institutions) provide opportunities for researchers to talk about the work they do and how they feel about it. Being in such a setting can help restore confidence and sense of empowerment. We hear the views and even the stories of other researchers, helping us see the connections between our own experiences, dilemmas, and difficult decisions and those of others. Talking to a supportive group about difficult craft issues, or about hard-to-handle feedback or confusing outcomes, and even about the personal costs of their work can sometimes serve to release someone who is stuck from pent-up stress and discouragement.

Mentors, too, are for many of us a crucial part of growing into a successful research career and of helping us get unstuck or to regain a sense of purpose and regained commitment to our work. Barbara recalls how Edgar Schein helped her gain access to business organizations in Boston when she was a visitor at MIT. She (as do others) singles out Lotte Bailyn as a mentoring influence on her career. The absence of such collegial mentoring was one factor in prolonging Joan Gallos's withdrawal from writing after receiving the initial reviews of her work and Anne Huff recalls similar difficulties in her first job. A key part of renewal for scholars is the quality of the responsiveness of colleagues at their institutions and, increasingly more globally, thanks to the reach of the internet. An essential aspect of getting connected is to discover and nurture a network of colleagues who will take the time to read one's work constructively, or help interpret feedback from journal editors and reviewers. One can see this proactivity demonstrated in the contributions of all the authors in this monograph.

Sometimes these colleagues become collaborators, as Jane Dutton finds. At other times they are members of a support boat that includes family and friends who have a keen understanding of the researcher's struggle, as Joanne depicts it. The connection can come through books. Karl communicating with Jane comments: "Your garden is full of people. My garden is full of books. Your relations are face to face. Mine are vicarious." Either way there is a connect with others who can make a difference to our capacity to endure and to renew. Barbara too makes vivid the connecting power of books and of their authors. On reading the book *Contingency, Irony and Solidarity*, by Richard Rorty, she writes, "When I came to the end of page 73 in Rorty's book, I began to cry. . . . It was the first time when somebody spoke about me, when somebody spoke directly to me, not to somebody who might be in some way similar to me."

Getting a Life

> Remember why you are doing it all.
>
> Joanne Martin

One common theme across the stories of renewal is that each of the authors has retained a passion for their work and for living, even though this feeling might have waxed and waned over time. Each of them makes reference to others outside the boundaries of their own work lives who keep them open to a life beyond their research endeavors which in turn enriches what they do. Jane, Joanne, Anne, and Karl talk affectionately about the lives they have with their families. Steve refers to his concern for an ailing father. Denny does not mention his family in his chapter but Ralph and Peter know, from conversations with him, how strong are his affections for his children and the role his family plays in taking him "away" from his work. This is true for Andy, given our knowledge of attention to family time (and, of course, his passion for breeding cattle). Barbara, though, in her own words, is "single, traveling, professor, instead of a journalist," makes it clear how important her family of friends is to her. They are an integral part of her life. You can count both Ralph and Peter in this set.

Getting a life is not necessarily about the link to a family or a partner. It is about finding meaning in a world apart from our work. The point here is that when we are engaged in relationships and activities outside of work or when we are simply "being," with no agenda to accomplish or goal to attain, we are more likely to let go of the preoccupations of work that might blind us to other pleasures, meanings, and benefits of life. It may be the happiness (or sadness) of our children that teases or jolts us out of our work agendas. Joanne notes: "tickling my son's belly, and hearing him grin, was a great reentry from work to home." It may be the beauty of a work of art we see or a photograph we create that lifts our eyes from the routines and rigors of our work regimes, as Denny finds. It might be the unhooking from thinking about anything but the dance, as Peter learns as he does, with his wife and with others, the intricate steps of Scottish country dancing and as Ralph discovers with the Monday evening Greek dancing group, where professional achievement counts for nothing.

When all is said and done, we do live privileged lives. But we need to work on ourselves and our institutions and our networks to get the most out of this condition. Finding ways to stay refreshed, to renew excitement for our craft ensures that we and our communities will remain healthy. The contributions of our eight story tellers and fourteen commentators provide a rich array of options for you to think about as you work out your own recipes for renewal. We hope you will do so playfully and with success and that you will pass your own hard-won lessons to others in the field. Also, like Barbara we believe in the institution of the university. We think her eloquent words on this matter are a fitting way to close: "Perhaps 'universitas'—a community of people working and living enthusiastically together in order to explore reality—never existed anywhere but in people's fantasy, or perhaps it is difficult to actualize in the mass education universities of today, but it does not matter. It is beautiful as an idea and should be cherished for that." We hope that this book makes a useful contribution to that idea.

Ralph and Peter

2003

References

AACSB. (2001a). *Guide to doctoral programs in business and management in the USA*. Download 30 October 2001. http://aacsb.edu/Publications/Publications/doctoral_ei.html

———. (2001b). *Newsline*. Winter 2001. Download 25 October 2001. http://www.aacsb.edu/publications/newsline/view.asp?year = 2001&file = wndegrees_t3.html

———. (2003a). Largest U.S. b-school's by enrollment. *ENewsline*. Accessed 4 February 2003. http://www.aacsb.edu/publications/enewsline/archive_data/survey-enrollment4.asp

———. (2003b). Projected doctoral supply/demand gap. *ENewsline*. Accessed 29 August 2003. http://www.aacsb.edu/publications/enewsline/archive_data/dd-doctoral-gap.jpg

Affleck, G., and Tennen, H. (1996). Construing benefits from adversity: Adaptational significance and dispositional underpinnings. *Journal of Personality 64*: 899–922.

Alvesson, M. (1993). *Cultural perspectives on organizations*. Cambridge: Cambridge University Press.

———, and Deetz, S. (1996). Critical theory and postmodernism approaches to organizational studies. In S. R. Clegg, C. Hardy, and W. R. Nord (Eds.), *Handbook of organization studies* (pp. 191–217). Thousand Oaks, CA: Sage.

Andre, R., and Frost, P. J. (1996). *Researchers hooked on teaching: Noted scholars discuss the synergies of teaching and research*. Thousand Oaks, CA: Sage.

Ashford, S. J. (1996a). Working with doctoral students: Reflections on doctoral work past and present. In P. J. Frost and M. S. Taylor (Eds.), *Rhythms of academic life* (pp. 153–58). Thousand Oaks, CA: Sage.

———. (1996b). The publishing process: The struggle for meaning. In P. J. Frost and M. S. Taylor (Eds.), *Rhythms of academic life* (pp. 119–27). Thousand Oaks, CA: Sage.

———, Rothbard, N. P., Piderot, S. K., and Dutton, J. E. (1998). Out on a limb: The role of context and impression management in selling gender-equity issues. *Administrative Science Quarterly 43*: 23–57.

Aspinwall, L. G. (1998). Rethinking the role of positive affect in self-regulation. *Motivation and Emotion 22*: 1–32.

Astley, W. G., and Van de Ven, A. H. (1983). Central perspectives and debates in organization theory. *Administrative Science Quarterly 28*, 2: 245–74.

Balogun, J., Huff, A. S., and Johnson, P. (2003). Three responses to the methodological challenges of studying strategizing. *Journal of Management Studies 40*, 1: 197–225.

Barker, J. R. (2003). Forum Introduction. *Management Communication Quarterly*, 17: 126-28.

Barley, S. R. (1983a). Codes of the dead: The semiotics of funeral work. *Urban Life 10*: 459–81.

———. (1983b). Semiotics and the study of occupational and organizational culture. *Administrative Science Quarterly 28*: 393–413.

———. (1986). Technology as an occasion for structuring: Evidence from observations of CT scanners and the social order of radiology departments. *Administrative Science Quarterly 31*: 78–108.

———. (1988). On technology, time, and the social order: Technically induced change in the temporal organization of radiological work. In F. A. Dubinskas (Ed.), *Making time: Ethnographies of high technology organizations* (pp. 123–69). Philadelphia, PA: Temple University Press.

———. (1990a). The alignment of technology and structure through roles and networks. *Administrative Science Quarterly 35*: 61–103.

———. (1990b). Images of imaging: Notes on doing longitudinal field work. *Organization Science 1*: 220–47.

———. (1996). Technicians in the workplace: Ethnographic evidence for bringing work into organization studies. *Administrative Science Quarterly 41*: 404–41.

———. (1998). What can we learn from the history of technology? *The Journal of Engineering and Technology Management 15*: 237–55.

———, Freeman, J., and Hybels, R. (1992). Strategic alliances in commercial biotechnology. In N. Norhia and R. G. Eccles (Eds.), *Networks and organizations: Structure, form and action* (pp. 311–45). Cambridge, MA: Harvard Business School Press.

——— and Knight, D. B. (1992). Toward a cultural theory of stress complaints. In B. M. Staw and L. L. Cummings (Eds.), *Research in organizational behavior* (vol. 14, pp. 1–48). Greenwich, CT: JAI Press.

——— and Kunda, G. (1992). Design and devotion: Surges of rational and normative ideologies of control in managerial discourse. *Administrative Science Quarterly 37*: 363–99.

——— and Kunda, G. (2001). Bringing work back in. *Organization Science 12*: 75–94.

———, Meyer, G., and Gash, D. (1988). Cultures of culture: Academics, practitioners, and the pragmatics of normative control. *Administrative Science Quarterly 33*: 24–60.

Barnes, W. (1989). *Managerial catalyst: The story of London business school 1964–1989.* London: Paul Chapman.

Barry, B. (1989). Management education in Great Britain. In W. J. Byrt (Ed.), *Management education: An international survey* (pp. 56–78). London: Routledge.

———, Dowling, P. J., and Tonks, G. (1995). Management education in Australia. Department of Management Working Paper Series, University of Tasmania.

Bateson, M. C. (1989). *Composing a life*. New York: Plume Book.

Baum, J. A. C., and Rowley, T. J. (2002). Companion to organizations: An introduction. In J. A. C. Baum (Ed.), *Companion to organizations* (pp. 1–34). Malden, MA: Blackwell.

Becker, H. S. (1998). *Tricks of the trade*. Chicago: University of Chicago Press.

Berlin, I. (2001). *Against the current: Essays in the history of ideas*. Princeton University Press.

Beyer, J. M., Chanove, R. G., and Fox, W. B. (1995). The review process and the fates of manuscripts submitted to AMJ. *Academy of Management Journal 38*, 5: 1219–60.

Bijker, W. E., Hughes, T. P., and Pinch, T. J. (Eds.). (1987). *The social construction of technological systems*. Cambridge, MA: MIT Press.

Bourdieu, P. (1980). *The logic of practice*. Stanford, CA: Stanford University Press.

Bozeman, D. P., Street, M. D., and Fiorito, J. (1999). Positive and negative co-author behaviors in the process of research collaboration. *Journal of Social Behavior and Personality 14*, 2: 159–77.

Brief, A. P. (2000). Still servants of power. *Journal of Management Inquiry 9*, 4: 342–51.

———. (2003). Editor's comments: AMR—the often misunderstood journal. *Academy of Management Review 28*: 7–8.

——— and Cortina, J. (2000). Research ethics: A place to begin. *The Academy of Management Research Methods Division Newsletter 15*, 1.

Burrell, G. (1996). Normal science, paradigms, metaphors, discourses and genealogies of analysis. In S. R. Clegg, C. Hardy, and W. R. Nord (Eds.), *Handbook organization studies* (pp. 642–59). Thousand Oaks, CA: Sage.

——— and Morgan, G. (1979). *Sociological paradigms and organisational analysis: Elements of the sociology of corporate life*. London: Heinemann.

Byrt, W. J. (1989). Management education in Australia. In W. J. Byrt (Ed.), *Management education: An international survey* (pp. 78–103). London: Routledge.

Calás, M., and Smircich, L. (1987). *Post-culture: Is the organizational culture literature dominant but dead?* Paper presented at the International Conference on Organizational Symbolism and Corporate Culture, Milan, Italy.

Cameron, K. S., Dutton, J. E., and Quinn, R. E. (Eds.). (2003). *Positive organizational scholarship*. San Francisco, CA: Berret-Koehler.

Campanario, J. M. (1998a). Peer review for journals as it stands today—1. *Science Communication 19*, 3: 181.

———. (1998b). Peer review for journals as it stands today—2. *Science Communication 19*, 4: 277.

Campbell, J. (1949). *The hero with a thousand faces*. New York: Pantheon Books.

Chanlat, J. F. (1996). From cultural imperialism to independence: Francophone resistance to American definitions of management knowledge in Québec. In S. R. Clegg and G. Palmer (Eds.), *The politics of management knowledge* (pp. 121–40). Thousand Oaks, CA: Sage.

Clark, J., Freeman, C., and Soete, L. (1984). Long waves, inventions, and innovations. In C. Freeman (Ed.), *Long waves in the world economy* (pp. 63–77). London: Frances Pinter.

Clawson, D., and Zussman, R. (1998). Canon and anti-cannon for a fragmented discipline. In D. Clawson (Ed.), *Required reading: Sociology's most influential books*. Amherst: University of Massachusetts Press.

Clegg, S. R. (1996). Creating a career: Observations from outside the mainstream. In P. J. Frost and M. S. Taylor (Eds.), *Rhythms of academic life* (pp. 37–54). Thousand Oaks, CA: Sage.

———— and Hardy, C. (1996). Conclusion: Representations. In S.R. Clegg, C. Hardy, and W. R. Nord (Eds.). *Handbook of organization studies* (pp. 676–708). London: Sage.

————, Hardy, C., and Nord, W. R. (Eds.). (1996). *Handbook of organization studies*. London: Sage.

————, Linstead. S., and Sewell, G. (2000). Only penguins: A polemic on organization theory from the edge of the world. *Organization Studies 21*: 103–17.

Clinton, G. L. (1995). The thrill of victory and the agony of defeat: Reflections of a psychiatrist. In L. L. Cummings and P. J. Frost (Eds.), *Publishing in the organizational sciences* (2nd ed., pp. 246–50). Thousand Oaks, CA: Sage.

Cohen, M. D., and March, J. G.. (1986). *Leadership and ambiguity: The American college president*. 2nd edition. Boston, Mass.: Harvard Business School Press.

Coombs, R. W. (1984). Innovation, automation, and the long-wave theory. In C. Freeman (Ed.), *Long waves in the world economy* (pp. 115–25). London: Frances Pinter.

Cooper, R., and Burrell, G. (1988). Modernism, postmodernism and organizational analysis: An introduction. *Organization Studies 9*: 91–112.

Cooperrider, D. L., and Dutton, J. E. (Eds.). (1999). *Organizational dimensions of global change: No limits to cooperation*. Thousand Oaks, CA: Sage Publications.

———— and Srivastva, S. (1987). Appreciative inquiry in organizational life. In W. A. Pasmore and R. W. Woodman (Eds.), *Research in organizational change and development* (vol. 1, pp. 129–69). Greenwich, CT: JAI Press.

Cronin, B., McKenzie, G., Rubio, L., and Weaver-Wozniak, S. (1993). Accounting for influence: Acknowledgments and contemporary sociology. *Journal of the American Society for Information Science 44*, 7: 406–12.

Crosby, F. (1982). *Relative deprivation and working women*. New York: Oxford University Press.

Culbert, S. A. (1996). *Mind-set management: The heart of leadership*. New York: Oxford University Press.

Cummings, L. L., and Frost, P. J. (1985). *Publishing in the organizational sciences*. Homewood, IL: Irwin.

Czarniawska-Joerges, B. (1998). *Narrative approach in organization studies*. Thousand Oaks, CA: Sage.

Davis, C. G., Nolen-Hoeksema, S., and Larson, J. (1998). Making sense of loss and benefiting from experience: Two construals of meaning. *Journal of Personality and Social Psychology 75*: 561–74.

Dreyfuss, H. L. (1995). *Being-in-the-World*. Cambridge, Mass.: MIT Press.

Dunnette, M. D. (1990). Blending the science and practice of industrial and organizational psychology: Where are we and where are we going? In M. D. Dunette and L. Hough (Eds.), *Handbook of industrial and organizational psychology* (2nd ed., vol. 1, pp. 1–27). Palo Alto, CA: Consulting Psychologists Press.

Dutton, J., Ashford, S. J., O'Neill, R. M., and Lawrence, K. A. (2001). Moves that matter: Issue selling and organizational change. *Academy of Management Journal 44*: 716–36.

Faris, R. E. L. (1967). *Chicago Sociology, 1920–1932*. Chicago: University of Chicago Press.

Feldman, M. (1991). The meanings of ambiguity. In P. J. Frost, L. Moore, M. Louis, C. Lundberg, and J. Martin (Eds.), *Reframing organizational culture* (pp. 58–76). Newbury Park, CA: Sage.

Fletcher, J. (1999). *Disappearing acts: Gender, Power, and relational practice at work*. Cambridge, MA: MIT Press.

Folkman, S. (1997). Positive psychological states and coping with severe stress. *Social Science Medicine 45*: 1207–21.

———, Moskowitz, J. T., Ozer, E. M., and Park, C. L. (1997). Positive meaningful events and coping in the context of HIV / AIDS. In B. H. Gottlieb (Ed.), *Coping with chronic stress* (pp. 293–314). New York: Plenum.

Frankl, V. E. (1959). *Man's search for meaning: An introduction to logotherapy*. New York: Simon and Schuster.

Fredrickson, B. L. (1998). What good are positive emotions? *Review of General Psychology 2*, 3: 300–319.

———. (2000). Cultivating positive emotions to optimize health and well-being, *Prevention and Treatment 3*, 1a: 1–28.

Frost, P. J. (2003). *Toxic emotions at work*. Cambridge, MA: Harvard Business School Press.

———, Moore, L., Louis, M., Lundberg, C., and Martin, J. (Eds.). (1985). *Organizational culture*. Newbury Park, CA: Sage.

———, Moore, L., Louis, M., Lundberg, C., and Martin, J. (Eds.). (1991). *Reframing organizational cultures*. Newbury Park, CA: Sage.

——— and Stablein, R. E. (Eds.). (1992). *Doing exemplary research*. Newbury Park, CA: Sage.

——— and Taylor, M. S. (Eds.). (1996). *Rhythms of academic life*. Thousand Oaks, CA: Sage.

Gagliardi, P. (1991). *Reflections on reframing organizational culture*. Paper presented at the International Conference on Organizational Symbolism and Corporate Culture, Copenhagen.

———. (1999). Theories empowering for action. *Journal of Management Inquiry 8*, 2: 143–48.

Gallos, J. V. (1996). On becoming a scholar: One woman's journey. In P. J. Frost and M. S. Taylor (Eds.), *Rhythms of academic life* (pp. 11–18). Thousand Oaks, CA: Sage.

Gass, W. H. (1999). *Reading Rilke: Reflections on the problems of translation*. New York: Alfred A. Knopf.

Gersick, C. J. G., Bartunek, J. M., and Dutton, J. E. (2000). Learning from academia: The importance of relationships in professional life. *Academy of Management Journal 43*, 6: 1026–44.

Gibbons, M., Limonges, C., Nowotny, H., Schwartzman, S., Scott, P., and Trow, M. (1994). *The new production of knowledge*. Thousand Oaks, CA: Sage.

Giddens, A. (1976). *New rules of sociological method*. London: Hutchinson.

———. (1984). *The constitution of society*. Berkeley: University of California Press.

Gilligan, C. (1982). *In a different voice*. Cambridge, MA: Harvard University Press.

Gioia, D. A. (1992). Pinto fires and personal ethics: A script analysis of missed opportunities. *Journal of Business Ethics 11*: 379–89.

——— and Chittipeddi, K. (1991). Sensemaking and sensegiving in strategic change initiation. *Strategic Management Journal 12*: 433–48.

——— and Corely, K. G. (2002). Being good versus looking good: Business school rankings and the Circean transformation from substance to image. *Academy of Management Learning and Education 1*: 107–20.

——— and Ford, C. M. (1996). Tacit knowledge, self-communication and sensemaking in organizations. In L. Thayer (Ed.), *Organization—communication: Emerging perspectives* (vol. 3, pp. 83–102). Norwood, NJ: Ablex Publishing.

——— and Pitre, E. (1990). Multiparadigm perspectives on theory building. *Academy of Management Review 15*: 584–602.

———, Schultz, M., and Corley, K. G. (2000). Organizational identity, image, and adaptive instability. *Academy of Management Review 25*: 63–81.

Glaser, B. G., and Strauss, A. L. (1967). *The discovery of grounded theory: Strategies for qualitative research*. Chicago: Aldine.

Golden-Biddle, K., and Locke, K. D. (1997). *Composing qualitative research*. Thousand Oaks, CA: Sage.

Gordon, R. A., and Howell, J. E. (1959). *Higher education for business*. New York: Columbia University Press.

Hall, E. T. (1969). *The hidden dimension*. New York: Anchor.

Hargadon, A., and Sutton, R. I. (1997). Technology brokering and innovation in a product development firm. *Administrative Science Quarterly 42*: 716–49.

Hassard, J., and Pym, D. (Eds). (1990). *The theory and philosophy of organization: Critical issues and new perspectives*. London: Routledge.

Hasse, J. E. (1993). *Beyond category: The life and genius of Duke Ellington*. New York: Simon and Schuster.

Hatch, M. J. (1999). Exploring the empty spaces of organizing: How improvisational jazz helps redescribe organizational structure. *Organization Studies 20*, 1: 75–100.

Hillman, J. (1999). *The Force of Character and the Lasting Life*. New York: Random.

Hochschild, A. (1983). *The managed heart: Commercialization of human feeling*. Berkeley: University of California Press.

———. (1989). *The second shift*. New York: Avon.

Hollway, W. (1991). *Work psychology and organizational behavior*. Newbury Park, CA: Sage.

Huff, A. S. (1999). *Writing for scholarly publication*. Thousand Oaks, CA: Sage.

———. (2000). Presidential address: Changes in organizational knowledge production. *Academy of Management Review 25*: 288–93.

——— and Pearse, J. (1999). A conversation on writing in English by nonnative speakers. In Huff, A. S. (1999), *Writing for scholarly publication*. Thousand Oaks, CA: Sage.

Inkson, K. (1988). Challenging hegemony in organizational behavior. *The Organiza-tional Behavior Teaching Review 13*: 1–9.

Isaacs, W. (1999). *Dialogue and the art of thinking together*. New York: Doubleday.

Jones, C. (2002). Foucault's inheritance/inheriting Foucault. *Culture and Organization 8*, 3: 225–38.

Kamoche, K., and Pina e Cunha, M. (2001). Minimal structures: From jazz improvi-sation to product innovation. *Organization Studies 22*, 5: 733–65.

Kanter, R. (1977). *Men and women of the corporation*. New York: Basic Books.

Kuhn, T. (1970). *The structure of scientific revolution*. Chicago: University of Chicago Press.

Kunda, G. (1992). *Engineering culture: Control and commitment in a high-tech corporation*. Philadelphia, PA: Temple University Press.

Lave, J., and Wenger, E. (1991). *Situated learning: Legitimate peripheral participation*. Cambridge: Cambridge University Press.

Lewis, J. D., and Smith, R. L. (1980). *American sociology and pragmatism: Mead, Chicago sociology, and symbolic interaction*. Chicago: University of Chicago Press.

Locke, R. R. (1989). *Management and higher education since 1940: The influence of Amer-ica and Japan on West Germany, Great Britain and France*. Cambridge: Cambridge University Press.

———. (1996). *The collapse of the American management mystique*. Oxford: Oxford University Press.

Ludema, J. D., Cooperrider, D. L., and Barrett, F. J. (2001). Appreciative inquiry: The power of the unconditional positive question. In P. Reason and H. Bradbury (Eds.), *Handbook of action research* (pp. 189–99). Thousand Oaks, CA: Sage.

———, Wilmot, T. B., and Srivastva, S. (1997). Organizational hope: Reaffirming the constructive task of social and organizational inquiry. *Human Relations 50*, 8: 1015–50.

Luthar, S. S., Cicchetti, D., and Becker, B. (2000). The construct of resilience: A crit-ical evaluation and guidelines for future work. *Child Development 71*: 543–62.

Maclean, N. (1992). *Young Men and Fire*. Chicago, Il.: University of Chicago.

March, J. G. (1965). Introduction. In J. G. March (Ed.), *Handbook of organizations* (pp. ix–xvi). Chicago: Rand McNally.

———. (1996). Continuity and change in theories of organizational action. *Admin-istrative Science Quarterly*, 41: 278–87.

Martin, J. (1981). Relative deprivation: A theory of distributive injustice for an era of shrinking resources. In L. L. Cummings and B. M. Staw (Eds.), *Research in organi-zational behavior* (vol. 3, pp. 53–107). Greenwich, CT: JAI Press.

———. (1982a). Stories and scripts in organizational settings. In A. H. Hastorf and A. M. Isen (Eds.), *Cognitive social psychology* (pp. 255–305). New York: Elsevier-North Holland, Inc.

———. (1982b). The fairness of earning differentials: An experimental study of the perceptions of blue-collar workers. *The Journal of Human Resources 17*: 110–22.

———. (1986a). The tolerance of injustice. In J. M. Olson, C. P. Herman, and M. P. Zanna (Eds.), *Relative deprivation and social comparison: The Ontario Symposium* (vol. 4, pp. 217–42). Hillsdale, NJ: Lawrence Erlbaum.

———. (1986b). When expectations and justice do not coincide: Blue-collar visions of a just world. In H. W. Bierhoff, R. L. Cohen, and J. Greening (Eds.), *Justice in Social Relations* (pp. 317–35). New York: Plenum.

———. (1990). Deconstructing organizational taboos: The suppression of gender conflict in organizations. *Organizational Science* 1: 339–59.

———. (1992). *Cultures in organizations: Three perspectives.* New York: Oxford University Press.

———. (1993). Inequality, distributive injustice, and organizational illegitimacy. In K. Murnighan (Ed.), *Social psychology in organizations: Advances in theory and research* (pp. 296–321). Englewood Cliffs, NJ: Prentice-Hall.

———. (1994). The organization of exclusion: The institutionalization of sex inequality, gendered faculty jobs, and gendered knowledge in organizational theory and research. *Organization* 1: 401–31.

———. (1995a). The style and structure of cultures in organizations: Three perspectives. *Organizational Science* 6: 230–32.

———. (1995b). Organizational culture, rituals, and taboos. Three entries in N. Nicholson, R. Schuler, and A. Van de Ven (Eds.), *The Blackwell Encyclopedic Dictionary of Organizational Behavior* (pp. 376–82, 494–95, 554). Oxford: Basil Blackwell Ltd.

———. (2002). *Organizational Culture.* Thousand Oaks, CA: Sage.

———, Brickman, P., and Murray, A. (1984). Moral outrage and pragmatism: Explanations for collective action. *Journal of Experimental Social Psychology* 20: 484–96.

———, Feldman, M., Hatch, M. J., and Sitkin, S. (1983). The uniqueness paradox in organizational stories. *Administrative Science Quarterly* 28: 438–53.

——— and Frost, P. J. (1996). The organizational culture war games: A struggle for intellectual dominance. In S. R. Clegg, C. Hardy, and W. R. Nord (Eds.), *Handbook of organization studies* (pp. 599–621). London: Sage.

——— and Harder, J. (1994). Bread and roses: Justice and the distribution of financial and socio-emotional rewards in organizations. *Social Justice Research* 7: 241–64.

——— and Knopoff, K. (1997). The gendered implications of apparently gender-neutral organizational theory: Re-reading Weber. In A. Larson and E. Freeman (Eds.), *The Ruffin series in business ethics:* (Vol. 3): *Business ethics and women's studies* (pp. 30–49). Oxford: Oxford University Press.

———, Knopoff, K., and Beckman, C. (1998). An alternative to bureaucratic impersonality and emotional labor: Bounded emotionality at the Body Shop. *Administrative Science Quarterly* 43: 429–69.

——— and Meyerson, D. (1988). Organizational cultures and the denial, channeling, and acknowledgment of ambiguity. In L. R. Pondy, R. J. Boland, and H. Thomas (Eds.), *Managing ambiguity and change* (pp. 93–125). New York: Wiley.

——— and Meyerson, D. (September 1997). *Executive women at Link. Com.* A set of eight teaching cases, with instructor's notes, Harvard University Press (#OB 33 in Stanford University series).

——— and Meyerson, D. (1998). Women and power: Conformity, resistance, and disorganized co-action. In R. M. Kramer and M. A. Neale (Eds.), *Power and influence in organizations* (pp. 311–48). Thousand Oaks, CA: Sage.

———— and Murray, A. (1983). Distributive injustice and unfair exchange. In K. S. Cook and D. M. Messick (Eds.), *Theories of equity: Psychological and sociological perspectives* (pp. 169–205). New York: Praeger.

———— and Murray, A. (1984). Catalysts for collective violence: The importance of a psychological approach. In R. Folger (Ed.), *The sense of injustice: Social psychological perspectives* (pp. 95–139). New York: Plenum.

———— and Powers, M. (1983a). Organizational stories: More vivid and persuasive than quantitative data. In B. Staw (Ed.), *Psychological foundations of organizational behavior* (2nd ed., pp. 162–68). Glenview, IL: Scott, Foresman.

———— and Powers, M. (1983b). Truth or corporate propaganda: The value of a good war story. In L. Pondy, P. J. Frost, G. Morgan, and T. Dandridge (Eds.), *Organizational symbolism* (pp. 93–107). Greenwich, CT: JAI Press.

————, Scully, M., and Levitt, B. (1990). Injustice and the legitimation of revolution: Damning the past, excusing the present, and neglecting the future. *Journal of Personality and Social Psychology 59*: 281–90.

———— and Siehl, C. (Fall 1983). Organizational culture and counter culture: An uneasy symbiosis. *Organizational Dynamics*: 52–64.

————, Sitkin, S., and Boehm, M. (1985). Founders and the elusiveness of a cultural legacy. In P. J. Frost, L. Moore, M. Louis, C. Lundberg, and J. Martin (Eds.), *Organizational culture* (pp. 99–124). Beverly Hills, CA: Sage.

McCall, M., and Bobko, P. (1990). Research methods in the search of discovery. In M. Dunnette and L. Hough (Eds.), *Handbook of industrial and organizational psychology* (vol. 1, pp. 381–418). Palo Alto, CA: Consulting Psychologists Press.

Mensch, G. (1979). *Stalemate in technology: Innovations overcome the depression.* Cambridge, MA: Ballinger.

Meyerson, D. (2001). *Tempered radicals: How people use difference to inspire change at work.* Cambridge, MA: Harvard Business School Press.

———— and Martin, J. (1986). Questioning the assumptions of value engineering: Alternative views of the culture change process. In R. Poupart (Ed.), *Proceedings: International Conference on Organization Symbolism and Corporate Culture: Cultural Engineering—The Evidence For And Against.* Montreal: ICOS.

———— and Martin, J. (1987). Culture change: An integration of three different views. *Journal of Management Studies 24*: 623–48.

———— and Scully, M. (1995). Tempered radicalism and the politics of ambivalence and change. *Organization Science 6*: 585–601.

Miles, R. E. (1996). Business schools in transition: A brief history of business education. In P. J. Frost and M. S. Taylor (Eds.), *Rhythms of academic life* (pp. 457–58). Thousand Oaks, CA: Sage.

Miller, J. B. (1991). The development of women's sense of self. In J. V. Jordon, A. G. Kaplan, J. B. Miller, I. P Stiver, and J. L. Surrey (Eds.), *Women's growth in connection.* New York: The Guilford Press.

Milliken, F. J., Morrison, E. W., and Hewlin, P. (2002). Choosing to stay silent: What people are silent about and why. Working Paper. Stern School of Business, New York University.

Mills, A. J., and Hatfield, J. (1999). From imperialism to globalization: Internationalization and the management text. In S. R. Clegg, E. Ibarra-Colado, and L. Bueno-Rodiquez (Eds.), *Global management*. Thousand Oaks, CA: Sage.

Mohr, L. B. (1982). *Explaining organizational behavior*. San Francisco, CA: Jossey-Bass.

Moldoveanu, M. C., and Baum, J. A. C. (2002). Contemporary debates and organizational epistemology. In J. A. C.Baum (Ed.), *Companion to organizations* (pp. 733–51). Malden, MA: Blackwell.

Morgan, G. (1983). In research, as in conversation, we meet ourselves. In G. Morgan (Ed.), *Beyond Method* (pp. 405–7). Beverly Hills, CA: Sage.

Morris, W. (Ed.). (1980). *The American heritage dictionary* (p. 707). Boston: Houghton Mifflin.

Muller, W. (1999). *Sabbath: Restoring the sacred rhythm of rest*. NewYork: Bantam.

Mumby, D. (1994). [Review of the book Culture in organizations: Three perspectives, by Joanne Martin.] *Academy of Management Review 19*, 1: 156–59.

Murnighan, J. K. (1996). Revising and resubmitting: Author emotions, editor roles, and the value of dialogue. In P. J. Frost and S. M. Taylor (Eds.), *Rhythms of academic life* (pp. 135–43). Thousand Oaks, CA: Sage.

Nadel, S. F. (1957). *The theory of social structure*. Glencoe, IL: Free Press.

Near, J. P. (1996). Stakeholders and you. In P. J. Frost and M. S. Taylor (Eds.), *Rhythms of academic life* (pp. 475–80). Thousand Oaks, CA: Sage.

Nelsen, B. J., and Barley, S. R. (1997). For love or money: Commodification and the construction of an occupational mandate. *Administrative Science Quarterly 42*: 619–53.

Nord, W. R. (1974). The failure of current applied behavioral science: A Marxian perspective. *Journal of Applied Behavioral Science 10*, 4: 557–78.

———. (1993). Alvin W. Gouldner as intellectual hero. *Journal of Management Inquiry 2*, 4: 350–55.

———. (2003). Editor's remarks: Augmenting the role books play in organization management studies. *Academy of Management Review 28*, 1: 154–55.

Northcraft, G., and Martin, J. (1982). Double jeopardy: Resistance to affirmative action from potential beneficiaries. In B. A. Gutek (Ed.), *Sex-role stereotyping and affirmative action policy* (pp. 81–130). Los Angeles: Institute for Industrial Relations, University of California at Los Angeles.

Oxford English Dictionary. (1971). (Vol. 1, compact ed.). New York and Oxford: Oxford University Press.

Perrow, C. (1986). *Complex organizations: A critical essay* (3rd ed.). New York: Random House.

Pettigrew, A. M. (1998). Catching reality in flight. *Management Laureates 5*: 171–206.

Pettigrew, T. (1967). Social evaluation theory: Convergences and applications. In D. Levine (Ed), *Nebraska Symposium on Motivation, 3*: 241–318.

——— and Martin, J. (1987). Shaping the organizational context for Black American inclusion. *Journal of Social Issues 43*: 41–78.

Pfeffer, J. (1982). *Organizations and organization*. Boston, MA: Pitman.

———. (1993). Barriers to the advance of organizational science: Paradigm development as a dependent variable. *Academy of management review, 18*: 599–620.

———. (1997). *New directions organization theory*. Oxford: Oxford University Press.

Pierson, F. C., et al. (1959). *The education of American businessmen*. New York: McGraw-Hill.

Platt, S. (1989). *Respectfully quoted: A Dictionary of quotations*. Washington D.C.: Library of Congress.

Polanyi, M. (1967). *The tacit dimension*. New York: Doubleday.

Poole, M., and Van de Ven, A. (1989). Using paradox to build management and organization theories. *Academy of Management Review 14*: 562–78.

Porter, L. W. (1996). Forty years of organization studies: Reflections from a micro perspective. *Administrative Science Quarterly 41*: 262–69.

——— and McKibben, L. E. (1988). *Management education and development: Drift or thrust into the 21st century?* New York: McGraw-Hill.

Prasad, A. (Ed.). (2003). *Postcolonial theory and organizational analysis*. New York and Basingstoke, UK: Palgrave Macmillan.

Putnam, L. L., and Mumby, D. K. (1993). Organizations, emotion, and the myth of rationality. In S. Fineman (Ed.), *Emotion in organizations* (pp. 36–57). London: Sage.

Pye, A. (1991). Managament competence: "The flower in the mirror and the moon on the water." In M. Silver (Ed.) *Competent to manage*. London: Routledge.

Quinn, R. E., O'Neill, R. M., and Debebe, G. (1996). Confronting the tensions in an academic career. In P. J. Frost and M. S. Taylor (Eds.), *Rhythms of academic life* (pp. 421–27). Thousand Oaks, CA: Sage.

Ragin, C. C., and Becker, H. S. (Eds.). (1992). *What is a case?: Exploring the foundations of social enquiry*. Cambridge and New York: Cambridge University Press.

Ragins, B. R., Townsend, B., and Mattis, M. (1998). Gender gap in the executive suite: CEOs and female executives report on breaking the glass ceiling. *Academy of Management Executive 12*: 28–42.

Reed, M. (1996). Organizational theorizing: A historically contested terrain. In S. R. Clegg, C. Hardy, and W. R. Nord (Eds.), *Handbook of organization studies* (pp. 31–56). London: Sage.

Rhodes, C. (2001). *Writing organization*. Amsterdam and Philadelphia, PA: John Benjamins Publishing.

Roethlisberger, F. J. (1968). *Man-in-organization: Essays of F. J. Roethlisberger*. Cambridge, MA: Harvard University Press.

———. (1977). *The elusive phenomenon: Boston: Division of Research*. Cambridge, MA: Graduate School of Business, Harvard University.

Rosen, M. (1981). Breakfast at Spiro's. In P. Frost, L. Moore, M. Louis, C. Lundberg, and J. Martin (Eds.), *Reframing organizational culture* (pp. 58–76). Newbury Park, CA: Sage.

Ryan, R. M., and Deci, E. L. (2000). Self-determination theory and the facilitation of intrinsic motivation, social development, and well-being. *American Psychologist 55*: 68–78.

Rynes, S. L., Bartunek, J. M., and Daft, R. L. (2001). Across the great divide: Knowledge creation and transfer between practitioners and academics. *Academy of Management Journal 4*, 2: 340–55.

Sampson, E. (1993). *Celebrating the other: A dialogic account of human nature*. Boulder, CO: Westview Press.

Sapir, E. (1921). *Language: An introduction to the study of speech.* New York: Harcourt Brace Jovanovich.

Schopenhauer, A. (1851/1970). On books and writing. In R. J. Hollinger (Ed. and translator). *Essays and Aphorisms.* London: Penguin Books, pp. 198–211.

Servan-Schreiber, J. (1967/1969). *Le Défi américain/The American challenge.* Harmondsworth, Middlesex, UK: Penguin.

Siehl, C., and Martin, J. (1984). The role of symbolic management: How can managers effectively transmit organizational culture? In J. G. Hunt, D. Hosking, C. Schriesheim, and R. Stewart (Eds.), *Leaders and managers: International perspectives on managerial behavior and leadership* (vol. 7, pp. 227–39). Elmsford, NY: Pergamon Press.

Siehl, C., and Martin, J. (1990). Organizational culture: A key to financial performance? In B. Schneider (Ed.), *Organizational climate and cultzelinure: Frontiers of industrial and organizational psychology* (pp. 241–81). San Francisco, CA: Jossey-Bass.

Silverman, D. (1970). *The theory of organization.* London: Heinemann.

Simon, H. A. (1991). Bounded rationality and organizational learning. *Organization Science 2,* 1: 125–34.

Sims, H. P. Jr., Gioia, D. A., et al. (Eds.). (1986). *The thinking organization.* San Francisco, CA: Jossey-Bass.

Spradley, J. P. (1979). *The ethnographic interview.* New York: Holt, Rinehardt, and Winston.

Stablein, R. (1999). Moving (a)head: A commentary on the Gagliardi, Frost, and Weick papers. *Journal of Management Inquiry 8,* 2: 148–49.

——— and Nord, W. (1985). Practical and emancipatory interests in organizational symbolism: A review and evaluation. *Journal of Management 11:* 13–28.

Starkey, K., and Madan, P. (2001). Bridging the relevance gap: Aligning stakeholders in the future of management research. *British Journal of Management 12* (Special issue): S3–S26.

Stern, R. N., and Barley, S. R. (1996). Organizations and social systems: Organization theory's neglected mandate. *Administrative Science Quarterly 41:* 146–62.

Strober, M., Brest, P., Brown, D., Chu, S., Gagnier, R., Goodman, J., Martin, J., Scott, W., Shapiro, L., Spudich, J., and Wack, M. (September 1993). *Report of the Provost's Committee on the Recruitment and Retention of Women Faculty.* Stanford University.

Taylor, S. E., and Martin, J. (1986). The present-minded professor: Controlling one's career. In M. P. Zanna and J. M. Darley (Eds.), *The compleat academic: A practical guide for the beginning social scientist* (pp. 23–60). New York: Random House.

Thomas, W. I., and Thomas, D. S. (1928). *The child in America: Behavior problems and programs.* New York: Alfred A. Knopf.

Thompson, J. (1967). *Organization in action.* New York: McGraw-Hill.

Time. (December 30, 2002–January 6, 2003). Persons of the Year. Nos. 51/52.

Van de Ven, A. H. (1999). The buzzing, blooming, confusing world of organization and management theory: A view from Lake Wobegon University. *Journal of Management Inquiry 8,* 2: 118–25.

———. (2002). Presidential address: Strategic directions for the Academy of Management: This academy is for you! *Academy of Management Review 27,* 2: 171–84.

Van Duijn, J. J. (1983). *The long wave in economic life*. London: Allen and Unwin.

Van Fleet, D. D., and Wren, D. A. (1982). The teaching of history in collegiate schools of business. *Collegiate News and Views XXXVI*, 2: 17–25.

Van Maanen, J. (1991). The smile factory: Work in Disneyland. In P. J. Frost, L. Moore, M. Louis, C. Lundberg, and J. Martin (Eds.), *Reframing organizational culture* (pp. 58–76). Newbury Park, CA: Sage.

Vaughn, D. (1996). *The Challenger launch decision*. Chicago: University of Chicago Press.

Walsh, J. P. (1996). Embracing change: We get by with a lot of help from our friends. In P. J. Frost and M. S. Taylor (Eds.), *Rhythms of academic life* (pp. 481–84). Thousand Oaks, CA: Sage.

Weaver, G., and Gioia, D. (1994). Paradigms lost: Incommensurability vs. structurationist inquiry. *Organization Studies 15*: 565–89.

Webster's Ninth New Collegiate Dictionary. (1987). Springfield, MA: Merriam-Webster, Inc.

Weick, K. E. (1979). *The social psychology of organizing*. (2nd ed.). Reading, MA: Addison-Wesley.

———. (1984). Small wins. *American Psychologist 39*: 40–49.

———. (1989a). Organized improvisation: 20 years of organizing. *Communication Studies 40*, 4: 241–48.

———. (1989b). Theory construction as disciplined imagination. *Academy of Management Review 14*: 516–31.

———. (1991). The vulnerable system. In P. J. Frost, L. Moore, M. Louis, C. Lundberg, and J. Martin (Eds.), *Reframing organizational culture* (pp. 90–103). Newbury Park, CA: Sage.

———. (1993). The collapse of sensemaking in organizations: The Mann Gulch disaster. *Administrative Science Quarterly 38*: 628–52.

———. (1995). *Sensemaking in organizations*. Thousand Oaks, CA: Sage.

———. (1996). Drop your tools: An allegory for organizational studies. *Administrative Science Quarterly 41*, 2: 301–13.

———. (1998). Wildfire and wisdom. *Wildfire 7*, 1: 14–19.

———. (2001). *Making sense of the organization*. Oxford and Malden, MA: Blackwell Publishers.

White, E. B. (1954/1975). The future of reading. In C. P. Curtis Jr., and F. Greenslet (Eds.), *The Practical Cogitator, or the Thinker's Anthology* (pp. 550–551). New York: Dell (Laurel).

Whorf, B. L. (1956). *Language, thought, and reality*. Cambridge, MA: MIT Press.

Whyte, D. (1996). *The heart aroused*. New York: Doubleday.

Willmott, H. (1995). Managing the academics: Commodification and control in the development of university education in the UK. *Human Relations 48*, 9: 993–1027.

Wong-MingJi, D., and Mir, A. H. (1997). How international is international management? Provincialism, parochialism and the problematic of global diversity. In P. Prasad, A. J. Mills, M. Elmes, and A. Prasad (Eds.), *Managing the organizational melting pot* (pp. 340–66). Thousand Oaks, CA: Sage.

Young, E. (1991). On the naming of the rose. In P. J. Frost, L. Moore, M. Louis, C. Lundberg, and J. Martin (Eds.), *Reframing organizational culture* (pp. 90–103). Newbury Park, CA: Sage.

Zabusky, S. E., and Barley, S. R. (1996). Redefining success: Ethnographic observations on the careers of technicians. In P. Osterman (Ed.), *Broken ladders*. Cambridge: Cambridge University Press.

————— and Barley, S. R. (1997). You can't be a stone if you're cement: Re-evaluating the emic identities of scientists in organizations. *Research in Organizational Behavior 19:* 361–404.

Zald, M. N. (1996). More fragmentation?: Unfinished business in linking the social sciences and the humanities. *Administrative Science Quarterly 41:* 251–61.

Contributors

Stephen R. Barley is the Charles M. Pigott Professor of Management Science and Engineering at Stanford's School of Engineering and a codirector of the Center for Work Technology and Organization. His research centers on the technical workforce and on the impact of technology on work.

David Barry is Professor of Creative Organization Studies at Victoria University, New Zealand; he works with arts-based organization studies and organizational aesthetics.

Jean M. Bartunek is Professor of Organizational Studies at Boston College and a past president of the Academy of Management. Her interests include social cognition, organizational change, and academic-practitioner interfaces.

Kevin Corley is Assistant Professor of Organizational Behavior in the College of Business at the University of Illinois, Urbana-Champaign. His research interests focus on organizational change, especially as it pertains to issues of organizational identity, image, reputation, identification, and learning.

Barbara Czarniawska holds the Skandia Chair in Management Studies at the Gothenburg Research Institute in Sweden. Her research focuses on control processes in complex organizations combining institutional theory and the narrative approach.

Jane E. Dutton is the William Russell Kelly Professor of Business Administration at the University of Michigan. She is excited about how her research contributes to Positive Organizational Scholarship. See http://www.bus.mich.edu/Positive/.

Peter J. Frost is the Edgar F. Kaiser Professor of Organizational Behavior at Sauder School of Business, University of British Columbia. His most recent book is *Toxic Emotions at Work* (HBS Press, 2003).

Dennis A. (Denny) Gioia is Professor of Organizational Behavior in the Smeal College of Business Administration at Penn State University. He fancies himself a scholar, writer, teacher, and artist and is flailing away at all four (ad)ventures.

Mary Jo Hatch, Professor of Commerce at the McIntire School of Commerce, University of Virginia, writes on organizational culture, identity, humor and aesthetics, corporate branding, and the jazz metaphor for organizing.

Paul M. Hirsch is the James Allen Distinguished Professor of Strategy and Organization at the Kellogg School of Management at Northwestern University. His research interests include careers and organizational change, the employment relationship and corporate takeovers, and mass communication and the sociology of culture.

Anne Sigismund Huff is Director of AIM, a U.K.-wide management research initiative with offices at the London Business School. Her research focuses on change at multiple levels of analysis, with particular concern for cognitive and sociopolitical contributions to change. She is a past president of the Academy of Management.

James D. Ludema is Associate Professor in the PhD Program in Organization Development at Benedictine University. His interests include global Organization Development, appreciative inquiry, sustainable development, the dynamics of hope in organizational life, organizational storytelling, large-group interventions, and qualitative research methods.

Sally Maitlis is Assistant Professor at the University of British Columbia. Her research interests include narrative and discursive approaches to emotion in organizational sensemaking and decision making.

Joanne Martin is the Merrill Professor of Organizational Behavior at the Graduate School of Business, Stanford University. Her most recent book is *Organizational Culture: Mapping the Terrain* (Sage, 2002).

Frances J. Milliken is Professor of Organizational Behavior at the Stern School of Business of New York University and Coordinator of the Doctoral Program in Management. Her interests include diversity, the dynamics of voice and silence in organizations, and how people think about and attempt to manage their time in work and nonwork lives.

Philip H. Mirvis is an organizational psychologist who studies and consults on large-scale organizational change. His most recent book is a business transformation story, *To the Desert and Back* (Jossey-Bass, 2003).

Walter R. Nord is Distinguished University Professor of Management at the University of South Florida. His coedited *Handbook of Organization Studies* received the 1997 George Terry Award, and he received the Academy of Management's 2002 Distinguished Educator Award.

Christine Pearson (Thunderbird, AGSIM) researches and teaches organizational crisis management and helps companies avert, contain, and learn from crises. She is currently writing her fourth book.

Leslie A. Perlow is Associate Professor of Organizational Behavior at the Harvard Business School. Her research interests include time use, the nature of work interactions, and work-family issues.

Michael G. Pratt is Associate Professor of Organizational Behavior at the University of Illinois. His research utilizes theories of identity/identification, symbolism, socialization, and sensemaking in examining the bond between the individual and various social groups.

Ralph Stablein is Professor of Management at Massey University in New Zealand. Both his research and teaching focus on inquiry in organization studies.

Kathleen M. Sutcliffe is Associate Professor at the University of Michigan Business School. Her research focuses on team/organizational resilience, high-reliability organizing, and the social/organizational underpinnings of medical mishaps.

Andrew H. Van de Ven is Vernon H. Heath Professor of Organizational Innovation and Change in the Carlson School of Management of the University of Minnesota. Since 1993 he has been conducting a longitudinal real-time study of changes in health care organizations. He is a past president of the Academy of Management.

Karl E. Weick is the Rensis Likert Distinguished University Professor of Organizational Behavior and Psychology at the University of Michigan. His current work includes an examination of distributed sensemaking in high-profile disease outbreaks, handoffs in wild-land fire tragedies, and organizing for high reliability in medical settings.

Index